The Wellness
Revolution

Other books by Paul Zane Pilzer

God Wants You to Be Rich
Other People's Money (with Robert Deitz)
Unlimited Wealth

The Wellness Revolution

How to Make a Fortune in the Next Trillion Dollar Industry

PAUL ZANE PILZER

WILEY

John Wiley & Sons, Inc.

Published by John Wiley & Sons, Inc., Hoboken, New Jersey.
Published simultaneously in Canada.

For general information on our other products and services please contact our Customer Care Department within the United States at (800) 762-2974, outside the United States at (317) 572-3993 or fax (317) 572-4002.

Wiley also publishes its books in a variety of electronic formats. Some content that appears in print may not be available in electronic books. For more information about Wiley products, visit our website at www.wiley.com.

Library of Congress Cataloging-in-Publication Data

Pilzer, Paul Zane.
    The wellness revolution : how to make a fortune in the next trillion dollar industry / Paul Zane Pilzer.
      p. cm.
    Includes bibliographical references and index.
    ISBN 0-471-20794-2; 0-471-43067-6 (pbk.)
    1. Health promotion. 2. Health products. 3. Entrepreneurship.
I. Title.
RA427.8.P554 2002   2001007199

Printed in the United States of America.

10 9 8 7

In memory of J. I. Rodale (1898–1971)

CONTENTS

The Wellness
Revolution

The Next Big Thing

In the twentieth century, our lives were revolutionized by things like the automobile, airline travel, the personal computer, and family planning. In those cases, initial discoveries led to the birth of empires and to unprecedented individual wealth for those entrepreneurs and investors who got in first. The next big thing of the twenty-first century has just begun, and it promises to similarly revolutionize our lives and offer opportunities for tremendous wealth building over the next 10 years.

This next big thing is the *wellness revolution.*

> **This book is not about a fad or a trend, it's about a new and infinite need infusing itself into the way we eat, exercise, sleep, work, save, age, and almost every other aspect of our lives.**

The desire for wellness already pervades our decisions, from which toothpaste and shampoo we use in the morning to what we eat throughout the day to the type of bedding and cosmetics we use at night. We demand more safety from our products; we want more prevention from them, too. And yet we are only at the beginning of the public consciousness of this growing need—because most people still aren't aware of how simple choices affect their wellness, and many wellness products and services aren't yet widely available in the marketplace.

This book explains the emerging wellness industry to arm you with the information that you need in order to profit from it, both financially and personally.

I show you how to stake your claim in this huge opportunity—how to find your place in this new total-life industry that not only can bring you riches, but also does incredible good.

The Next Big Thing

When Henry Ford first invented a mass-produced automobile that was affordable to the common person, many scoffed at the thought that people would buy it. There were few paved roads on which to travel, gasoline stations were nonexistent, and most people lived within walking distance of their workplaces. But the need grew along with proliferation of the product. People moved to suburbia and needed cars. At the same time, gasoline stations sprung up. Soon the car became a necessity just to get to work or shop for daily necessities.

What if you had been told back then that Henry Ford's Model T wasn't just another new product, but the beginning of a whole new trillion dollar sector of the world economy—that in 100 years there would be 500 million cars on the road, necessitating ancillary trillion dollar industries in gas stations, road construction, replacement tires, suburban homes, and fast-food restaurants?

Would you have accepted this notion? In addition to the limitations of no roads, no gasoline stations, and conveniently nearby workplaces, people typically worked six days a week for little pay and with little time off for Sunday drives in the country. To accept this notion you would also have had to foresee the coming five-day, 40-hour workweek and the rise in discretionary income.

But suppose you overcame your skepticism and saw the new autopowered vehicles of Henry Ford and others as the beginning of a trillion dollar industry. As an entrepreneur or an investor, where would you have placed your bet? Would it have been on gasoline-powered cars or on electric or diesel ones? Would it have been on road construction, on replacement parts like tires, or on residential land development? And just as significantly, once you picked one of these areas, what specifically would you have done to stake your claim?

More recently, in 1981 a surprise mega-industry was born from the newly minted personal computer, the IBM PC, along with competitive models by Apple and RadioShack. Perhaps most people were similarly unable to predict that these were not just new products, but the harbingers of another trillion dollar sector of the world economy—a sector growing so fast that personal computer sales would surpass U.S. automobile sales in only 10 years, by 1991.

In our modern economy, changes that used to take place over the span of 100 years or more now take place in 10 years or less. Had you been able to foresee the rise of the trillion dollar personal computer business like Bill Gates (Microsoft, software), Michael Dell (Dell Computer, hardware), Jeff Bezos (Amazon, distribution), and countless others, in what part of the personal computer industry would you have placed your bet?

The self-powered vehicle and the personal computer were the oxymora of their times. After all, in the days of the horse and buggy, the public had a difficult time accepting that a vehicle could be self-powered. Similarly, in the days of room-size mainframe computers, who could easily visualize that a computer could be "personal"?

Historically, pivotal new products became available because of scientific breakthroughs that allowed their invention and affordable manufacture.

People didn't need the automobile and the personal computer before they became available—any more than today we need interplanetary travel. Yet once they became available, they quickly went from being simply new products to becoming absolute necessities for daily work and life.

What was it about these two new products, and several others, that made them so immediately successful? Was there something evident about them that foreshadowed how pervasive they were about to become in almost every aspect of our lives? Knowing those traits could perhaps help you predict other new industries from which to profit.

There are actually five distinct characteristics of emerging pervasive industries, which I will tell you about in a moment. But first I want to share with you a crucial way of thinking about wellness and understanding the causes of its inevitable growth.

Defining the Trillion Dollar Wellness Industry

We are now at the very beginning of the next trillion dollar industry—an industry that will impact almost every aspect of our lives and achieve $1 trillion in sales within 10 years, but one that is as unknown today as the automobile industry was in 1908 or the personal computer industry was in 1981.

The automobile industry was spawned by scientific breakthroughs in chemistry, metallurgy, and mechanics. The personal computer industry was spawned by scientific breakthroughs in physics and binary mathematics.

This next trillion dollar industry is being spawned by scientific breakthroughs in biology and cellular biochemistry.

The wellness industry is tackling one of the most profound issues of life, solving one of the few remaining mysteries of human existence—age and vitality—on which technology has yet to make its mark.

In order to define the wellness industry and identify its opportunities, we must first distinguish it from a related industry based on some of the same technology—the current $1.5 trillion (U.S.) healthcare industry.

Approximately one-seventh of the U.S. economy, about $1.5 trillion, is devoted to what is erroneously called the "healthcare" business. *Healthcare* is a misnomer, as this one-seventh of the economy is really devoted to the *sickness* business—defined in the dictionary as "ill health, illness, a disordered, weakened, or unsound condition, or a specific disease."[1]

The sickness business is *reactive*. Despite its enormous size, people become customers only when they are stricken by and react to a specific condition or ailment. No one really wants to be a customer.

In the next 10 years, an additional $1 trillion of the U.S. economy will be devoted to the yet-unnamed *wellness* business—defined in the dictionary as "the quality or state of being in good health *especially as an actively sought goal* [emphasis added]."[2]

The wellness business is *proactive*. People *voluntarily* become customers—to feel healthier, to reduce the effects of aging, and to avoid becoming customers of the sickness business. Everyone wants to be a customer of this earlier-stage approach to health.

From this point forward I use the following definitions:

> **S**ickness industry   Products and services provided *reactively* to people with an existing disease, ranging from a common cold to existing cancerous tumors. These products and services seek to either treat the symptoms of a disease or eliminate the disease.
>
> **Wellness industry**   Products and services provided *proactively* to healthy people (those without an existing disease) to make them feel even healthier and look better, to slow the effects of aging, or to prevent diseases from developing in the first place.

How to Read This Book

Throughout this book I highlight important points you need to know in order to explain the importance of this new industry to your family, associates, clients, customers, investors, and partners.

> **I also highlight points essential to helping you stake your claim through entrepreneurship, investment, distribution, and/or by using this information to change your existing business today.**

In Chapter 1, I share with you my vision for the wellness industry over the next 10 years. When I began the research for this book, I thought the existing items in the wellness industry—fitness clubs, vitamins, and the like—might already total a few billion dollars in U.S. sales. I was very surprised to find that sales have already reached approximately $200 billion—including $70 billion for vitamins and $24 billion for fitness clubs—and yet only a small percentage of the population even know about wellness. Imagine what will happen as more people understand the potential that wellness can add to the quality and longevity of their lives!

In Chapter 2, I explain the notion of demand, how it operates in relation to wellness, and how controlled growth of demand can occur. I show why the $200 billion in proven demand today is only the tip of the iceberg and why these new products and services represent the beginning of a *new* $1 trillion sector of our economy (as opposed to offshoot products in existing industries like agribusiness or medicine).

In Chapter 3, you learn how our $1 trillion existing agribusiness and food industry targets overweight and obese consumers for ever increasing consumption—causing a health crisis in the United States that finds 61 percent of the population currently overweight and 27 percent clinically obese. These numbers have doubled since 1980 and increased 10 percent in the last four years. Other developed nations, especially in the European Community, are not far behind. Then, in Chapter 4, you learn how this has created one of the greatest business opportunities of our time—educating consumers and providing healthy food and the necessary vitamins and supplements that are no longer contained in our modern food supply.

In the past, a significant part of the health and sickness industry was concerned with wellness. At the beginning of the last century, technological breakthroughs in inoculation and antibiotics allowed medicine to develop preventive measures for many diseases (smallpox, typhoid, tuberculosis, polio) that had been the scourge of humankind for millennia.

That was the past.

Most of the one-seventh of the U.S. adult population that work in the healthcare industry today focus on treating the symptoms of disease rather than on preventing disease. This is because it is more profitable for medical companies to research and develop products that create customers for life.

It is also because the third parties paying for most medical treatments—insurance companies and ultimately employers—no longer have a long-term financial stake in the health of their employees. If you are among this one-seventh of the workforce in the healthcare field, Chapter 5 examines some of the entrepreneurial opportunities arising in the wellness industry for medical professionals. Providing wellness products and services that people will voluntarily purchase with their own funds works better than providing bureaucratic procedures to unhappy consumers without choice who are financed by distant third parties.

In Chapter 6 you learn why our existing employer-based healthcare insurance system is on the verge of collapse and what you can do to protect yourself and your family. Despite a steadily rising economy in the past decade, U.S. personal bankruptcy filings doubled—from approximately 750,000 in 1990 to 1.5 million in 1999—with much of the increase resulting from family medical catastrophes. Then in Chapter 7 you learn how opting out of the existing sickness-based system (i.e., getting Wellness Insurance™ today) can save you thousands of dollars a year and pay for the wellness products and services you need to invest in your long-term health and vitality.

The entrepreneurial opportunity to convert households from sickness to wellness insurance is as great an opportunity as is the entire wellness business itself.

As exciting as some of these developments may seem today, they all pale in comparison to the coming new wellness products and services. As with automobiles in 1908 and personal computers in 1981, the best new products and services are still in the laboratory and will be coming onto the market in the next few years. Already today, with a simple swab on the inside of the mouth, it is possible to examine a person's DNA and predict his or her probability of developing certain diseases. Using this information, a wellness entrepreneur could target specific exercise, food, vitamin, and supplement-based therapies—adding years in both quantity and quality to the life of a customer.

Even this immediate opportunity pales in comparison to what is coming next—for we are getting close to cracking the genetic code for aging itself, and once we do, the wellness industry will be at the forefront in distributing the resultant products and services.

In any industry based on new technology, the greatest entrepreneurial fortunes are consistently made by those who distribute products and services rather than by those who make them. This is partly because, in any area of rapidly advancing technology, today's CD-ROM disc is tomorrow's eight-track tape, and only distributors unbeholden to a specific technology are able to quickly shift to new and more efficacious products. But it is mostly because of the following, as you learn in Chapter 8:

Today, 70 to 80 percent of the cost of most retail products is in distribution—which explains why the world's greatest individual fortunes between 1970 and 1999 were made by people focused on distributing things rather than on making things.

You also learn in Chapter 8 how the nature of the opportunity within distribution has recently changed—from the physical distribution of products themselves to the intellectual distribution of information about them. Sam Walton (Wal-Mart) became the richest man in the world in 1991 by physically distributing to customers what they already knew they wanted; however, by 1999 Jeff Bezos (Amazon) became *Time* magazine's Man-of-the-Year by teaching customers about products that they didn't know even existed. Nowhere is this more true than in the emerging wellness industry—an industry in which most of the costs of products and services lie in their distribution and in which the overwhelming majority of future customers do not yet know that the products even exist.

Suppose I told you in 1845 about the gold rush that would be coming to California in 1849. No matter how motivated you were to get rich and no matter how hard you worked once you got to California, you wouldn't have made a dime unless you knew where to stake your claim once you got there. In reality, very few of the wanna-be miners who spent their lives searching for gold actually made it. Many of the fortunes of the California gold rush were made by individuals using skills and relationships they had already developed elsewhere to provide products and services for the gold rush industry—men like Henry Wells (1805–1878) and George Fargo (1818–1881), who formed the Wells Fargo Company to provide banking and express transport services for miners.

Each of us has generic abilities, functional skills, and personal relationships based on what we have done in our lives until now. In Chapter 9 you learn where you should stake your claim to your share of this emerging $1 trillion wellness industry.

From providing services to distributing products to investing in wellness companies, there are numerous opportunities, but the best ones for each of us are the ones that best use the assets we already have.

The Five Distinct Characteristics of Pervasive Industries

The most successful investors and entrepreneurs know how to distinguish between a passing fad and a long-term trend—the five distinct characteristics of pervasive industries that I promised to tell you about. Let's take a look at these characteristics and analyze each one with respect to the emerging wellness industry.

Most people think of Henry Ford as the inventor of the automobile in 1908 with his Model T. However, cars were actually around for decades earlier as recreational toys for the wealthy.[3] Ford's real "invention" was to use various new technologies to produce, in his own words, a car "so low in price that no man making a good salary will be unable to own one."[4]

A similar story can be told about radios, televisions, restaurants, jet airplane travel, VCRs, fax machines, personal computers, e-mail, and many other inventions that have become ubiquitous and changed the way we live.

All of these products, like the automobile, started out as products for the rich. Then, once technology advanced to the point where they could be produced at a price affordable to working people, they became ubiquitous. Why did they become so popular? What else did these products or services have going for them in addition to being first enjoyed by the rich?

Each of these now-ubiquitous products or services had five distinct characteristics at the time they traveled from the classes to the masses.

Experienced entrepreneurs and investors look for all five of the following characteristics to be present before they launch a new mass-market business: (1) affordability, (2) legs, (3) continual consumption, (4) universal appeal, and (5) low consumption time.

---

1. *Affordability.* When the VCR first came out in 1976, every household wanted one, but few could afford the $1,500 price. As advancing technology lowered the price to less than $100, so many VCRs were sold that by 1990 there were 121 million VCRs in 110 million U.S. households. In some cases, such as with the automobile or single-family homes, rapidly advancing technology couldn't make them cheap enough to be affordable—but then another new industry, consumer finance, emerged to spread out the cost on an affordable monthly basis.

2. *Legs.* No amount of marketing will make a product or service ubiquitous unless it has legs—the ability to walk off the shelf without promotion once a critical mass of people own it. Cars, televisions, and PCs are all products that consumers immediately want once they see them being enjoyed by others. Marketing graveyards are filled with products that stopped selling the minute their promotion had stopped.

3. *Continual consumption.* It costs more than $100 today in promotion and advertising expenses to get consumers to try a new product, and that's just to see if they like it. If they do like it, to succeed it must be part of a business with products or services that they will continue to purchase. With television or radio, continual use leads to more advertising sales, which leads to more shows, which leads to more televisions and radios. While a consumer might purchase a VCR for $100 only once every five years, each VCR creates hundreds of dollars in annual sales and rentals of prerecorded tapes. Once people buy a new PC, they typically then want a new printer, a better monitor, a faster Internet connection, and so on. Ubiquitous products must be continually consumed in order to succeed.

4. *Universal appeal.* In order to become a mass-market business that changes the way in which we live, especially with the high cost today of customer education, the product or service must be one wanted by virtually everyone who learns about it. Virtually everyone today wants a car, a radio, or a PC—but not everyone wants a kayak, a bicycle, or a luxury cruise. However, just because a business has universal appeal doesn't mean that there is such a thing as a universal product—each consumer has different needs that must be served within the same product family. Henry Ford initially made his Model T affordable by making a single universal model, often boasting that he would sell you a car "in any color you want, so long as it's black." Yet Ford lost out in the 1920s to General Motors when GM appealed to the Model T owner who wanted to trade up to a higher-quality model with a wide choice of colors and with annual model changes to stimulate recurring demand.

5. *Low consumption time.* This is the greatest challenge today for new products and services seeking to become ubiquitous—busy consumers must have time to enjoy them. At the time they became widespread, most of today's ubiquitous products, in addition to being enjoyable, actually saved the consumer time. The automobile and jet plane got them there faster, the VCR let them watch a movie in less time than it took to go to the theater (or gave them more time with their families while they watched their favorite show over dinner), and the PC produced finished letters in a fraction of the time it took using a typewriter.

Wellness Is a Pervasive Industry
That Won't Go Away

Until recently, many wellness products and services were available only to the rich. I first became aware that such products and services existed when we built our family beach house in Pacific Palisades, California, and I noticed how my wealthy and celebrity neighbors approached the subject of food and health. After I became a wellness consumer, I found it difficult to obtain many of the products and services I wanted when I traveled outside of my upscale community—from restaurants serving healthy food to exercise facilities at hotels.

Today things are beginning to change. Every day more restaurants serve healthy food, new exercise facilities open, and more vitamins and supplements are being touted in mainstream advertising. But have things changed enough for the wellness industry to be ready to jump from the classes to the masses? To answer that question, let's take a closer look at the five characteristics of ubiquitous products and how the wellness industry relates to each of them.

First, are wellness products and services affordable? It used to be that the only way to get fresh, healthy food was to make it yourself. Restaurants served either expensive, heavy cuisine or prepackaged processed food. Today, healthy food is available not only in health-food restaurants, but in most eating establishments, as they add affordable, healthy alternatives to their menus. As we examine later in more detail, a similar lowering of prices is occurring in other wellness areas: Personal trainers now work by the hour for dozens rather than for only one celebrity, and quality vitamins and supplements are now readily available without having to grow or mix them up yourself. Moreover, as we discuss in Chapter 7, when it comes to making wellness affordable, new health insurance plans are emerging that will pay for wellness expenses, if for no other reason than to save money on sickness expenses.

Second, do wellness industry products have legs to "walk off the shelf on their own" without continued promotion? Every time successful wellness consumers mention their age, adeptly perform some physical activity, or lose weight, their friends and associates ask what they are doing to look so young, become so strong, or get into such good shape. Invariably, their response leads to the purchase of a similar item by the person asking the question.

Wellness industry products and services have perhaps the strongest legs of any product or service, as people

**immediately notice when someone has a wellness experi-
ence and are anxious to duplicate their results.**

Third, are wellness industry products and services continually
consumed? By their very nature, vitamins, exercise, food, and
other wellness products and services are perhaps the most continually consumed products and services in our economy. When wellness consumers find something that works for them, they typically
become fanatic consumers of that product or service and become
open to trying other wellness items. For example, once people start
exercising to lose weight, they often start taking dietary supplements and seeking out healthier cuisine.

Fourth, do wellness products and services have universal appeal?
Every human being, no matter how healthy or fit, wants to be even
healthier and more fit. This is partly because there is no limit to
how well and strong we can feel, but mostly because only the wellness industry offers solutions to the universal problem of human
aging rather than just telling aging consumers to blindly accept
their deteriorating physical condition.

Last, and perhaps most important in assessing both the short-
and long-term prospects for the wellness industry, do consumers
have available the time it takes to consume most wellness products
and services? The answer to this question bodes well for our entire
economy as well as for the wellness industry.

As explained in Chapter 2, the growth of our modern economy
depends on consumers spending their increasing disposable
income on luxury goods that soon become necessities—often on
new products and services that didn't exist when they were born.
However, a close examination of some of these new products and
services yields a paradox that could limit this growth in the future.

Most new luxury products, from Harley-Davidson motorcycles
to garden tractors, have one major drawback: They take time to
enjoy. This is one of the great paradoxes of modern life. Each
year, consumers seem to have more and more disposable income
but less and less time to enjoy it. In contrast to the "idle rich" and
"working poor" stereotypes of the past, disposable income today is
inversely proportional to leisure time for almost every class level.
When you asked people years ago why they hadn't bought a particular new item, a typical response might have been that they
couldn't afford it. Today, a more likely response might be that they
haven't had time to play with the new item they bought a week or
month ago.

Moreover, an increasing amount of the growth in consumer demand today is for entertainment and services rather than for physical products. These time-consuming purchases, ranging from massages to luxury cruises to opera tickets, have their own limitation on demand—the 24-hour day and the 365-day year. Some consumers report that their main time constraint today comes from other leisure activities rather than from their work.

Our modern economy could grind to a halt because of such a nonmonetary limit to consumer demand—unless, of course, technology could come up with products and services desired by consumers that do not take time to enjoy.

Wellness products and services represent perhaps the only sector of consumer spending that does not take time to enjoy. Money spent to make a person feel stronger, smile better, look younger, or feel healthier yield rewards that are enjoyed every moment of every day—on the job, at home, and at every moment in between.

It is clear that wellness is about to change our lives as much as did the automobile or the personal computer. Before I explain how you, the entrepreneur, can benefit from this pervasive and eternal industry with tremendous growth potential, let's examine how the wellness industry got started and how pervasive it is about to become.

CHAPTER I

Why We Need a Revolution

First, let's check out the definition:
rev·o·lu·tion[1]
I *a: a sudden, radical, or complete change*
   b: a fundamental change in political organization
   c: activity or movement designed to effect fundamental changes in the socioeconomic situation
   d: a fundamental change in the way of thinking about or visualizing something : a change of paradigm <the Copernican revolution>
   e: a changeover in use or preference esp. in technology <the computer revolution> <the foreign car revolution>

The seventeenth-century English writer John Milton saw revolution as the right of society to defend itself against abusive tyrants—creating a new order that reflected the needs of the people. To Milton, revolution was the means of accomplishing freedom.[2]

The eighteenth-century German philosopher Immanuel Kant believed in revolution as a force for the advancement of humankind—a "natural" step in the realization of a higher ethical foundation for society.[3]

The nineteenth-century German philosopher G. W. F. Hegel saw revolutions as the fulfillment of human destiny, and he saw revolutionary leaders as necessary to instigate and implement reforms.[4]

These insights aptly apply to the wellness revolution.

Entrepreneurs and revolutionaries are really the same kinds of people born into different circumstances. Both see the status quo in need of change, and both

are willing to take the risks, and reap the rewards, of changing it.

The emerging wellness industry is as much a reaction to the tyranny of the sickness and the food industries as it is to every person's desire for the freedom wellness offers. Wellness is the next natural step forward in our destiny and in the advancement of humankind. By extending your years of strength and wellness, you can accomplish those things you want to accomplish.

The revolutionary leaders in wellness are the entrepreneurs who grow and procreate wellness, the inventors who instigate wellness services and products, and the practitioners and distributors who carry the wellness message throughout society. Take your pick of how you want to be a leader of this new industry.

Revolutions and entrepreneurial journeys often begin with an epiphany—an illuminating discovery by an individual that typically sets him or her out on a quest. For everyone, this trigger will be different. For you, it could be what you learn from this book, or it could be a sickness experience—your own or that of a loved one—that could have been prevented. My epiphany occurred during a speech I was giving in 1996.

How Wellness Became My Cause

When I was growing up in the 1950s, economic issues seemed to dominate 95 percent of our waking lives. My father left for work at 5:30 A.M. and returned home after dinner, just as my mother was putting my brother and me to bed. He did this six days a week. All our neighbors and relatives lived a similar existence, except those unlucky enough to be out of work. And, although everyone talked mostly about economic issues (how to make money, where to find work, etc.), no one seemed to have solutions for how to achieve economic success. This is why I became an economist, to find these solutions—solutions to what then seemed to be the most important problems facing my society.[5]

Twenty-five years later, while giving a speech in the Midwest, I realized that I was now in the wrong profession.

It was Saturday, September 7, 1996, at the RCA Dome in Indianapolis. I was getting ready to go onstage as the keynote speaker before 45,000 people to discuss my latest book, *God Wants You to Be Rich*. My speaking fee had just been handed to me in a sealed envelope—more money for a 45-minute speech than I used to make in a full year when I graduated from Wharton and started working at Citibank.

I should have been elated. But instead I felt guilty. As I watched the audience file into the stadium and began my speech, I felt as if I were about to rip them off.

Like much of America, half of the audience was unhealthy and overweight, a direct consequence of diet and lifestyle evidenced by the fatigued look on their faces and the size of their waistlines. Nothing I was about to say about economics was going to improve the quality of their lives until they first learned how to care for their bodies.

A strange urge seized me to scrap my prepared speech and tell my audience that good health was more important than any riches they might acquire, but I chickened out. I didn't want to offend my hosts. And truthfully, I didn't know back then what actions would allow most people to take control of their health.

On the flight home early the next morning I began to wrestle with this question: Why would intelligent people spend time and money to improve their lives in every area *except* the one in which they most obviously needed improvement? And, more significant, what should a person who is unhealthy and overweight do to begin taking control of their life?

Why We Need a Revolution: Two Nations Divided by Great Want[6]

I arrived in Los Angeles around 10 A.M. that Sunday morning and rushed to Pacific Palisades to meet the contractor who was renovating our family beach house. As we stood outside discussing the construction, neighbors jogged or biked by on their way to the beach. I was struck by how fit and healthy everyone appeared. Compared to some of the people I had just seen in Indianapolis, these neighbors seemed to be inhabitants of a different planet.

That week, as I began the research that led to this book, I became excited about why an economist needed to write about health and weight.

I quickly discovered that the major reason so many people are unhealthy and obese has more to do with economics than with biology.

> **Incredibly powerful economic forces are preventing people from taking control of their health and actually *encouraging* them to gain weight—forces so powerful that nothing short of a revolution will be able to stop them.**

For many individuals, it may be impossible to take control of their health until they first understand the $1 trillion food and $1.5 trillion medical industries that represent a quarter of our national economy.

I discovered that the effects of obesity and poor health go far beyond a person's mere appearance. In our new millennium we have replaced racial and gender discrimination with a new kind of discrimination based on a person's weight and appearance. Whereas in the past poverty was associated with thinness and obesity with wealth, most people who are overweight today occupy the lower rungs of the economic ladder. *Rich fat man* has become an oxymoron, and *poor* and *fat* have become synonymous.

Incredibly, despite the fact that we are enjoying the greatest economic prosperity ever known to humankind, 61 percent of the U.S. population is overweight, and a staggering 27 percent are clinically obese. Both of these figures increased 10 percent in just five years (from 1994 to 1999), and obesity has almost doubled since the 1970s.[7]

Weight and appearance now define social and economic opportunities just as family name and birth did in the nineteenth century. When a person is fat—not just 15 pounds overweight, but clinically obese—it is hard to find a job, a relationship, or the energy to stay on top of the everyday demands of even a simple life.

Even most people of normal weight are unhealthy, although they often don't know it. Modern medicine tells them to accept headaches, stomach distress, body pain, fatigue, arthritis, and thousands of other common ailments as inevitable symptoms that afflict an aging population. Yet these ailments, like being overweight and obesity, are the direct result of a terrible diet.

How Economics Perpetuates Obesity and Malnutrition

Economics is largely to blame for this state of affairs. A powerful trillion dollar food industry bombards us with messages calculated to make us eat more and more of the worst possible food.

Understanding how the food industry works today is critically important for entrepreneurs wanting to lead and/or participate in the wellness revolution.

Packaged food companies, such as General Foods and Procter & Gamble, employ some of the best and brightest minds to study customer psychology and demographics. In trying to decide what sorts of foods to sell us, they invariably apply one of the great unwritten laws of marketing: It is easier to sell more product to an existing customer than to sell that same product to a new customer. In other words, it is easier to influence a regular customer to eat four additional bags of potato chips per month than it is to persuade a new customer, who may never have tasted potato chips, to buy even one bag of this exotic new substance.

Most processed food sales, products such as Hostess Twinkies, Oreo cookies, and McDonald's Happy Meals,[8] are governed by what those in the business call a "potato chip marketing equation." According to this law, more than 90 percent of product sales are made to less than 10 percent of their customers. In the case of processed foods, that coveted 10 percent consists largely of people weighing more than 200 pounds and earning less than $25,000 per year. The targeting of overweight customers is especially lucrative since these unfortunate individuals typically consume twice the amount per serving as a person of normal weight.

Each company studies its 10 percent, known as the *target market,* like rats in a laboratory. Customer surveys reveal their likes, dislikes, hopes, dreams, heroes, and desires. High-consumption customers are recruited to take part in focus groups, where they are asked to sample new products, view advertising, and offer opinions.

No expense is spared to hit every psychological button that matters to the target market. If people in that market like a particular actor or singer, that very celebrity will soon appear on radio or television, praising the product. If a certain look, feel, or lifestyle appeals to people in that market, legions of stylists and designers will descend on the studio to simulate it. Like a deer caught in the telescopic sight of a hunter at close range, the target never has a chance.

At times, the ruthlessness of the process troubles the consciences of the $200,000-per-year marketing executives in charge of it. Some actually refuse to attend their own focus groups. Rather than confront their future victims in person, they prefer to review transcripts in the safety of their offices. Imagine the table talk in the homes of such executives. "Today, I met ten 200-pound women who barely had the energy to participate in the group," they might report to their families over dinner. "If my team can get each of them up to 210 pounds by April by increasing their consumption of our potato chips, we'll make our first-quarter sales numbers and I'll get the bonus we need to take that vacation in Barbados."

This executive is probably eating a healthy meal, even as he speaks these words.

One of the great scandals of the junk-food culture is the extent to which its most enthusiastic promoters personally avoid the very products they are pushing. Moreover, many of the emotional and medical challenges some people face today, from controlling one's temper to depression to cancer, are as much products of these junk-food companies as are frozen pizza and low-fat cookies.

These food companies do something even worse than targeting lower-income, unhealthy, overweight consumers for their products. Once the target actually tries the product and becomes a customer, company chemists ensure they will never be satisfied with eating just a healthy amount of it.

Say, for example, I give you an apple, a banana, a stalk of asparagus, or almost any food in its natural state. After eating two or three apples or bananas, your body begins craving a different type of food as the pleasure you feel in your taste buds lessens with each bite. But if I give you a chocolate bar, a McDonald's french fry, a can of cola, or almost any other item of processed food, you almost always crave more and more of the same item because the chemical flavorings have been altered to ensure that "nobody can eat just one" of them. This chemical alteration causes great over-consumption, promoting obesity and destroying the natural tendency of our taste buds to seek variety in what we eat.[9]

The human body requires a daily intake of 13 essential vitamins,[10] most of which the body cannot manufacture on its own. These vitamins, along with certain minerals, are necessary to sustain the millions of chemical reactions our bodies perform each day. Eating a variety of fresh fruits and vegetables throughout the day gives us all of what we need, and our bodies are naturally programmed to seek out the different types of natural foods we require. But, the majority of Americans are not getting the minimal amount of these vitamins and minerals that their bodies require because of the chemical alteration of the processed and fast foods they consume.[11]

Over the short term, these deficiencies manifest themselves as mood swings, lack of energy, joint pain, failing eyesight, hearing loss, and thousands of other ailments that medical science tells us to accept with advancing age. Over the long term, these deficiencies cause major illnesses like cancer and heart disease.

In the twentieth century, U.S. tobacco companies altered the chemical composition of their products to increase consumption—creating lifelong customers by getting children addicted to specific brands of processed tobacco. Recent legislation has forced Big Tobacco to curb some of these activities when it comes to promoting cigarettes, but they are not letting their acquired expertise go to waste—they have been purchasing the major brands of addictive processed foods. In 2001, Philip Morris, the world's largest tobacco company, purchased some of the most popular children's processed-food brands, including Oreo cookies, Ritz crackers, and Life Savers candies.[12] This makes Philip Morris, which produces everything from Oscar Mayer bacon to Post cereals to Philadelphia cream cheese, the world's second largest food company after Nestlé, Inc.[13]

How Economics Perpetuates Sickness

As my research led me to the medical industry, I encountered large multinational companies whose nefarious practices made those of the food companies pale by comparison. It quickly became apparent to me why an economist needed to write about obtaining good medical care along with how to obtain food for a healthy lifestyle.

Understanding how the medical (i.e., "sickness") industry works today is critically important for entrepreneurs wanting to lead and/or participate in the wellness revolution.

When patients go to see a physician, they believe they are receiving a prescription for the best drug or treatment available for their specific ailment. Not likely.

Just as obese consumers are the target market of the food companies, physicians are the target market of the medical and pharmaceutical companies. Patients receive the drug or treatment that is most profitable for the supplier of the treatment, the health insurance company, and, in some cases, even the individual physician. This may or may not represent the best medical treatment available. In the United States, doctors typically prescribe completely different treatments for the same ailment depending on which drug company has the dominant market share in their region.

Medical technology and pharmaceuticals change so fast today that what physicians learn in medical school is often obsolete by the time they graduate. In practice, doctors learn about new drugs and treatments from a special type of salesperson, called a *detail person* in the medical industry. Detail person is actually a euphemism for "a very attractive, highly paid young person of the opposite sex." Detail people lavishly hand out free samples and handsomely reward physicians and their staff in proportion to the amount of prescriptions they write for their company's product. Physicians and their families receive expensive dinners, cruises, and tax-free trips to resorts, where they "learn" more about such products at taxpayers' expense.

Although the ethical (prescription) pharmaceutical companies around the world justify the very high prices of their drugs by citing the high cost of research and development, drug companies actually spend much more money marketing drugs than they do on research and development. Moreover, a considerable amount of the research and development that leads to the creation of new drugs is funded by the federal government through grants to nonprofit entities such as research labs at universities and medical schools and the National Institutes of Health.

When your wellness customers pay staggering prices for prescription drugs, they are also paying for the marketing campaign that successfully induced the doctor to check the box on the prescription form that reads "DAW"—*dispense as written,* meaning the prescription will be the more expensive name brand rather than the cheaper generic that is available for about 90 percent of all prescriptions. Drug company profits often come from outdated name-brand drugs taken on an ongoing basis by patients prescribed years before when they first developed the condition. Prescription drug companies limit informing customers and physicians of improved products in cases where they could lose existing customers to competitive brands when patients visit their doctors for revised prescriptions. Generic drugs are sometimes safer or better than the brand-name products they replace because they have been prescribed more recently and thus contain improved formulas.

There are enormous business opportunities in educating consumers about the prescription drugs they are already taking: how to obtain alternative prescription drugs that are more effective, less expensive, have fewer side effects, or all three.

In recent years the pharmaceutical companies have hired the same advertising firms as the food companies and have begun direct image-based advertising to consumers. In these advertisements for prescription-only items that may be legally dispensed only on the written recommendation of a doctor, the patient is *directly* urged to demand the product and told to "ask your doctor" for a DAW prescription—with the knowledge that if the doctor refuses to write the prescription, the presold patient will simply find another doctor who will.

Sadly, most physicians have become "technology dispensers" for the products and services of the large multinational medical companies—companies that always seem to tip the scale between profits and patients in favor of profits.

These practices have pushed the price for U.S. drugs so high that patients cannot afford to fill approximately 22 percent of the prescriptions written each year. Prescription drugs now represent the single largest monthly expense for most over-65 U.S. citizens, approximately $300 per month, and millions of people are forced to make the terrible choice between purchasing food or medicine. Medicare pays for doctor visits but generally does not pay for prescriptions.[14]

This and hundreds of other examples are symptoms of the two underlying problems with medical care in the developed world today—both of which are almost entirely economic rather than scientific.

---

1. **It is more profitable for medical suppliers to produce products consumers use for the rest of their lives than to make products that a consumer might use only once. Invariably, *this means spending research and development funds on products that treat the symptoms of diseases rather than the causes or the cures.***

2. **The third parties paying for most medical treatments—insurance companies and, ultimately, employers—do not have a long-term financial stake in the health of their employees. Individuals bear little or no direct responsibility for their medical expenses, and almost all expenses to prevent illness (e.g., exercise, vitamins, nutritional supplements) are disallowed for reimbursement.**

As I discuss in Chapter 6, the American health insurance system is really a disguised payment and discounting mechanism designed to extract the most out of those who can often afford the least.

No Solution in Sight

The more I pursued my research, the more distressed I became that there might not be a solution to this plague of obesity and ill health that afflicted the majority of our population.

Although there was obviously no direct conspiracy between the $1 trillion food industry (which causes most of the problems) and the $1.5 trillion medical industry (that treats just enough of the symptoms to get the target consumers back to work and consumption), the economic effect was the same as if these two industries were conspiring against the American consumer in the most sinister fashion.

On a microeconomic level, each time consumers got real information that could help them take control of their health, the food and medical industries, acting in their own economic self-interest, manipulated this information against them.

For example, prior to 1990, consumers were told that eating too many calories caused obesity. When the public became aware that the amount of fat in their diets was a major cause of obesity, the food industry reacted with enticing low- and nonfat foods, advertising that consumers could now eat as much as they want without gaining weight. The food industry went so far as to repackage many products that *never* had fat in them, like sugarcoated candies and pretzels, to suggest that they had created new, healthy, nonfat versions of these products.

What their massive advertising didn't tell consumers was that these low- and nonfat products had extremely high levels of sugar and carbohydrates, which turn to fat once ingested into the body, not to mention more addictive chemicals that made them worse in the long run than the "fattening" products they replaced. Throughout the 1990s, obesity, as well as the sales of low- and nonfat foods, steadily increased.

On a macroeconomic level, it seemed as if there would be no escape.

When it comes to attempting to control our federal, state, and local governments, the food and medical companies follow their own Golden Rule: He with the gold makes the rules.

Lobbyists for the food industries have created mandatory school lunch and milk programs that hook children on addictive processed foods. Pharmaceutical companies have helped create government-sponsored programs that put millions of children on dangerous drugs to combat the effects of their terrible diets. In some cases, such as when Ritalin is used to control hyperactive children, parents are threatened with losing custody of their own children if they refuse to force them to take such drugs for alleged disorders.[15]

The U.S. Food and Drug Administration, originally designed to protect consumers from unhealthy products, now often protects the very companies it is supposed to regulate by keeping out competition and prolonging the economic life of the drug companies' government-sanctioned patents.

Typically the news media, acting in its own self-interest for publicity and ratings, leads society in exposing such heinous activities. But in this case the media is all too often ineffective. As consumers themselves, the members of the media are subject to the same disinformation and thus largely unaware of the problem. Moreover, a major funding source for the media—especially network television advertising revenue—comes from food and drug companies.

For example, the detrimental health effect of drinking cow milk has been widely known for years in the medical community but has rarely been covered by the media, which reaps fortunes each year running ads for the American Dairy Association. Imagine the hypocrisy of celebrities who sport milk mustaches in paid advertisements but themselves drink only soy-based milk products.

The scandal of these celebrities goes even deeper than endorsing products that they would never consume themselves. Leading actors, singers, and models make literally millions of dollars each year on their looks. Most of them lean toward vegetarian diets lacking in processed and addictive fast foods. Yet these societal role models for fitness and beauty are cautioned by their managers not to let their elite dining habits become known to the press, lest they be boycotted by television producers in an industry where most of the revenue comes from advertisements for processed foods and fast-food restaurants.

Despite the fact that many young people admire them for more than just their professional talents, celebrities today have learned not to take positions on controversial issues that could affect their careers. As one Hollywood manager once told me, no one wants to become the "Jane Fonda of healthy eating"—referring to the talented actress who was boycotted by some theatergoers in the 1970s because of her controversial left-wing political views.*

In a free-enterprise system, when people want something that can't be provided by profit-seeking entities, they typically turn to government ("the provider of last resort") for assistance. This worked well in the 1970s, when consumers demanded that government restrict the actions of businesses that were destroying the environment.

But in this case, government seems helpless. Like the media, our elected officials are consumers who are subject to the same disinformation and thus unaware of the health issues. Take a look at the waistlines and the diets of most politicians if you want to know what they think of food and health! Our politicians have been effectively controlled by the food and drug companies for so long that our government is now a large part of the problem rather than poised to be part of a solution.

It seems incredible to me that although we won the cold war and democratic ideals are more universally cherished than ever before in history, we also must admit that half of our people have become personally enslaved to a lifestyle that limits their daily lives, dreams, and happiness as much as would any authoritative government or dictatorship.

The thousands of companies that comprise the $1 trillion U.S. food industry and the $1.5 trillion U.S. medical industry are governed by universal laws of economics that cause them to act in concert as though they were part of a vast nefarious conspiracy.

While I was conducting most of my research, between 1996 and 2000, the percent of the U.S. population who are overweight and obese increased by an additional 10 percent, to 27 percent obese

*One notable exception is the talented Alicia Silverstone (born in 1976), star of *Clueless* (1995), *Batman & Robin* (1997), and 13 other major films. Although there are many famous vegetarian actors (Brad Pitt, Kim Basinger, Richard Gere, Alec Baldwin, Drew Barrymore, Paul Newman, Liv Tyler, William Shatner, David Duchovny, Daryl Hannah, Dustin Hoffman), Ms. Silverstone, to the detriment of her career, is one who consistently uses her celebrity status against the dairy and processed food lobbies in trying to teach healthy eating to her young fans.

and 61 percent overweight, and medical costs rose from $1.0 to $1.5 trillion. It became depressing to me to think of these numbers in terms of human suffering—77 million Americans clinically obese and 184 million overweight and unhealthy because they lacked the resources, information, and motivation to safeguard their most precious asset: their wellness.

It seemed only a question of time before virtually everyone in the United States would be overweight, and more than half of the population would be obese and unhealthy. I decided to take a closer look at the healthy, nonoverweight 39 percent of the U.S. population to see how much time we had left.

When I began examining the 39 percent of our population that was not overweight, I stumbled across the seeds of the revolution about to take place.

An Economic Solution to an Economic Problem

When I looked closer at the nonoverweight 39 percent of the population, I found a growing group of millions of Americans who are eating and living healthier than ever before in history. This wellness-based group includes most of the movers and shakers in our society as well as celebrities who literally make their living on how they look. This group has quietly embraced a revolutionary new approach—to diet, to exercise, to vitamins, to nutritional supplements, to medical care, and, most important, to the aging process itself.

In ancient Greece, physical strength, health, and beauty were just as central to one's *arete,* or "excellence," as were creative talents, intellect, industriousness, or moral character. Indeed, outward beauty was believed to reflect the beauty within. For obvious reasons, the people today most dedicated to *arete* are the "professionally beautiful," those people who economically depend on maintaining their health and appearance. Movie stars, talk show hosts, entertainment professionals, and many leading business executives inhabit a secret world in which the physical fundamentals of life (food, exercise, vitamins, nutritional supplements, medical care, and aging) are seen from a perspective radically different than that of most human beings.

To the wellness elite, each act of apparent pain or denial, from sessions with their personal trainers to

> navigating through menus at exclusive restaurants, is a positive, almost religious experience.

These people focus on how they will feel hours later *because* of each laborious exercise, or they focus on how much stronger they will feel that evening *because* of what they are not eating for lunch or dinner. Thus, what may seem painful to others becomes to them a euphoric experience with its own almost immediate rewards.

> At first I thought that this revolutionary way of forward thinking about the impact of food on your health might be only a Hollywood or West Los Angeles phenomenon. But further research quickly showed this to be a world-wide movement with revolutionaries throughout the globe.

The reason is simple. Everyone, no matter how healthy or fit, wants to be even healthier and more fit. Everyone wants to look and feel more youthful. However, until recently, there was very little anyone could do to obtain efficacious wellness services and products. Until now, the few wellness products and services available were affordable only by the very rich. Now that they are becoming widely available and affordable, entrepreneurs are rushing in to provide wellness products and services to a delighted public—creating an economic solution to what is essentially an economic problem.

When I was growing up, mealtime conversation seemed to center around personal economic issues. Today, mealtime conversation is becoming more and more centered around wellness issues—which foods to eat, which supplements to take, how to exercise, and how to avoid getting sick and to limit the effects of age. This is only the beginning of a huge new wave of wellness.

The First $200 Billion

When I began the research that led to this book, I had two objectives in mind: (1) exposing the nefarious practices of the food and medical industries and (2) teaching people the correct choices to make in order to be healthy and obtain good medical care. Explaining a new business opportunity that would allow people to make money was not one of my objectives.

The more my research progressed into obesity and sickness, the more upset I became with the status quo. The more upset I became, the more I felt that nothing short of a revolution was needed in the way we think about health, eating, and the practice of medicine. I could see that this revolution might eventually take place, but the most surprising part of my initial research was how far the revolution had already progressed.

The nascent wellness industry today encompasses some of the following businesses:

Vitamins

Nutritional supplements

Cosmetic plastic surgery

Voluntary eye surgery (LASIK™, radial keratotomy)

Cosmetic dermatology

Genetic engineering (sex selection and fertility enhancement)

Cosmetic and reconstructive dentistry (caps, implants)

Preventative medicine

Medical Savings Accounts

High-deductible (wellness) health insurance

Fitness clubs (including trainers)

Fitness and athletic equipment

Voluntary pharmacy: Viagra (for impotence), Rogaine (for hair growth)

Health food products

Health food restaurants

Weight loss products

Although most of these businesses did not exist at an economically significant level just two or three decades ago, by 2000 they already totaled approximately $200 billion in annual sales, about half the amount spent to purchase U.S. automobiles.[16]

When I saw that wellness had already achieved sales of this magnitude, I knew that the wellness industry had already jumped far beyond being products for only the wealthy or the "professionally beautiful." I began to focus on which segments of our society were consuming most of this $200 billion and on the potential demand for future consumption.

It became apparent that wellness would reach sales of $1 trillion or more over the next 10 years and that wellness would be the industry in which the greatest fortunes of the new century would be created—fortunes eclipsing even those of the Internet billionaires of the late 1990s.

However, before we examine in the next chapter why this is so and where the wellness industry is headed, it is important to understand where the wellness industry has been and why the concept of wellness has come so late to our food and medical industries. The wellness industry really began when entrepreneurs were legally allowed to explain the benefits of their products and services in the late 1970s.

Our wellness industry today exists in large part thanks to a historic battle won in the 1970s by the greatest wellness revolutionary of our time: the late J. I. Rodale, founder of *Prevention* magazine and Rodale Press (*Men's Health, Runners World*).

How Rodale Paved the Way for the Wellness Revolution

In 1954, entrepreneur and author J. I. Rodale had a lot to lose. His company, Rodale Press, was just getting his fledgling *Prevention* magazine off the ground. *Prevention* was dedicated to teaching readers how to prevent disease versus just treating the symptoms of disease.

Rodale had concluded that eating large quantities of red meat and dairy products dramatically increased the risk of heart disease and that physical activity actually decreased the risk of having a heart attack. This was at a time when the U.S. government was spending millions encouraging Americans to eat more red meat and dairy products at every meal, three meals a day. Doctors were telling patients with heart disease to reduce or eliminate physical activity entirely. No wonder heart disease was the leading cause of death in the United States!

Rodale wrote about his new findings in two books: *How to Eat for a Healthy Heart* and *This Pace Is Not Killing Us*. He was convinced that this information could save millions of lives. But, like many writers in the 1950s, he was not on an approved list drawn up by Senator Joseph McCarthy's House Un-American Activities Committee, so his publisher refused to publish his new books.

This situation forced Rodale to print the books himself and try to sell them through bookstores along with his other Rodale publications. But many booksellers refused to distribute his new books. Undaunted and convinced that the public needed this information as soon as possible, Rodale took full-page advertisements in national publications and offered his new books via mail order at a special price.

The Federal Trade Commission ordered Rodale to stop advertising and selling the books, claiming that the medical advice given in his books was unsubstantiated. The FTC had successfully taken similar action against other publishers who had promulgated then-unconventional medical advice.[17]

Rodale was furious! He felt that the FTC action was a blatant violation of the First Amendment guaranteeing freedom of the press.

The FTC scheduled hearings in 1955 at which Rodale was ordered to present proof that people who purchased the books and followed their advice would, indeed, reduce their risk of heart disease. Rodale refused to attend, claiming that the First Amendment gave him the right to publish any information he wanted, regardless of its efficacy.[18]

At these hearings, the nation's most respected medical professionals testified that (1) there was no correlation between heart disease and eating large quantities of red meat and dairy products and (2) following Rodale's advice on increasing physical activity to avoid heart disease could be injurious, if not fatal. The FTC ordered Rodale to "cease and desist" from claiming, directly or indirectly, that readers of any of his publications would improve their health.[19]

Rodale appealed the case, mainly on the grounds that the First Amendment prohibited the FTC from regulating information-based products. His legal battles with the federal government dragged on for almost two decades, at times putting his entire personal net worth at risk. Over the years, the FTC, fearing that they would lose their case on constitutional grounds, attempted to settle with Rodale. But despite financial hardship, Rodale refused to back down unless the FTC agreed to acknowledge that the First Amendment prohibited them from regulating books and printed material.

In the later years of the case, Rodale's lawyers introduced new

testimony from some of the same leading medical experts that the
government originally used at the initial FTC hearings almost 20
years earlier. One by one, these "experts" refuted their original testimony, claiming they "didn't know back then," and admitted that
many of Rodale's original claims had since become established
medical facts. Rodale felt that there could never be a better example
of what our Founding Fathers had in mind when they made freedom of the press the very first item in the Bill of Rights.

Then, in 1971, while describing his legal problems with the federal government on national television, J. I. Rodale dropped dead.
Until he actually stopped breathing and turned blue, everyone
watching *The Dick Cavett Show* thought Rodale was facetiously
faking a heart attack in order to make a point about his troubles
with the FTC.

The case never reached the Supreme Court.

**Soon after wellness pioneer J. I. Rodale passed away,
the U.S. government reversed its position, stating that
the FTC would no longer require advertisers of information-based products to establish the efficacy of their
claims. This policy change opened the door for the free
flow of wellness information, allowing the vitamin,
nutritional supplement, fitness, and alternative medicine industries to grow to their current level, laying the
foundation for the wellness revolution.**

Today *Prevention* magazine has 12 million readers, and Rodale
Press is the largest health-oriented publisher in the world, publishing over 100 new wellness titles each year that sell a combined 20
million copies per annum.

Why We Often Reject New Ideas

**One of the greatest challenges facing Rodale, and facing
many entrepreneurs like you today who base their businesses on a new technology, is human rejection of the
new or unknown, especially when the new technology
forces people to rethink established beliefs.**

Understanding the cause of this phenomenon, and how to sur-
mount it, is crucial for the entrepreneur seeking success.

The human quest for knowledge, in both religion and science, is really the quest for order in our lives. Once people believe they have found such order, they will often risk heaven and hell to preserve their beliefs, even in the face of irrefutable evidence to the contrary. For example, until roughly the fourth century B.C., it was commonly believed that the mysterious lights in the sky were gods wandering about the heavens. In fact, the word *planet* comes from the Greek word meaning "wanderer." This is how most people explained the disorder in their daily lives. The gods (planets) wandered about in the heavens, and their wanderings caused the crops to grow, the rain to fall, and the tragedies and joys of a disorderly human existence.

The Greek philosopher Aristotle refuted this belief. Aristotle believed that there was an order to things that people could understand and use to bring order to their lives—particularly in the area of understanding the seasons and their effect on agricultural production. In 340 B.C., Aristotle theorized that the planets and every other object in the heavens were not gods, but were simply spheres that revolved in fixed paths on a schedule around a stationary earth.

The Aristotelian geocentric view of the world, although wrong in its fundamental assumption that the earth, rather than the sun, was at the center of our solar system, became the bedrock of civilization for the next 1,800 years. Looking back, we can see that its endurance was hardly surprising, as it agreed with the evidence of one's senses. After all, from our vantage point on earth, it certainly looks as if everything revolves around us.

But the Aristotelian-Ptolemaic calendar was not accurate, because it incorrectly placed the earth at the center of the universe. Every 100 years or so it would snow in Rome in July, and the pope would have to set the calendar back about six months. This led to a great quest among astronomers to discover a working model of the universe that could more accurately track the months and predict the beginning of the seasons—the use of which could greatly increase agricultural and economic output.

It wasn't until the early sixteenth century that the Polish astronomer Nicolaus Copernicus succeeded in this quest. By manipulating mathematical equations, Copernicus determined that the sun was at the center of the solar system and that the heavenly bodies—including the earth—revolved around it. Fortunately for Copernicus, his *De Revolutionibus Orbium Coelestium* was not published until he was on his deathbed in 1543, and his heliocentric view of the universe did not become known for over half a century.

In 1609 the Italian mathematician and physicist Galileo Galilei began observing the heavens through his new invention, the telescope. He was able to see that the sun rather than the earth was at the center of our universe, and he wrote a treatise about Copernicus's theory in colloquial Italian, which could be read by the masses, rather than in the traditional Latin of academia. This treatise soon attracted widespread support for the heliocentric model of the universe.

The bulk of that support, however, came from outside the establishment. The reaction from inside was quite different. Galileo was bitterly attacked by both scholars and theologians, and in 1616 the Church commanded him, under penalty of death, never again to "hold, teach, or defend the Copernican system in any way whatsoever."

Nine years later, in 1623, Galileo's childhood friend Maffeo Barberini became Pope Urban VIII. Emboldened by his friendship with the pope, Galileo again began to write about the heliocentric theory. The reaction from the Church was swift. Galileo was forced to kneel in front of the Inquisition and recant his belief in the Copernican system. While his friendship with the pope probably saved him from being burned at the stake, Galileo was condemned to life in prison for having disobeyed the 1616 order. His works were placed on the pope's *Index of Prohibited Books,* and only in 1992 did the Roman Catholic Church formally reexamine the case and admit its mistake.

Looking back, it seems difficult to understand why the pope thought it was his duty, as God's emissary on earth, to so vigorously defend the geocentric model of the universe. After all, what does believing in Jesus Christ have to do with whether God put the earth or the sun at the center of our universe? Yet surprisingly, and perhaps on a different scale, most people today behave similarly in clinging to their established beliefs.

As children, people are typically taught beliefs about religion by their parents, then spend their adult lives looking for reinforcement of those beliefs—including outright rejection and avoidance of anything that might challenge them. When was the last time you visited a different church, synagogue, or mosque than the one you were brought up to believe in to see what they had to offer? When was the last time you read a book by someone you knew held political opinions opposite from yours?

The reason we do not embrace opposing views is that our human mind fears disorder—and automatically

avoids or rejects new ideas that challenge the existing order.*

A lawyer friend of mine who tries death-row cases believes that some trials are decided the very instant that the jury first sees the accused. Individual jurors, particularly in high-profile capital crime cases, are anxious to solve their own personal "disorder" problem of guilt or innocence as soon as possible. To do so, they sometimes make up their minds on first seeing the accused enter the court-room. Then, throughout the trial, they nod and listen attentively to evidence that supports their prejudicial decision, rolling their eyes when a conflicting view is being presented.

When presenting a new hypothesis that might challenge the status quo, it is important to be able to explain the history behind an established belief and to be able to explain where our society may have gone wrong when such a belief was first established.

Here's how most people developed incorrect views of many wellness treatments.

How Traditional Western Medicine Rejected Wellness

Throughout history, people, especially the very rich, have sought wellness. In every civilization from ancient Egypt to medieval Europe, alchemists believed that gold dissolved in *aqua regia* was the elixir of life, and they consumed fortunes trying to discover the correct formula.[20] In the sixteenth through nineteenth centuries, monarchs backed expeditions like those of Ponce de León to find the mythical Fountain of Youth.[21] While some of these quests proved fruitful in other areas (like the alchemists' discovery of chemistry or Ponce de León's discovery of Florida), they all failed miserably in their quest for wellness, and wellness practitioners were often characterized as charlatans.

Then, in the twentieth century, scientific discoveries linked disease

---

*This also explains why direct selling (person-to-person versus television-to-person or store-to-person) is often the best way to explain a new product or service that challenges an established belief. When most people are confronted with such a challenge, they simply change the channel or continue to walk down the aisle—something that politeness prevents when listening to a friend or acquaintance.

and aging to food and exercise. In 1908, Polish-born biochemist Casimir Funk discovered that there were four ammonia-based substances vital for life, which he called "vital amines" or "vitamins."[22] Studies of longshoremen and other laborious occupations showed that physical exercise was beneficial to overall health and to the avoidance of chronic disease. But for the most part, these and other now-accepted wellness discoveries were rejected by the Western medical community. Here's why.

Prior to the nineteenth century, doctors administered the few medicines that existed, and by trial and error observed which medicines cured which diseases. Medical knowledge was accumulated like this over centuries and occasionally diffused between cultures.[23]

But when a medicine or treatment worked, doctors didn't know *why* it worked. The underlying theories that explain infections, and the inoculations and antibiotics that these theories produced, had to await the widespread use of the compound optical microscope (which was invented at the beginning of the seventeenth century but didn't become ubiquitous until the late nineteenth century). The microscope led to the discovery of cells and bacteria and allowed scientists to actually see how they worked.

In the late nineteenth and early twentieth centuries, scientists became international heroes as they eliminated, one after another, the major diseases that had been the scourge of humankind (e.g., smallpox, tuberculosis, typhoid, polio).

Emboldened by this success, and partly to distinguish themselves from charlatans practicing magic more than medicine, Western medical science began arrogantly rejecting age-old treatments and cures whose function could not be scientifically explained by the then-current level of technology.

The basic unit in biology, the cell, is about 20 micrometers in diameter. It takes about 10,000 human cells to cover the head of a pin. For physical reasons, an optical microscope cannot resolve two points that are closer together than approximately one-half of the wavelength of the illuminating light—and an individual bacterial cell, for example, is approximately one-tenth the wavelength of visible light.[24]

Today we know that the critical biochemical functions performed by exercise, vitamins, minerals, and nutri-

tional supplements take place on a molecular versus a cellular level. And because each cell is composed of trillions of molecules, these functions cannot even be detected with an optical microscope.

Until the relatively recent invention of the electron microscope, which is still not as widespread as the optical microscope was in the 1800s, scientists were unable to study the molecular structure of cells and how they function.

This led most Western medical school training to virtually ignore, still to this day, the importance of nutrition and the effect of vitamins, minerals, and natural supplements.

Meanwhile, during the twentieth century, while Western medicine was ignoring the importance of diet and exercise in preventing disease and aging, the amount of exercise performed by individuals declined due to labor-saving devices in the home and to machines in the workplace. The quantity and variety of vitamins and minerals in our diets declined as food became more processed and less varied. And the percent of fat in our diets increased by 75 percent—from about 20 percent of our calories in 1910 to about 35 percent of our calories today. These and other factors contributed to the epidemic in obesity and ill health we have today in the United States, sowing the seeds for the wellness revolution that is about to take place.

The Wellness Revolution Is about More than Just Making Money

In the rest of this book we will examine the increasing size of the wellness industry and the thousands of fortunes that will be created through wellness.

As you read ahead and start to think about your place in this emerging industry, keep in mind that there is something even more important than your personal economic reward—your impact on the world in which we live.

Economically, we live in halcyon days that have far surpassed the wildest dreams of our forebears, who fought so hard and lost so

much to create what we have today. Yet due to our plague of obesity and ill health, we begin this millennium with more human
unhappiness than at any time in our history.

Fully 61 percent of Americans are trapped within their own
prison of being malnourished and overweight, and almost half of
those, about 27 percent, are clinically obese—overweight to a point
where they are hopeless and have no idea where to turn for help.

These Americans are malnourished to the point where they live
with constant headaches, body pain, stomach distress, heartburn,
fatigue, arthritis, and hundreds of other ailments—ailments that
medicine wrongly tells them to accept as symptoms of advancing
age. Medical companies sell them billions of dollars worth of products (e.g., aspirin, laxatives) that treat only their symptoms while
ignoring their cause. A similar situation exists in Western Europe,
Taiwan, and most other developed nations.

However, all of this is about to change, thanks to the wellness
revolution. Never before in history has a business opportunity had
the potential to have such an incredibly positive impact on the lives
of its customers.

Before Proceeding to the Next Chapter

Action Plan for Entrepreneurs, Investors, and Distributors

1. Make a list of 10 potential wellness businesses that interest you.

2. Assess how you could participate in each of areas:
   a. Entrepreneur
   b. Investor
   c. Distributor

3. Analyze each business area with respect to the five characteristics of pervasive industries (outlined in the Introduction).

4. Choose the three best areas for you to pursue based on your prior skills and experiences.

5. Analyze why each of these three areas of wellness business opportunity does or does not yet exist. For those that do exist, analyze your potential competition and the opportunity for growth in each area.

6. Rethink your choices of your three best areas of wellness business opportunity, and perhaps choose a different three based on your analysis thus far.

Now read Chapters 2 through 9, and at the end of each chapter, think about dropping and replacing any or all three of your chosen areas of wellness business opportunity.

CHAPTER 2

Understanding and Controlling the Demand for Wellness

The current boom in wellness products and services is being driven by another boom that occurred between 1946 and 1964—the baby boom—which represents about 28 percent of the U.S. population but accounts for about 50 percent of our $10 trillion economy. Boomers are just discovering the potential of the wellness industry to preserve what they hold dearest: their youth. But even this is only the beginning, thanks to the nature of demand in our modern economy, to our current economic expansion due to advancing technology, and to our unlimited propensity to consume more wellness products and services once we have had a positive wellness experience.

Practice What You Preach

Like many people of my generation, I barely knew what wellness was when I turned age 40 in 1994. Managing my health then used to consist only of skipping meals when I felt I was putting on weight—often with disastrous results.[1]

Since then, I have spent thousands of dollars a year, and part of each day, consuming wellness products and services. I choose my food based on how I will feel afterward rather than on my immediate sensory gratification. I take vitamins, minerals, and supplements on a daily basis. My family has a health insurance program that allows us $3,000 per year for wellness expenses and lets us put an additional $3,800 per year into an IRA-type Medical Savings Account for our future healthcare needs. I work out lifting weights twice a week, and depending on the weather, I mountain-bike, surf, or snowboard for one to two hours almost every day. When I first began writing this book, I thought that the U.S. market of individuals like me, who were already practicing wellness, might amount to a few billion dollars a year.

As noted earlier, I was very surprised to find out that wellness spending had already reached $200 billion a year by 2000. And I was even more surprised to discover that this $200 billion represented just the tip of the iceberg for the wellness industry over the next decade. Here's why.

The Baby Boom Generation Is the First Wellness Generation

The birth rate of American citizens increased dramatically after World War II. Between 1946 and 1964, approximately 78 million children were born in the United States. In contrast, in the same amount of years just prior to 1946, only 50 million births were recorded. And in the same amount of years immediately following 1964, despite a much larger population base, only 66 million births were recorded.

This huge bulge in the U.S. population is generally referred to as the *baby boom,* or the baby boom generation. We define it as a *boom* because birth rates rapidly declined after 1964; had this not occurred, the postwar birth rate increase would simply have represented a long-term trend rather than a distinct population group.

The significance of this fact cannot be overstated.

> In any society, there is a limit to the number of topics that can occupy public concern at a specific period in time. With a normally expanding population, these topics are typically dominated by the concerns and tastes of the younger members of the society, since there are simply more (and more) of them. However, the bulge in the U.S. population of those born between 1946 and 1964 has caused our topics of concern to be dominated by this group rather than by the concerns of the next generation.[2]

This phenomenon initially manifested itself in the late 1960s and early 1970s when certain oldies radio stations became more popular than contemporary ones—as the first baby boomers entering adulthood continued to listen to the music of their youth.

Beginning in the 1970s we saw boomers increasingly returning to the fashions of their youth in clothing, automobiles, housing, furniture, industrial design, and commercial architecture. A new word was coined to define this phenomenon, *retro,* which entered our vernacular (and our dictionary) in 1974.[3]

Now, as the baby boom generation (currently ages 38 to 56) is entering its most economically productive years, this phenomenon of catering to their concerns will accelerate even more. Their economic dominance will continue until sometime after 2010, when the first boomers turn 65 and their economic power and social influence begin to wane.

The economic impact of the baby boomers on wellness is even stronger than their numbers suggest—because this group is behaving differently than any prior generation. Boomers are refusing to passively accept the aging process.

A recent book by Cheryl Russell explains it best from a marketing perspective:

> One of the most important truths about boomers is that they are still the youth market. In their teens and twenties . . . boomers created the youth market. As they enter their forties and fifties . . . boomers are proving the youth market to be a state of mind rather than a stage of life. Most boomers still live in that state, refusing to adopt the attitudes and lifestyles of their parents. . . . Businesses savvy enough to determine what boomers want will catch a wave of consumer demand that will be the ride of a lifetime.[4]

Boomers are already responsible for the largest stock market rise in history, the housing boom, the rise of international airlines, the personal computer, the Internet, the sport utility vehicle—in short, boomers are responsible for roughly $5 trillion of our $10 trillion national economy. But, it is even more important to know which consumer products boomers are purchasing most. From the 2002 T-Bird convertible that looks like the 1956 model, to retro furniture and clothes, boomers flock to purchase products and services that remind them of their youth.

If baby boomers are spending all this money on things that simply remind them of when they were young, think of how much these boomers will soon spend on

> **wellness products and services that actually make them young or slow the effects of aging. It's easy to see why boomers are about to add an additional $1 trillion to our economy as they seek to preserve what they hold dearest.**

Moreover, most of our current $200 billion in wellness sales are to boomers born closer to 1946 rather than to those born closer to 1964. Over the next 10 years alone, boomers will increase their spending on existing wellness-based services from approximately $200 billion to $1 trillion or more. This growth will come partly from the demographic expansion of the market (age range of boomers shifting from ages 38 to 56 to ages 48 to 66) and partly from sales growth due to improvements in the efficacy of wellness-based products and services.

> **Hundreds if not thousands of better wellness-based products and services are coming out of the laboratory during the next 10 years. This list includes improved types of vitamins and minerals, new supplements like echinacea that ward off colds and diseases, and natural hormone and soy-based antiaging creams that truly retard wrinkles and impart youthful vitality to the cells they touch.**

And this fivefold increase is only the beginning. Just as boomers now set the pace for the desires of the next generation, from retro tastes in music to housing and independent lifestyles, boomers will set the pace for the wellness industry for generations to come.

> **By 2010, Generation X, those born between 1965 and 1982, will be entering their most productive and highest-spending years. This and subsequent generations will take the boomer-established proactive approach to wellness and aging as standard medical procedure.**

Moreover, as we examine in more detail in Chapter 7, the current sickness-based health insurance system is being replaced for many Americans by a new wellness-based system that will pay for weight reduction, exercise plans, nutritional advice, vitamins, minerals, smoking cessation, and hundreds of other wellness-related or preventative treatments.

But the main reason that wellness sales are growing so fast is because of what happens once consumers of any age have their first wellness experience—they typically become voracious customers with an unlimited appetite for more wellness products and services.

Before we examine these powerful developments, which will take the U.S. wellness industry to $1 trillion and beyond by 2010, it is important to understand the nature of demand in our modern economy and what is fueling the economic expansion of both the past and the current decade that will allow us to afford this new $1 trillion industry.

The Mistake Many People Make Misunderstanding Consumer Demand

During the Great Depression of the 1930s, the economist John Maynard Keynes foresaw that advancing U.S. technology would one day be able to supply the American people with everything they could want.

Lord Keynes made the optimistic prediction to U.S. president Franklin D. Roosevelt that one day soon most American families would have a telephone, an automobile, and a four-bedroom one-bathroom house with indoor plumbing. However, the economist warned the president, once people had fulfilled this American dream, they would lose their incentive to work. These productive Americans would stop spending their increasing income and start saving it, bringing the economy to a halt—a victim, as it were, of its own success.

Therefore, Keynes suggested that the U.S. government adopt progressive income taxation to keep the most productive people in society from hoarding more and more of their earnings as their income increased.

This was radical thinking back then. When the (flat rate) federal personal income tax was first established in 1913, many people thought it unfair that a person earning $100,000 a year should pay 10 times the amount of federal taxes as a person earning $10,000 a year—yet both had equally only one vote. Now Keynes was advocating raising federal income tax rates on a progressive scale so that the more a person was earning, the higher (and higher) his or her percentage income tax rate would be.

Thanks to Keynes and the U.S. policymakers who followed his

advice, individual federal income tax rates rose throughout the twentieth century, reaching peak marginal rates of 92 to 94 percent by 1964 before stabilizing at 70 percent until the 1980s.[5]

As Chapter 6 shows in detail, to avoid these insidious rates of taxation, and also to get around government wage and price controls, employers and unions lobbied Congress for the right to pay employees with nontaxable perks such as company-provided medical care for them and their immediate families. This, more than any other single economic factor, has led to the problems we face in the United States today in regard to escalating medical costs.

We can sometimes learn more by studying the mistakes of history's greatest minds than by studying their successes. Although Keynes's theory that increasing affluence breeds complacency and oversaving seems logical, today we know that it is incorrect. The very opposite of what Keynes predicted has come to pass.

Looking back at the time when Keynes developed his landmark theory of oversaving, it is easy to see where he went wrong. During the 1930s, an insufficiency of consumer demand was the root cause of the continued depression—nothing the government did seemed able to get consumers spending again. Keynes was convinced that doom was inevitable unless the government established graduated income tax rates on personal income and then injected this money back into the economy through increased government spending.

Over the past century, and especially the past two decades, upscale consumer demand has proven itself insatiable. The more we earn, the more we spend; the more we spend, the more we get; the more we get, the more we want; and the more we want, the harder we seem to be willing to work to earn it.

If any segment of our society has lost the incentive to work, it is the very poor whom we seem unable to help over the hurdle of purchasing their first cars or their first houses—purchases that lead to the never-ending cycle of unlimited consumer demand.

In the world we live in today, advancing technology has been able to meet the basic primary needs for most Americans.

Advancing technology is constantly creating its own demand—offering new products and services that before too long become considered basic primary needs by the majority of the population.

Before the invention of the first electric washing machine around the time of World War I, few Americans cared how many times they wore a shirt before they washed it, and clothing was constructed to require a minimum number of washings. Shirts, for example, came with detachable collars and cuffs—the parts that got dirty most quickly.[6] Once the washing machine became available on a widespread basis, every American had to wear a clean shirt every day—and detachable collars and cuffs went the way of the horse and buggy.

When Henry Ford first invented a mass-produced automobile that was affordable to nearly everyone, people scoffed at the thought that anyone would buy it—there were few paved roads available; gasoline stations were nonexistent; and most people lived within walking distance of where they worked. Then, thanks to the automobile, most people actually moved to suburbia—gasoline stations proliferated, and soon the car became a necessity just to get to work or shop for daily necessities.

When the telephone first became available to businesses, most businesspeople communicated through hand-delivered written messages that they originated by dictating to their secretaries. Many were convinced that using the telephone was a waste of time. After all, who wanted to dictate a message to a secretary, have it transcribed, then read by the secretary over the telephone to the recipient's secretary, then transcribed by the recipient's secretary into a written message for the recipient. Of course, before long the telephone changed the way in which businesspeople communicated: speaking directly to one another rather than through notes transcribed by their secretaries. Inevitably, the telephone, like the fax machine in the 1970s and e-mail in the 1990s, became an absolute necessity for every business.

The story of how the telephone was initially rejected by businesspeople contains an important lesson for us today. Most people use computers and other new inventions merely to modify existing obsolete ways of doing things rather than to reengineer the work itself to fit the ability of newly available tools. Many entrepreneurs launching new wellness products and services will inevitably make this same mistake.

Today, almost 95 percent of the things we spend our money on—which most of us think of as necessities— were not even around when many of us were born: television sets, airline travel, Disneyland vacations,

> high-fashion clothing, stereos, DVDs, air conditioners, personal computers, day care, movies, fast-food restaurants, dry cleaning, Internet access, to name a few. The same will happen with wellness.

Even basic necessities like food, clothing, and housing are no longer necessities in the traditional sense because we consume quantities of them far in excess of our basic needs. In 1935 the average American lived in 136 square feet of living space; today it's in excess of 750 square feet per person.

The reason that consumer demand is so unlimited has to do with the nature of the two types of demand in our technological society: *quantity demand* and *quality demand*. This is critically important for the entrepreneur to understand, especially an entrepreneur with a long-term plan for success.

Quantity Demand and *Quality Demand*

> **Quantity demand** is the consumer's desire for more of what he or she has already purchased: another television set, a second car, a bigger house, an extra suit of clothing—even if he or she has just made their first purchase of such an item.

Consider a young person entering the workforce after graduation, possibly for the first time in his or her life needing business attire to wear to work. He or she proudly goes to the store and purchases a first suit. But on the first day of work it becomes clear that what's needed is more suits so they don't have to wear the same thing every day—not to mention ties, scarves, shirts, and shoes to match.

Or think of a young couple buying their first automobile. The automobile changes everything for them: where they work, how they travel, where they dine, and so on. But they soon realize their new need for something they hadn't even dreamed of before: a second car, so they can each independently get to work and go shopping. Similarly, a couple might purchase a second television set for their bedroom, only to quickly discover the need for a third set in a child's room or the kitchen.

A first house may seem to be the ultimate purchase for many young people starting out, yet it's actually just the beginning, as the home acquisition ignites never-ending demand for furniture, kitchen appliances, entertainment equipment, and so on. New home construction is the most important indicator in forecasting most types of retail sales.

Savvy retailers of every product or service know that a purchase by a satisfied customer is just the beginning, rather than the ending, of their relationship.

A men's clothing store might sell 100 suits a year to first-time purchasers just entering the workforce, but 2,000 suits a year to consumers who already own one or more. The most important marketing information to an automobile dealer is what type of car the potential consumer already owns. And for every first-time home buyer in the United States each year there are at least five homes sold to existing homeowners moving on to (typically) larger ones.[7]

But at some point, a classical economist like Keynes might argue, demand must be sated. After all, how many new suits, cars, homes, and televisions can a consumer own? The seemingly obvious answer to this question has confounded many merchants.

When *quantity demand* is satiated (as it is these days among a majority of people in the developed nations), *quality demand* kicks in. When you have all the food, clothing, and TVs you need—you start wanting *better* food, *better* clothing, and *better* TVs.

Whereas *quantity demand* reflects the consumer's demand for a larger supply of an existing product, *quality demand* reflects the appetite for a different or improved kind of product.

In the case of TV sets, *quality demand* reflects a consumer's more sophisticated yearning for a *better* TV (say, a high-definition color receiver with picture-in-picture capability and six-channel sound) as well as for related but otherwise entirely new products (such as a TIVO satellite receiver or a DVD player).

A typical middle-class couple would probably have little if any interest in buying a third sedan to add to the two they already own. But they might jump at the chance to get rid of one of the sedans and upgrade to a new sport utility vehicle (SUV). A young executive whose closet is filled with eight $200 suits would probably have little interest in purchasing a ninth one. But he or she might jump at the chance to purchase a new $400 designer suit.

Moreover, this flip in the nature of demand goes both ways. As the consumer begins to satisfy his or her desire for higher quality, *quantity demand* once again begins to work its magic. Now the couple wants *two* SUVs so they don't argue over who has to drive the sedan. Now the young executive wants *seven* $400 designer suits because he or she no longer "feels right" wearing the older $200 ones. Theoretically, of course, the demand for more and better goods will be satiated when the consumer finally owns a sufficiently large number of the best cars or best suits on the market. But as long as technology continues to advance, there will never be a best car or a best suit—at least not for very long. Each year a better one will be developed, and the process will start all over again.

The more emotionally detached you are from your entrepreneurial marketplace, the easier it can sometimes be for you to understand *quantity demand* and *quality demand* and how to navigate between them to create constant, ongoing demand.

For example, when it comes to riding the shift between *quantity demand* and *quality demand* for American and European consumers, no one has been able to do it better than the Japanese. In the 1960s, the Japanese overwhelmed many of the world's markets with inexpensive products—in effect, satiating *quantity demand*. But in the early 1970s, they turned their attention to increasing the quality of their goods, riding the shift from *quantity demand* to *quality demand* (leaving the now unprofitable market for cheaper goods to their imitators). In less than 20 years, they went from being known as the lowest-cost producer of almost everything consumers could want to being known as the highest-quality (and usually the highest-priced) producer of almost everything.

In the 1990s the Japanese also dumped many of their traditional brand names like Datsun and Toyota in favor of new ones like Nissan and Lexus. And they left General Motors in the dust, wondering why GM's satisfied Chevrolet customers weren't buying any more Chevrolets.

Ignoring *quality demand* is one of the biggest mistakes made by new entrepreneurs, particularly in areas of new technology like wellness. Many entrepreneurs begin

> with a lower-quality item—hoping to improve the qual-
> ity and increase the price as they build their business.
> This is shortsighted.

If you begin with a lower-quality item, it may be difficult or
impossible for you to retain clients when your once-satisfied customers begin demanding a higher-quality product or service. When
a business or distributor becomes known for having lower prices,
which is often correctly equated with lower quality by the consumer, it is sometimes impossible to change this perception.

> The most successful wellness companies today manufac-
> ture or distribute the highest-quality (which often
> means the highest-priced) wellness products and ser-
> vices.

The consumer's continual desire for higher-quality items is so
incorporated into our marketplace that it is often transparent. Each
year, as advancing technology lowers the cost of products and services, smart producers and providers recognize that they want to
keep existing customer relationships. To do so, they automatically
improve the quality of their products rather than lowering the price.

Suppose you spent $600 on a 27-inch color television in 1990
and went out in 2000 to buy its replacement at the same store. You
would have found that virtually the same television now costs only
$300 (actually $229 in 1990 dollars after adjusting for inflation).
But rather than purchase the same television, you would probably
have elected to spend $600 again ($458 in 1990 dollars) to purchase a 36-inch model—or perhaps $1,500 ($1,144 in 1990 dollars) on a superdeluxe high-definition model with six-channel
sound and picture-in-picture channel displays. Moreover, you
might not even find the $300 model at your local store, as your
merchant, aware that satisfied customers want increasing quality
rather than lower prices, no longer carries the (now) lower-end
models.

Or suppose in 1995 you entered medical school hoping to purchase a new $45,000 convertible automobile on completing your
residency in 2002. When you go to the dealer in 2002, you find
that the car with all the features you wanted back then now costs
only $25,000. But rather than purchasing this car and pocketing
the $20,000 savings, you decide to "trade up" to a $45,000 car
that has twice the features of the car you wanted back in 1995.

This consumer-driven phenomenon of choosing increasing quality over lower price is so prevalent today that most people don't realize how much the material quality of their lives has steadily increased—thanks to the improved quality, safety, and lower prices of their products. Whether you are talking about TVs or toys, automobiles or air conditioners, blue jeans or bedding, digital cameras or convertible sofas, refrigerators or MP3 recorded music, people today invariably enjoy better-quality goods at a lower real cost than they did at any time in history.

Wellness *Quantity* and *Quality Demand*

All of this has great implications for the wellness industry.

The majority of consumers today are not even aware that there *is* a wellness industry. Yet each of us knows someone who has recently had a wellness experience:

1. A single mother who changed her diet and lost 35 pounds
2. A boy with a new vitamin regimen who now focuses twice as hard in school
3. A father using magnetic therapy who has eliminated chronic pain
4. A girl taking echinacea who no longer misses school because of colds
5. A former athlete using glucosamine who has returned to bicycling without knee problems
6. A patient with an enlarged prostate who avoided painful surgery by taking saw palmetto

The list goes on and on.

Now think for a moment what else may happen in this person's life after an initial wellness experience:

1. The single mother probably has a new schedule that includes regular athletic activity like jogging.
2. The boy is trying out for sports since his academics are under control.
3. The father wants something to develop more energy to keep up with his children since pain no longer dominates his thoughts.
4. The girl's parents want to know what supplements they should be giving their other children.

5. The former athlete wants products to improve his memory since he now believes in nutritional supplementation.

6. The former prostate patient has completely changed his diet and now wants to learn everything about alternative medical treatments.

For each of these people, the initial purchase of a single wellness product or service ignited *quantity demand*—the demand for more of what they had just purchased—even though they were unaware such a product existed before they purchased it.

Even more important, when the wellness product or service had worked its magic, it ignited *quality demand*—the demand for different and/or better wellness products and services.

Thanks to *quantity demand* and *quality demand*, satisfied wellness customers are beginning a lifetime consumption of products and services that have the potential to improve every aspect of their lives for every moment of their lives. More than any other factor, this unlimited propensity to consume wellness products and services will take the industry to $1 trillion and beyond by 2010.

How Some Prospective Entrepreneurs Misunderstand Our Economy

It wasn't too long ago that the most common culprits of being late for a meeting would be either a flat tire or a flooded carburetor—problems that advancing technology (radial tires and electronic fuel injection) have eliminated from our daily concerns.

Sometimes, potential entrepreneurs are dissuaded by economic indicators that regularly appear in our media, particularly in times of recession or economic contraction. But because of advancing technology, these economic indicators are often misinterpreted as reasons *not* to start a business when in reality they are actually *good news* for the budding entrepreneur.

For example, lower prices and better-quality products are sometimes reported in our media as a decrease rather than an increase in our material wealth. This is because our most common economic indicators, such as gross domestic product (GDP) and retail sales, are not indexed for either increasing quality or for price deflation caused by the ability of technology to lower prices. When the medical student purchased his $45,000 car with twice the features of the one he originally wanted, he experienced a $20,000 unreported increase in his material lifestyle. If he had purchased his $45,000 original dream car for $25,000, it would have been reported in the media as a $20,000 decrease in GDP or retail sales.

Similarly, when the average cost of a new home is reported by the U.S. government, this figure is not indexed for the fact that it is more than twice the size of the average new home in the 1960s or that it contains features and appliances that alone make it worth twice as much to the consumer. Most of us were raised in a typical middle-class house of 1960—about 900 square feet without a dishwasher or air conditioning, which today could be considered a fairly primitive standard of living compared to a new home in 2001, which averages about 2,300 square feet and contains a host of modern appliances and conveniences.

> **Yet probably the most misunderstood economic indicator in our society is unemployment—particularly the type of unemployment we mostly experience today, which comes from technological change, or what economists sometimes call *structural unemployment*.**

As we will see in a moment, such unemployment, caused by the substitution of technology for labor, is actually the first sign of true economic growth. And as we shall also see, it is because of structural unemployment that the labor force is available to develop and grow new industries.

This brings us to our next topic underlying the growth of the next $1 trillion industry: What has been fueling the economic expansion of the past and current decades that allows us to afford all of these new products and services, and is it going to continue?

How Unemployment Leads to Economic Growth

Imagine a self-sufficient island with 10 men, all of whom make their living by fishing with poles from a communal boat. One day, a missionary shows the men a new, technologically better way of fishing—using a large net instead of 10 individual lines. Two fishermen, one to pilot the boat and one to throw the net, can now catch the same number of fish as ten fishermen could with lines.

On the surface, unemployment on the island has risen from 0 to 80 percent, since 8 of the 10 fishermen are now out of a job. Yet, although eight of the men are no longer working, the island society as a whole remains just as prosperous because two fisherman using the net catch as many fish as ten did with lines.

Now the island society must decide what to do with the eight unemployed fishermen and their families. They have three options: (1) They can pass a law making the use of fishing nets illegal; (2) they can tax the two working fishermen 80 percent of their earnings and redistribute this 80 percent to the unemployed; or (3) they can help the eight unemployed fishermen develop new jobs in new industries (e.g., education, medicine, food preparation) that will add to the wealth of the entire community.

What civilized society would deliberately stunt economic growth by limiting the use of new technology? What society would tax 80 percent of the earnings of their best producers (i.e., the ones with the nets)? Yet these have been the traditional responses when the implementation of technology made certain people richer than their neighbors.

Throughout the nineteenth and twentieth centuries, governments passed pro-union legislation limiting the ability of private companies to substitute technology for labor. Between 1913 and 1960, the United States and Western Europe instituted highly progressive income taxes, increasing the personal marginal income tax rate to 91 percent and more on their most efficient citizens (i.e., the ones with the nets). Eastern Europe and China chose communism (effectively 100 percent taxation), removing the individual's incentive to implement new technological methods and devastating their economies.

In the United States in 1930, there were approximately 30 million farmers, producing just enough food to feed a population of about 100 million people. Technological breakthroughs in agriculture over the next 50 years made farming so efficient that by 1980 only 3 million farmers produced enough food for a population of more than 300 million[8]—and the displaced 27 million farmers, or their children, moved on to producing new products and services that added to the total wealth in the economy.

This is how our economy has evolved since the beginning of civilization.

New technology makes workers more efficient, causing structural unemployment, but over time, the displaced workers end up producing new products and services that add to society's overall wealth. The only thing new about this process today is the speed with which it is occurring.

Changes that used to take place over millennia or centuries now take place in years, months, or even days—as was the case in our island example with the fishing net. This increased speed underlies our employment challenges today, as individuals must often change careers and/or professions several times within a single lifetime rather than slowly over several generations.

The 27 million farmers who were displaced were relatively fortunate. They had 50 years to grow old, retire, and watch their children develop new careers as carburetor mechanics or vinyl record manufacturers—careers that were then on the cutting edge of new technologies. Their children, who left the family farm to pursue these new careers, weren't nearly as fortunate, as they had only five years or less to adjust to similar changes.

In 1980, approximately 300,000 people in the United States were employed in the manufacture and repair of mechanical carburetors. In just five years, by 1985, virtually all of these jobs disappeared as automakers replaced $300 mechanical carburetors with much more efficient $25 computerized electronic fuel injectors. The rest of society greatly benefited from fuel injectors, which halved effective fuel cost (by doubling fuel economy) and halved harmful automobile emissions.

In 1985, approximately 100,000 people in the United States were employed in the manufacture of vinyl records. In just five years, by 1990, these jobs disappeared when the music industry replaced the vinyl record, costing $2.50, with the digital compact disc, costing 25 cents. (Today it is the music industry's turn to cry, as consumers press their own CDRs and download free music from the Internet via MP3 files.)

Similar examples in the past century made total economic growth in the United States the envy of the world—so much so that the cold war ended in the 1990s when the people of Eastern Europe and China democratically decided to become free-market economies.

Today, most leaders worldwide realize that they cannot stop structural unemployment without devastating their economies.

This is especially true in a free-trade environment, where multinational employers can simply take jobs overseas if they try. While this has resulted in much greater total economic output and greater overall prosperity, it has made employment much less stable for individuals, who must now be ready to retrain themselves on short notice.

Economic Implications for the Wellness Industry

Because of misunderstood economic indicators, our economy is actually growing at a higher rate than is reported. Despite some media reports to the contrary, most of the unemployment we are experiencing is *structural unemployment,* which is actually the first sign of true economic growth. These facts bode well for the wellness industry.

There is more than enough growth in the economy to support a new $1 trillion industry.

Just as U.S. GDP increased from roughly $5 trillion to $10 trillion between 1990 and 2000, even the most conservative growth estimates forecast U.S. GDP hitting $15 trillion by 2010.

Despite the existence of relatively low levels of unemployment (even with the economic downturn caused by the September 11 World Trade Center disaster), the labor force is available today to support a new $1 trillion industry.

The $5 trillion in economic growth we have had and will continue to experience almost invariably starts with structural unemployment, as technology displaces productive individuals and frees them for new jobs in new areas of the economy.

The main question for us, as businesspeople and entrepreneurs, is, "Which sectors of the economy will attract the greatest share of this growth and employ these displaced employees?"
The wellness industry is poised to become the next $1

trillion sector of our economy because everyone, no matter how fit or how healthy they are, wants to be more healthy and more fit.

The wellness industry is poised to become the next $1 trillion sector of our economy because it contains the five distinct characteristics of pervasive industries: (1) affordability; (2) legs; (3) continual consumption; (4) universal appeal; and, most important, (5) low consumption time. Wellness products and services represent perhaps the only sector of consumer spending that does not take time to enjoy.

This may seem obvious when stated, but it is often overlooked because consumers have only recently had the option to purchase wellness products and services. Until now, *most people were told to accept their wellness deficiencies as part of the aging process, as though there were nothing they could do about them.*

How the Vitamin Business Shifted from Sickness to Wellness

One of the fastest growing sectors of the wellness industry today is the vitamin and nutritional supplement business. But until very recently this business was limited almost entirely to treating sickness.

Scurvy, or vitamin C deficiency, is one of the oldest known nutritional disorders, and its symptoms were written about in Crusader history. It was the major cause of disability and mortality among British sailors until Scottish physician James Lind noted that the Dutch employed citrus fruits to eliminate scurvy. In 1795 the consumption of lime juice became mandatory on all British naval vessels—and people of British descent are still called "limeys" to this day.

Rickets, or vitamin D deficiency, was noted throughout history and caused skeletal deformities, especially in children. Beginning in the eighteenth century it was treated with cod-liver oil and sunlight.[9]

Beriberi, or vitamin B$_1$ deficiency, is caused by the unnatural removal of this vitamin from processed rice and other grains. Beriberi literally means "extreme weakness" in Sinhalese and has been noted in Asian countries since polished white rice became a staple more than 1,000 years ago.[10] In all of these cases, scientists recognized these nutritional deficiencies only when they manifested themselves as terrible sickness.

In the twentieth century it was discovered that there are 13 essential vitamins required to maintain good health that generally cannot be manufactured in the body.[11] More recently, it has been discovered that these same vitamins can prevent disease from developing, make us feel "better than well," and even slow the aging process itself.[12]

Today, almost 50 percent of Americans take some sort of nutritional supplement, and industry sales for these products exceed $70 billion. Yet the vitamin and mineral industry has barely scratched the surface of what is possible, for we are just beginning to understand the biochemistry that explains how vitamins, minerals, and other supplements work.

As explained in Chapter 1, when it comes to understanding how our cells function on a molecular level, we are where the sickness industry was prior to the nineteenth century—we know that many wellness products and services work, but we do not yet fully understand *why* many of them work. Yet medicine established itself as a major science long before the optical microscope was able to explain so many of its mysteries, and wellness will do the same.

Similarly, we have already seen the wellness industry garner about $200 billion in U.S. annual sales even though science does not yet understand the molecular secrets behind much of its efficacy. Even if we don't uncover these secrets in the near future, this $200 billion is just the beginning.

Many potential customers have never even heard of wellness products and services, let alone tried them. As we have seen, customers who try a wellness product or service and have a positive experience usually open their minds to trying other wellness products and services.

In my case, between the ages of 35 and 43 I had pain in my left knee—the result of years of competitively racing down mogul-laden ski slopes. Each orthopedic surgeon I visited came to the same conclusion—surgery. One young orthopedic surgeon even joked that he expected my left knee to finance his grandchildren's college education as, even after the surgery, I would probably be his patient for life. At age 43, I was finally considering scheduling the surgery.

I started taking glucosamine and the pain in my knee disappeared within two months. One year later the same orthopedic surgeon asked me who had operated on my knee. When I told him about the glucosamine, he took some X rays and asked me not to publicize my experience, as it could put him out of business—only this time he wasn't joking. I was amazed that I, an economist, was teaching an orthopedic surgeon about glucosamine.

This experience opened my mind to thinking about what else the medical practitioners in my life might not know. After completing some research, I started taking the daily vitamins and mineral supplements I take today, and I became open to taking other dietary supplements in the future.

For too long, medical science has told people to expect and accept chronic pain, declining health, and reduced energy levels as they age—partly because many doctors have only rudimentary training in nutrition and partly because the ultimate payors or providers of medical services (employers) do not have the proper financial incentives to pay for wellness. We examine both of these phenomena in Chapters 5 and 6.

But first, let's examine in Chapter 3 the changes in our food supply that created most of the sickness problems we have today and, in Chapter 4, the opportunity to fix these problems using the same entrepreneurial skills that created them.

Before Proceeding to the Next Chapter

Action Plan for Entrepreneurs, Investors, and Distributors

1. Make a list of what you and your family currently spend on wellness that you weren't spending 10 years ago. Your own personal accounts of wellness activity are powerful tools when explaining the emerging wellness industry to others.

2. Analyze the items on this list with respect to your three current areas of potential wellness businesses. Are you already a customer of any of these three areas? Why or why not?

3. Analyze your three current areas of potential wellness businesses with respect to the baby boom market (customers age 38 to 55).

4. Analyze your three current areas of potential wellness businesses with respect to the Generation X market (customers age 20 to 37).

5. For each of your three current areas of potential wellness businesses, make a list of products that you would offer to satiate *quantity demand*—the initial customer demand for more of each product.

6. Now analyze each product to see how you can make the eventual transition to *quality demand*—the demand for a different or higher-quality product.

7. What areas in your region of the world are experiencing structural unemployment (displacement due to technology), and how could these displaced people work in each of your three areas of wellness business opportunity?

Based on your answers to these questions, think about dropping and replacing any or all of your three individual areas of wellness business opportunity.

CHAPTER 3

What You Need to Know about Food

Most of the immediate demand for wellness, and most wellness products themselves, exist today because of two major problems with food. To understand the wellness industry, you are going to have to understand why we need food and the origin of these two major problems with our supply of food.

Once you start your wellness business, you will need to go beyond simply understanding the problems with our food supply—you will have to be able to explain and teach the origins of these problems to your customers, your associates, and your investors. Thus, you will probably read this chapter more than once.

If you are still choosing which wellness business opportunity to pursue, you should carefully read this chapter, noting each of the problems with food and my personal suggestions for improving your own diet—then analyze how you might be able to turn one or more of these suggestions into a profitable wellness business opportunity.

What Is Food and Why Do We Need It?

Adam and Eve didn't worry too much about food. According to the Bible, the Garden of Eden freely contained "every tree that is pleasant to the sight, and good for food."[1] Then, because Eve tasted the apple, the ground was cursed so that it would yield food only with hard labor.

Ever since then, the search for food has dominated our existence. But what is food, and why is it so necessary for human existence?

In addition to enjoying food because it tastes good, human beings require food for three purposes:

1. *Energy.* Fuel (calories) necessary to perform external work and to simply allow the heart, lungs, and other organs to function.

2. *Building blocks.* Raw materials (e.g., proteins, most minerals) used to manufacture blood, skin, bones, hair, and internal organs; the human body is constantly replacing and renewing every cell on a daily to monthly basis.

3. *Catalysts.* Chemical compounds (e.g., vitamins, enzymes, and some minerals) necessary to facilitate the chemical reactions that convert food into energy and into bodily organs.

Human beings require food for energy every few hours and require specific foods that function as building blocks and catalysts on a daily or semidaily basis. Our bodies are biologically programmed to immediately sense when energy is needed—we experience hunger pain. Unfortunately, we usually become aware of missing building blocks or catalysts only when our bodies become ill from these deficiencies.

Our bodies are also biologically programmed to seek out foods containing the highest amounts of energy. Foods containing the highest amounts of energy (e.g., sugar, fat) taste the best.

The successful exploitation of our biological programming by the entrepreneurs and commercial providers of our food supply is the major cause of obesity and ill health in the developed world today.

The United States is the poorest of the developed nations when it comes to health—U.S. citizens are the most obese and spend three times as much money on medical care than their European or Asian counterparts. This massive difference, not just in the cost of medical care but also in the unhappiness caused by poor health, is the result of our having a terrible diet.

The Two Major Problems with Our Food Supply

There are two major problems with the diet of most people in the United States:

1. We eat too much. Fully 61 percent of our citizens are overweight.

2. Most of us are not getting the minimum amounts of building blocks and/or catalysts that our bodies need.

To understand how these two problems of overeating and poor nutrition were created, and to understand the entrepreneurial opportunity to cure these problems (Chapter 4), it is first necessary to understand how our bodies process food into energy and living matter.

How Our Bodies Process Food into Energy and Living Matter

All food consists of one or more of six nutrient categories:

1. Water
2. Carbohydrates (contained in sugars, breads, etc.)
3. Lipids (contained in fats, oils, etc.)
4. Proteins (contained in meat, fish, eggs, vegetables, etc.)
5. Vitamins (contained in fruits, vegetables, etc.)
6. Minerals (contained in fruits, vegetables, etc.)

Digestion begins when food enters your mouth and starts being broken down by your teeth and the enzymes in your saliva. Then chemicals in your stomach go to work digesting the food into its six nutrient categories.

The Opportunity in Water

The human body is composed of about 60 percent water and requires a minimum of two quarts of fresh water per day. It is estimated that 75 percent of Americans are chronically dehydrated and that 37 percent mistake thirst for hunger. A mere 2 percent drop in body water can trigger fatigue and mental dysfunction. As a preventative measure, drinking five glasses of water daily decreases the risk of colon cancer by 45 percent, the risk of breast cancer by 79 percent, and the risk of bladder cancer by 50 percent.

If possible, and if it will not interfere with getting your minimum daily water requirement, you should try to avoid drinking this water during mealtimes. The chemicals in your stomach become less efficacious when diluted, and this can cause valuable nutrients to wash through versus being absorbed by your body.

To ensure that I drink enough water each day, and especially not just at mealtimes, I travel with a small, soft backpack called a Camelbak™. My Camelbak contains three liters of distilled drinking water in a refillable plastic sack attached to a plastic tube. This lets me drink safely while biking, driving, walking, or in almost any situation. In my home and office, I make sure there is a water filter or reverse osmosis unit at every sink so that clean drinking water is always available and in sight.

One of the simplest wellness business opportunities is providing consumers with clean, healthy water at convenient times and locations throughout their day.

How We Obtain and Burn Calories

The energy contained in specific portions of food and the energy needs of the body are both measured in units called *calories*. The number of calories in a particular food can be measured by burning a weighed portion of the food and measuring the amount of heat produced. It is also possible to measure the number of calories burned by a particular physical activity, from sleeping to jogging up a steep hill.

Of the six nutrient categories, only carbohydrates (4 calories per gram), lipids or fats (9 calories per gram), and proteins (4 calories per gram) provide energy.[2]

The human body requires approximately 2,200 calories of energy per day for a woman and 2,900 calories per day for a man. A person doing daily athletic exercise requires more calories per day than a sedentary person. The following chart shows the amount of calories burned per half hour by different types of activities. At any level of activity, the human body uses about 65 percent of its energy for basal metabolic functions like breathing and pumping blood.

Calories Burned per 30 Minutes of Activity[3]

Activity (30 minutes)	120-lb. person	175-lb. person
Bicycling 14–16 mph	288	420
Skiing, downhill	238	346
Bicycling, mountain	230	336
Jogging	191	278
Swimming, moderate	166	242
Tennis, singles	166	242
Golf, carrying clubs	166	242
Walking 4 mph	140	205
Weight lifting, general	94	136
Golf, using a cart	94	136
Sitting	29	42
Sleeping	25	37

When your daily intake of calories exceeds your daily bodily requirements, the body converts these excess calories into fat, which is then stored throughout the body. A normal amount of fat, typically between 15 and 25 percent of body mass, is important for hundreds of bodily functions. These functions range from maintaining temperature to absorbing fat-soluble vitamins to cushioning vital organs. If you have too little fat in your system, the body will begin destructively breaking down muscles and internal organs to meet its requirements for energy.

However, when you consume more calories than the body uses over a period of time, your body starts to store excess fat in visible places. This excess fat often first appears in the stomach on a man and in the thighs on a woman. Excess fat is associated with fatigue, heart disease, cancer, and hundreds of other life-threatening diseases.

Four Reasons It's Difficult to Lose Fat

Excess stored fat should be converted back into calories when the body next requires more energy. This does not typically occur today for four main reasons:

1. We consume available carbohydrate calories before fat calories.
2. Our bodies tell us to look for more food before using stored reserves.

3. Readily available food causes our metabolism to stabilize at the higher fat level.

4. The type of food we eat today is different than it was when our biological formula for energy storage was developed.

First, just as a hungry person consumes the most readily available source of food, the human body always consumes the most easily convertible source of energy. Of the nutrients containing calories, molecules of carbohydrates are the simplest in form and thus are the easiest for the body to quickly convert into energy. This is why people crave carbohydrates when they haven't eaten for a while or immediately after performing strenuous exercise.

In contrast, molecules of fat are more complex and require additional energy and additional time to be converted into energy (or burned). The body always looks to available carbohydrates first for energy before it begins to break down ingested and then stored molecules of fat.

Second, when a person needs energy, he or she experiences hunger (typically for more carbohydrates) long before the body turns to its stores of excess fat. This biological programming served us well in prehistoric times—telling prehistoric humans to keep eating (and eating and eating) when food was plentiful before drawing on his stored reserves.

We are biologically programmed to eat each meal as though it were the last one we are going to get for a long time—and in many cases it was, before humankind learned how to preserve foods, to farm, and to domesticate animals.

The ability to make conscious choices contrary to our biological programming is what separates us from most of the animal kingdom. Humans and animals have virtually the same biologically driven appetites and desires, which yield pleasure when satisfied, with one all-important difference: Humans have a mind and soul that is superior to and can control their biological desires. Unfortunately, this seems true for most people today in every area except their dining habits.

Some animals have learned how to supersede their biological programming in our world of abundant food. Many people with pets today use dried food and leave it out to be consumed on a leisurely basis rather than waiting until their pet begs for its next meal. Veterinarians and pet owners have learned that if you feed your pet only when it gets very hungry, it will eat the full amount given even if its body no longer requires it. However, if food is continuously available, most pets will adjust their appetites and eat only what they need for optimum health. Sadly, this is a lesson that most doctors and U.S. citizens have yet to learn for themselves and their own children.

We also eat much faster today than our parents did—when people often sat around the table for long time periods to share conversation.

It typically takes 10 to 15 minutes from the time we ingest food until our hunger becomes sated—this is why you are sometimes no longer hungry at a restaurant when an entrée arrives late.

When you take time between courses or bites to digest your food, your hunger becomes satisfied with only the amount of calories you require. But when you eat quickly at your desk between appointments or at fast-food restaurants, you often think you are hungry and keep eating even though you have already ingested more than enough calories.

Third, when people put on additional fat, say 15 pounds of weight during a vacation with lavish meals, their daily basal metabolic requirement for calories increases. Where their hunger used to be sated with 2,500 calories per day, these people now require approximately 3,000 calories in order not to feel hungry—their body and appetite having reached a new equilibrium at the heavier, 15-pound level. As long as food is readily available and people listen to their stomachs (hunger) regarding how much to eat, their increased amount of weight will remain.

Once a person puts on excess weight he or she will most likely have to take proactive measures (e.g., diet) to lose it.

And fourth, the main reason that this stored excess fat may not be converted into energy calories is because our food today is very different than food was when our biological program for storing energy was developed—it contains much more fat. When our biological programming for food was developed, our ancestors ate mostly a low-fat vegetarian diet, with some game meats. And even those foods that contained fat had much *less* fat than they do today—game meats contain about 5 percent fat by weight versus the 30 percent fat by weight contained today in commercially produced and hormonally treated domesticated animals.

Back then, fat was so rare and so useful that our taste buds evolved to crave it and the parts of the animals that contained most of it. Today, unfortunately, this sensory craving has been exploited by our food suppliers. Like the first victim in the movie *Seven,* which is about the monastic seven deadly sins, we are literally eating ourselves to death.

In just the past century we have almost doubled the percent of fat in our diets—from 20 percent of our calories in 1910 to about 35 percent today.[4]

This 35 percent average number belies the fact that our nation is divided when it comes to health: Millions of upscale Americans eat diets that have 20 percent or less of their calories from fat, and millions more eat diets that have 50 percent or more of their calories from life-threatening fat. Most experts agree that our bodies are biologically programmed for a diet requiring about 20 percent of our calories from fat.

The Critical Importance of Proteins, Vitamins, and Minerals

The second major problem with the diet of most U.S. citizens is that they are not getting the minimum amounts of building blocks and/or catalysts that their bodies require.

The first book of the Bible, Genesis, which is common to Judaism, Christianity, and Islam, speaks of the Garden of Eden, where God made "every tree that is pleasant to the sight, and good for food."[5] This reference to a wide variety of food has more than just aesthetic significance.

Although most adults think of their bodies as fully grown, the individual cells that comprise their organs actually replace themselves on a daily to monthly schedule.

Our bodies manufacture 200 billion red blood cells each day, replacing all the blood in our body every 120

days. Skin is completely replaced every 1 to 3 months. It takes 90 days for old bone to be broken down and replaced by new bone.

The cells that comprise these replacement organs contain over 100,000 different proteins made up of 20 different amino acids. Food supplies us with plant and animal proteins containing the amino acids that our bodies require as the building blocks of this living tissue.

Without a daily supply of proteins, vitamins, and minerals, no matter how much energy we get in the form of calories, our bodies and minds deteriorate because we are not able to fully replace the dying cells in our internal and external organs.

Food also supplies us with certain minerals we require as building blocks to repair and regenerate our living matter. There are 14 essential minerals, some of which are required as catalysts rather than as building blocks. Seven of these are *major minerals,* defined as those of which we need more than 100 milligrams per day—calcium, chloride, magnesium, phosphorus, potassium, sodium, and sulfur. The remaining seven are called *trace minerals,* such as iron and zinc.

In addition to supplying proteins and minerals as building blocks, food contains the 13 essential vitamins our bodies require as catalysts to convert food into energy and to convert amino acids into bodily tissue. A catalyst is a substance that must be present, typically in a very small quantity, for a specific chemical reaction to occur.[6] For example, without vitamin B_3, which is contained in green leafy vegetables and unprocessed grains, our bodies cannot break down plant and animal proteins into basic amino acids. It doesn't matter how much protein you eat if your body can't convert it into the building blocks of your living tissue.

When we don't get enough protein, vitamins, and minerals, our initial symptoms include mood swings, fatigue, nervousness, headaches, confusion, and muscle weakness. Over the longer term, such poor nutrition can cause cancer, hypertension, Alzheimer's disease, and many other diseases that we used to just accept as part of our aging process.

Modern medicine typically treats these problems with drugs that focus on each symptom rather than on the underlying problem, which is what we eat, or more correctly in the case of poor nutrition, what we don't eat.

Before you become alarmed that you're never going to get enough of all these critical nutrients, here is some good news. Our bodies require only a small amount of protein and a minuscule amount of minerals and vitamins on a daily basis.

The human body requires approximately 46 grams (1.6 ounces) of protein per day for women and 58 grams (2.0 ounces) of protein per day for men. This is less than most people believe they need, thanks to successful but misleading advertising campaigns by the beef and cattle industry. Ironically, meat and milk products are actually a poor source of protein because they contain high amounts of harmful fats compared to other protein sources such as fish, nuts, breads, and vegetables.

The human body requires 13 essential vitamins in dosages ranging from 60 milligrams per day for vitamin C to 200 micrograms per day for vitamin B_8 (folic acid). These quantities are naturally abundant in commonly available fresh foods.

Similarly, the 14 minerals we require are contained in fresh foods in more than adequate quantities—100 milligrams is only $\frac{3}{1,000}$ of an ounce.

Now here's the bad news.

Despite the relatively small amounts of proteins, vitamins, and minerals we require on a daily basis, and despite their abundance in natural foods, our biologically programmed need for these substances is not being met by our modern food supply.

How the Green Revolution Changed the Economic Opportunity within Food Production

When our ancestors were hunter-gatherers they subsisted on a plant-rich diet of nuts, fruits, beans, grains, and roots, with some game meats. Because no single type of food was found in abundance, while they searched primarily for calories they automatically consumed the variety of foods containing the different proteins, vitamins, and minerals that their bodies required. (Conversely, their bodies adapted to the nutrients in the variety of foods they consumed.)

Over time, these hunter-gatherers became farmers. Using human ingenuity and the economic abundance that results from specialization, they learned how to efficiently produce large quantities of specific foods that they could then trade for other foods. They learned how to produce the foods that naturally tasted the best and could last the longest—foods rich in fat like dried meats and aged cheeses. World population rose steadily from around 200 million at the time of Jesus Christ to about 1 billion by the end of the nineteenth century.

In the twentieth century, rising agricultural technology finally eliminated the age-old problem of food scarcity—with a vengeance. Thanks to the green revolution, India and China went from starvation economies to net exporters of food. World population rose from 1 billion to almost 6 billion. Thanks to advances in agrarian technology led by the United States, between 1930 and 1980 the United States went from 30 million farmers, barely producing enough food for a domestic population of 100 million people, to 3 million farmers producing more than enough food for 300 million people. Farm production became more and more efficient, with no end in sight.

The U.S. Department of Agriculture (USDA) was originally created to safeguard the economic interests of farmers, particularly in times of drought and famine. During this period of rising agricultural efficiency, the USDA budget was shifted to government "farm income stabilization" programs that paid farmers billions of dollars each year *not* to grow more food, thus keeping food prices higher, thus safeguarding the farmers' economic interests. Today, in addition to forcing consumers to pay higher prices for food, these subsidies keep many farmers from learning how to use new technology and from switching to crops that consumers really want. Worst of all, this subsidy encourages many young people to become farmers even though our economy no longer needs more farmers.

Yet despite efforts to the contrary by the USDA, the relative prices for farm produce fell steadily throughout the second half of the twentieth century as supply far exceeded demand.

As the price farmers received for basic food fell, the profit opportunity in agriculture shifted from producing raw foodstuffs (e.g., wheat, milk, fruit, cattle) to manufacturing these foodstuffs into name-brand foods with

long shelf lives (e.g., cereals, condiments, processed cheeses, canned foods, frozen foods, and junk or snack foods).

It became particularly profitable to make junk or snack foods, products that initially consumers didn't know they wanted, but which they developed a seemingly unlimited propensity to consume.

Additionally, in the postwar U.S. economy, the supply and demand for a new type of food arose—a food type defined not by its taste, price, or availability, but by its long shelf life and speed of service: *fast food*.

How Food Economics Created the Wellness Food Opportunity

During this period of great technological advances in our food supply, our knowledge of basic nutrition was just evolving. Many of our food scientists and engineers, let alone the consuming public, didn't know enough about the need for proteins, vitamins, and minerals. Each food company concentrated on making each product taste better than that of the competition, last longer, and be safe from contamination by microorganisms.

Looking back, they did an admirable job in fulfilling their mission. Processed and fast foods effectively didn't exist for most Americans at the end of World War II. By the end of the twentieth century, processed and fast-food sales had risen to dominate the U.S. $1 trillion food industry.

Despite making basic calories affordable for everyone, our food industry unwittingly injured the health of much of the nation.

In order to make their products taste better, they added fat. The better it tasted, the more customers ate their products. The more customers ate their products, the fatter they became. The fatter customers became, the more food products they were able to consume on a daily basis—and so on, and so on, and so on.

In order to make their products safe from contamination, they pasteurized and/or heated them.[7] Today, all canned foods and virtually all milk and juices are pasteurized. Unfortunately, the application of heat to food, as well as its storage over time in cans and other airtight containers, destroys many of the vitamins and some of the minerals. In general, canning and most other types of food processing do not affect proteins, fats, and carbohydrates.

In order to increase the shelf life of their products (as well as to add to their safety), food producers added preservatives ranging from enormous amounts of sodium to a dizzying array of chemical compounds in supposedly "safe" amounts. While a typical adult requires about 500 milligrams a day of sodium, which is found naturally in common foods, salt is so widely added to most processed foods that the typical U.S. adult consumes 10 to 14 times this amount per day. In addition to desensitizing our taste buds so that natural, unprocessed foods no longer taste good, salt is the primary cause of high blood pressure, which leads to increased risk of stroke, heart disease, and kidney failure.

In order to get people to consume more of their product, producers chemically altered the flavorings so that people would continually crave more and more of their single product rather than naturally seeking the variety in foods that their bodies require.

Empty Calories: The Core of the Food Supply Problem

The end result is that today the U.S. food supply is dominated by what nutritional experts call *empty calories*—food containing high amounts of caloric energy but low (or empty) in essential vitamins, minerals, and proteins.

The human body can consume only 2,200 to 2,900 calories per day for energy without becoming obese, but it must get the required amounts of protein, vitamins, minerals, and healthy fats along with these calories. Just a quick glance at the nutritional facts printed on any processed food label shows us what we are *not* getting along with our calories.

A typical can of soda contains 140 empty calories (38 milligrams of sugar, 70 milligrams of sodium, added caffeine, various preservatives, and 0 milligrams of proteins, vitamins, and minerals). A typical fast-food meal contains an incredible 1,000 calories or more with few essential vitamins or minerals. One 1-ounce serving of Lay's potato chips ("Betcha Can't Eat Just One")[8] contains 230 empty calories (plus 270 milligrams of sodium).

But these foods are even worse for what they *do* contain than for what they are missing: Most empty-calorie foods have incredibly high levels of fat, which is added to make them taste better. A healthy food should yield about 20 percent of its calories from fat (each gram of fat contains 9 calories) and the rest from carbohydrates and proteins. Just one deluxe McDonald's burger contains 810 calories, with an incredible 490 calories (55 grams, or 61 percent) from fat. Even without the medium-size french fries (containing 450 additional calories and 22 grams of additional fat), *55 grams of fat is the full amount you should consume in an entire day, not the amount you should consume from a single item of food.*[9] The typical American now eats three hamburgers and four orders of french fries each week.[10]

In contrast, foods in their natural (unprocessed) state are packed with caloric energy, vitamins, minerals, and low levels of fat.

Fruits are high in carbohydrates, vitamins, and minerals and contain virtually no fat. A banana contains 103 calories of energy with 0 grams of fat. Fresh vegetables contain enormous quantities of vitamins, some protein, and almost no fat. A single stalk of broccoli contains 5 grams of protein with no fat, and a single medium-size potato containing 100 calories has 6 grams of protein and no fat. Moreover, when eating a natural food, people typically tire of its taste and automatically seek out different natural foods—containing the different vitamins and minerals that their bodies require on a daily basis.

Fish, beef, and chicken are loaded with protein, vitamins, minerals, no carbohydrates, and widely varying amounts of fat. A 6-ounce serving of fish (halibut) contains 35 grams of protein with 2 grams of fat. A 6-ounce steak (rib eye) contains about the same amount (39 grams) of protein—but an incredible 55 grams of fat as well. A 6-ounce serving of chicken (light and dark meat) contains 46 grams of protein with 25 grams of fat.

Unfortunately, we no longer eat as our ancestors did, or even as our parents did. Meals used to be prepared at home primarily using fresh foods and without adding much fat, salt, or chemical preservatives.

Today, most of us are too busy to prepare foods from fresh ingredients, so we purchase foods that are partially or fully ready to serve—foods processed with much added fat, sugar, sodium, and chemical additives.

The percentage of meals eaten or prepared away from home (restaurants, take-out) has increased more than 50 percent since 1970. Meals prepared outside the home are much higher in fat and sodium and lower in vitamins and minerals than meals prepared at home—even when compared to meals at home made from highly processed foods.[11] Ironically, as we will see in a moment, being biologically programmed to like the taste of fat—a trait that was responsible for our very survival in prehistoric times—has now become the cause of our worst medical problem.

Economics versus Avarice and Our Food Supply Problems

Wellness entrepreneurs should keep in mind that as insidious as the manipulation of our food supply may seem in hindsight, none of it was done with insidious intent.

Entrepreneurs and businesspeople added fat to our food to make it taste better, not to create a nation of overweight and obese individuals. Entrepreneurs and businesspeople canned and processed our food to increase its shelf life, not to reduce the amount of vitamins and minerals and decrease wellness. And, as you'll see in a moment, entrepreneurs and businesspeople hydrogenated oils to make foods look better and last longer in the supermarket, not to turn good fats into bad fats and increase heart disease. Unfortunately, compounded by laws of economics that led thousands to imitate their behavior, the effect on our food supply is the same as if this manipulation had been carried out for the worst of insidious purposes.

These actions were taken in response to often misguided or uninformed consumer demand. Chapter 4 examines how the new consumer demand for wellness, by well-guided and informed consumers, is leading entrepreneurs and businesspeople to fix the problems created by their predecessors. Moreover, the same laws of economics that compounded our wellness problems will now be applied to fix them, as virtually every provider in our food supply chain will be forced to embrace the wellness industry or get out of the way for those who do.

> **As sad as the problems with our food supply may seem, the creation of these problems has also created the greatest opportunity within the wellness industry—the opportunity to provide consumers with healthy foods and dietary supplements to fix the problems with our modern food supply.**

Before we examine these wellness food opportunities, some readers, particularly those focusing on obesity, may want more information on the wellness needs of the 61 percent of the U.S. population that is overweight or obese. Since this is a book on entrepreneurship and not biology, I am including the biological background on obesity in Appendix A at the back of this book. If you are personally or economically focusing on obesity, I suggest you read it now. If not, proceed.

Before Proceeding to the Next Chapter

Action Plan for Entrepreneurs, Investors, and Distributors

1. Analyze how each of your three individual areas of wellness business opportunity will change our food supply. More specifically, what impact will each of these areas have on the following:

   a. Water

   b. Carbohydrates

   c. Lipids (fats)

   d. Proteins

   e. Vitamins

   f. Minerals

2. Analyze how the obesity epidemic impacts each of your three individual areas of wellness business opportunity.

3. Analyze the impact of each of your individual areas of wellness business opportunity on calories—both the calories your customers consume and the calories they burn.

4. Consider the impact of each of your three areas on educating people about what's missing from their food.

   Based on your answers to these questions, think about dropping and replacing any or all of your three individual areas of wellness business opportunity.

CHAPTER 4

Making Your Fortune in Food

Retroactively in response to consumer demand and potential government regulation, companies in the food industry will begin fixing the problem that they created. But the greatest riches await those entrepreneurs who jump ahead of the consumer demand for wellness—entrepreneurs like Steve Demos and Paul Wenner who each built $100 million businesses by proactively getting their products and distribution in place and waiting for the market to come to them.

The wellness fortunes to be made in food lie in two basic areas:
1. Growing, finding, harvesting, transporting, and preparing healthy foods
2. Teaching consumers how to choose healthy foods and how to limit their overall consumption of food

---

Some of the business opportunities in fixing our food supply are economically distorted because of cultural preferences in choosing the foods we eat and massive government subsidy programs that distort the true cost of producing the foods we eat. Our religious and government institutions have fallen behind the consumer in embracing wellness. Before we examine specific wellness food opportunities, it is important for the entrepreneur to understand how this has occurred and to understand the components of our existing $1 trillion food industry.

As you read this chapter, each time a problem with food is discussed, whether it is based on religion, government, or a specific type of food, you should stop and think how you might be able to turn this problem into a profitable wellness business opportunity.

How Religion and Government Fell Behind on Wellness

The history of human civilization is mostly the history of obtaining food—where humans originally migrated to find it and, later, how they cultivated and preserved it. Growing, finding, harvesting, preserving, transporting, preparing, and eating food dominated our daily existence, and the world economy, until the beginning of the twentieth century.

Then, almost overnight, the green revolution and other technologies shifted our major dietary issues from the problems of starvation and cleanliness to the problems of overeating and malnutrition. This happened so fast that our religious and government institutions have still not had the opportunity to catch up.

Today, in developed nations where food is plentiful, most religious people begin meals with prayers thanking God for providing them with food—as opposed to thanking God for giving them the knowledge of what to eat to be healthy. Gluttony is denounced from Exodus through Jude and is one of the seven deadly sins of early Christianity.[1] The Old Testament predicts that gluttons will become poor (Proverbs 23:21). Yet today gluttony is virtually ignored by most religions. Even those religions that focus heavily on diet, such as Orthodox Judaism and Islam, focus on biologically archaic laws of cleanliness (eating kosher) versus the true dietary needs of most of their congregants (eating healthy food, ingesting sufficient vitamins and minerals, and avoiding obesity).

Even today in the United States, the main mission of the U.S. Department of Agriculture (USDA) is to protect the incomes of farmers, not to protect the food supply of consumers. This may have been good policy in 1776 when George Washington called for the establishment of a National Board of Agriculture—farmers then represented more than 95 percent of the population and farm sales comprised more than 90 percent of the nation's economy. But it is an outdated mission now, when farmers represent less than 2 percent of the U.S. population, farm sales are less than 0.5 percent of our economy, and the majority of our citizens are overweight and malnourished.

In the past century, advancing technology in producing, preserving, and distributing food decreased relative food prices so much that food industry sales now represent less than 10 percent of the U.S. economy, or about $1 trillion ($1,000 billion) each year of our $10 trillion gross domestic product. This breaks down roughly as follows:

$1 Trillion U.S. Food Industry

Agriculture	$ 45 billion[2]
Food processing and distribution	$ 500 billion
Restaurants	$ 400 billion[3]
Diet supplementation	$ 70 billion[4]
Other	$ 30 billion
Total U.S. food sales	$1,000 billion*

*Total excludes the $45 billion in agriculture, as it is all either exported or is included as a subcomponent of the other categories.

In the previous chapter we saw how this same advancing technology caused the empty-calorie crisis we have today—our food contains high amounts of fat and caloric energy but is low (or empty) in essential vitamins, minerals, and proteins. This is about to change as consumers become educated and begin demanding healthier foods of all types.

Agricultural Subsidy Programs

Two major areas of agriculture should rapidly change in response to consumer demand for wellness: (1) which foods (healthier) farmers produce and (2) how farmers produce these foods (e.g., organic farming and genetic engineering).

I say *should* because which foods farmers choose to produce and how they produce them are often determined today by obsolete government subsidy programs written almost a century ago rather than by consumer choice and sound economic decisions. Although entrepreneurial opportunities for farmers in the wellness industry still exist, there are fewer opportunities than there would be if farmers were more free from government interference to serve consumer demand.

Even if you are not interested in becoming a wellness farmer, it is important to understand these government subsidy programs for the following reasons:
1. You are paying for them as a taxpayer.
2. Subsidized produce will compete with your wellness food products.

3. They keep farmers producing unhealthy foods, which increase the demand for more wellness products and services.

Agriculture today represents a very small part of our food industry and a minuscule part of our $10 trillion economy, yet farmers and their economic issues occupy a great part of the national stage. This is because too much federal power is now concentrated in several low-population agricultural states. The combined population of any 20 mostly agricultural states like North Dakota (634,000) and Wyoming (480,000) is less than the population of any one industrial state like Texas (20,044,000) or California (33,145,000), yet these agricultural states have 20 times the political power of Texas or California in the U.S. Senate[5]—power that is unfortunately controlled and abused by rich farmers and powerful special interests like the American Dairy Association (ADA).

Beginning in the 1920s, when most voters were farmers, the federal government sought to stabilize farm prices to protect individual farmers from falling prices. Over the years, dozens of different government programs evolved into the system we have today, where farmers (or their children who do not want to farm anyway) are paid corporate welfare *not* to grow certain crops—$24 billion in 1999 alone.[6]

In one county in Texas, federal subsidies make up more than one-third of all farm income, and the top 10 percent of subsidy recipients were paid an average $396,131 from 1996 to 1999—with several farmers receiving more than $2 million each over this period.[7] These subsidy programs are cloaked in names like the "Freedom to Farm Act," suggesting that they benefit consumers and family farms, but most of the money ends up in the hands of a very few rich individuals and corporations who can afford to employ lawyers and lobbyists who are experts in processing government subsidy applications. Unlike virtually every other entitlement or welfare program, federal farm subsidies have no requirements regarding income, assets, or debts.

Even worse than just paying out $24 billion in corporate welfare, these subsidies incentivize production of certain outdated foods that should no longer be produced for wellness reasons.

The Dairy Deception

The worst of these foods, receiving $7 billion in government subsidies, are dairy products. But dairy products cost U.S. consumers many times more than just the $7 billion federal subsidy given dairy producers as corporate welfare.

Milk and milk by-products are leading contributors to the $1.5 trillion sickness industry—milk causes allergies, gas, constipation, obesity, cancer, heart disease, infectious diseases, and osteoporosis.

Yes, milk causes osteoporosis, despite the massive deceptive advertising campaign by the ADA stating that milk prevents osteoporosis.

Several studies have concluded that drinking milk is more likely to *cause* than to prevent osteoporosis, which is the result of calcium leaching out of the bones and is not directly associated with calcium intake, because the amount and type of protein (casein) in milk results in a great loss of calcium in the bones. For those who believe that taking calcium as an adult will help them have strong bones, calcium contained naturally in vegetables is much healthier, easier to absorb, and more abundant. A cup of the latest Tropicana calcium-enriched orange juice contains more calcium than fortified milk—350 milligrams versus 302 milligrams in a cup of milk. Moreover, whatever benefit calcium intake may have in avoiding osteoporosis probably stops in adulthood when bone mass stops increasing—despite the fact that ADA milk advertising promoting calcium intake to avoid osteoporosis is targeted toward adults and older Americans.

But of far more concern than contributing to osteoporosis, milk contains hormones and carries infectious diseases. A typical cow in nature can produce up to 10 pounds of milk per day, whereas today's tortured modern dairy cows produce up to 100 pounds of milk per day. This is because cows today are given massive amounts of specialized hormones like bovine growth hormone (BGH) to increase milk production—making their udders so large they often drag on the ground. This results in frequent infections and the need for constant antibiotics—the USDA allows drinking milk to contain from 1 to 1.5 million white blood cells (that's *pus* to a nonbiologist) per milliliter. These growth hormones, antibiotics, and pus remain in the milk after processing, which causes dire medical consequences for people, especially children, who consume dairy products.

Any U.S. brassiere manufacturer will tell you that sales have been good the past few decades since the introduction of BGH in milk, because BGH and other hormones have increased the size of the average teenage human female breast and have decreased the age of menarche.[8] But what the brassiere manufacturer may not be able to tell you is that these same hormones are also a major cause of the increase in breast cancer in adults—as they cause malignant tumors in the human breast to grow as though they were tortured cows' udders filled with BGH. Despite the fact that numerous consumer groups have called for milk containing BGH and other hormones to be banned or at least labeled as such, the FDA continues to bow to the ADA lobbyists and refuses to ban such hormones or to require milk to be so labeled.

Milk production is also terrible for the environment and for the cows themselves. A dairy cow may produce 100 pounds per day of milk, but it also produces 120 pounds per day of waste—equivalent to the waste produced by 24 people, but with no toilets, sewers, or treatment plants. Each cow consumes 81 pounds of grains and vegetables, plus 45 gallons of water—per day. Although natural cows may live 20 to 25 years, cows in dairy production typically live only 4 to 5 years—burning out from the hormones and constant artificial pregnancies that turn them from living creatures into grotesque milking machines.

The worst thing about dairy products is not the disease they cause, the torture for the animals involved, or the terrible impact on the environment—the worst thing about dairy products is that they are the major cause of more than 61 percent of our population being overweight and obese.

Although drinking milk and eating cheese may *possibly* give a young girl the breasts of Britney Spears (the latest celebrity proudly sporting a milk mustache), drinking lots of milk and eating cheese will *definitely* give a young girl the thighs and hips of the late Mama Cass.*

---

*"Mama" Cass Elliot (1941–1974) of The Mamas and The Papas, was one of the greatest singers and warmest people in history. Unfortunately, as was sometimes noted affectionately in the group's songs, she was terribly obese and died tragically of a heart attack at age 33 while performing at the London Palladium.

The average American eats over four pounds of food per day, and nearly 40 percent of that food is milk and dairy products. Milk contains no fiber and is filled with saturated fat and cholesterol. A glass of milk is 49 percent fat, and cheeses are more than 65 percent fat. Milk really should be called "liquid meat"—one 12-ounce glass contains as much saturated fat as eight strips of bacon. When it comes to obesity and being overweight, milk is even worse than beer—a 12-ounce glass of milk contains 300 calories and 16 grams of fat, whereas a 12-ounce glass of beer contains 144 calories and no fat. Just four tablespoons of half-and-half added to a cup of coffee contain 15 grams of saturated fat—about 80 percent of the saturated fat you should consume in an entire day. To counter the undisputed truth of these facts, the dairy industry came up with the deception of "2 percent" and "low-fat" milk. In reality, 2 percent milk contains 24 to 33 percent calories of fat and is only slightly less fattening than whole milk (which contains 3 percent fat by weight). Milk producers even had the audacity to label cottage cheese, which contains 20 percent calories of fat, "low fat"—which prompted the FDA to recently order dairy producers to stop promoting milk products as low- or nonfat foods.

How did we get to where we are today—where most Americans drink milk and eat milk by-products every day? Historically, milk was valued by our pioneer ancestors because it could be processed at home into high-energy foods like butter and cheese that could last through the winter.

Because milk was perceived to be so valuable, innovative entrepreneurs figured out ways to produce milk at an amazingly low price, then used their profits to build a self-perpetuating marketing and political organization now known as the ADA.

The ADA lobbied the federal government to subsidize overproduction, then forced milk into the diets of children through mandatory school lunch programs. I say *forced* because, though it is widely known that 95 percent of Asians are lactose intolerant, I suspect that most adult humans of every race are similarly intolerant. Caucasians, who comprise most of the milk market, have sadly learned to accept the accompanying allergic reactions, heartburn, upset stomach, diarrhea, gas, and diabetes as facts of everyday life—and to treat only the symptoms of these diseases, taking addictive over-the-counter remedies on a continual basis.

As consumers become educated about the detrimental effects of drinking cow milk, they will develop a voracious appetite for a wellness substitute. This will occur not only for milk, but for the thousands of unhealthy food products that currently dominate our modern food supply. And, as we see in a moment, the greatest rewards will be for the entrepreneurs who get there first.

The Soy Solution: A New Opportunity Born from Wellness

Fortunately, there is a high-energy low-fat substitute for milk that lasts longer, is incredibly healthy, prevents disease, is great for the environment, and costs less: soy milk and other foods made from soybeans. Unfortunately, few people in the United States and other Western countries know about it. This is ironic considering that, although containing less than 5 percent of the world's population, the United States produces about 50 percent of the world's soybeans. Of the 3 million bushels of soybeans grown in the United States each year, 98 percent is for animal feed or industrial uses and only 2 percent for direct human consumption—with the overwhelming majority of this 2 percent sold to Japan and other countries where consumers already enjoy a soy-rich diet.

Converting more farms from producing soybeans for animal feed to soybeans for human consumption is one of the largest wellness opportunities for agriculturally based entrepreneurs.

Soybeans first came to North America in the early 1800s, not as food, but as ballast aboard clipper ships. In 1904, George Washington Carver, the famous African-American chemist, discovered their high-protein value for animal feed and also discovered that farmers could produce higher-quality cotton and other plants by rotating them with soybeans every one to three years. Henry Ford used soybeans to make the plastic parts for many Ford cars—using 60 pounds of soybeans in every Ford by 1935.[9]

But soy's greatest benefits, which could make soy the largest staple in a wellness diet, have only recently been discovered. For human beings, soy is the best low-fat source of proteins, carbohydrates, fibers, vitamins, and minerals we know about today. Moreover, soy has great medicinal qualities that can prevent many of the diseases caused by dairy products, from osteoporosis to heart disease and cancer.

Soy is high in calcium and, unlike milk, does not contain the casein proteins that result in calcium loss in the bones. Soy has even been shown to reverse osteoporosis, as the isoflavones found in soybeans can increase bone mineral content and bone density.[10] An *isoflavone* is a colorless organic compound (ketone) occurring in a plant in sufficient amounts to affect the endocrine system of animals. Another soy isoflavone, genistein, stops cancer cells from growing when added to live cancer cells in laboratory test tubes. Other soy isoflavones reduce the frequency and intensity of hot flashes in menopausal women, similar to estrogen-replacement therapy. And the protein in soy has such a preventive effect on heart disease that in October 1999 the FDA announced that soy producers may claim that "consuming 25 grams of soy protein a day may help consumers lower their (bad) cholesterol and reduce their risk of heart disease." The American Heart Association endorsed the same claim one year later.

Soybeans contain more protein by weight than beef, fish, or chicken, with no cholesterol and little saturated fat. Moreover, for those individuals wanting to limit or eliminate their consumption of animal proteins, soy protein is the only "complete" vegetable protein. As noted earlier, human beings require 20 basic amino acids from proteins, 11 of which can be produced by our bodies. The remaining nine we must get from the foods we eat. Soy protein provides all nine missing amino acids, making it as complete as the protein in milk or meat products—but without the hormones, the saturated fat, the calories, and the devastating effect on our environment.

Soybeans and soy beverages have been cultivated and produced in China for 5,000 years and enjoyed throughout Asia for centuries. In the West, the term *milk* has been used since the twelfth century to define "a fluid secreted by the mammary glands of females for the nourishment of their young, or the contents of an unripe kernel of grain."[11] But all this didn't stop the cow milk producers from having the audacity in February 2000 to file a trade complaint with the FDA requesting that soymilk producers be prohibited from using the term *milk* in their advertisements—claiming "that 'milk' has a standard of identity dictating that it must come from dairy cows."[12] If the FDA insisted on the truth about cow milk and milk advertising, it should rule that cow milk be labeled "cow pus" and carry warnings on each carton similar to the warnings now required on individual packs of cigarettes (e.g., "The Surgeon General has determined that the human consumption of cow milk causes allergies, constipation, gas, bacterial infections, osteoporosis, obesity, heart disease, and cancer").

Many upscale Americans who dine in expensive sushi restaurants already love soybeans but don't know it. The green "snap beans" often served as complimentary appetizers in upscale sushi restaurants, called *edamame,* are nothing more than pure boiled (or steamed) soybeans. Edamame (pronounced ed-ah-MAH-may) is technically the name of a specialty soybean harvested just before the beans reach maturity. While most sushi diners think of them only as something to nibble on while waiting for their fish, edamame is incredibly healthy and actually contains more proteins and nutrients than the fish itself—an amazing 22 grams of protein per cup. Although the farming of edamame is currently a very minor part of U.S. soybean agriculture, it is extremely profitable, and its cultivation is expected to grow exponentially as it becomes more widely known.

From a scientific standpoint, soy foods should already be widely touted as the wellness wonder products of our time. Unfortunately, science has very little to do with the Western diet. When it comes to food, we are ruled by convention, taste, and convenience.

Many people are unwilling to try new foods, seeking out the familiar and expected glass of milk in the morning or the cheeseburger for lunch. Those of us eager to try new foods are often ruled by the immediate sensory gratification of taste rather than the longer-term benefit of how we will feel afterward. Even if soy products were familiar to us and tasted good, they would have to be as conveniently available as McDonald's Big Macs or Coca-Cola to make a real impact on the average diet.

A few wellness revolutionaries are poised to achieve exactly this result in all three areas—convention, taste, and convenience. Some of these revolutionaries are already entrenched in the largest part of our food industry, the $500 billion food processing business. Fortunately for the wellness entrepreneur just getting started,

these successful entrepreneurs are barely scratching the surface of what is possible in developing wellness substitutes for many of our unhealthy foods.

The Soy Wonder: Building a "Right Livelihood"

In 1970, when Steve Demos graduated from Bowling Green University in Ohio, he knew everything he *didn't* want to do to make a living. However, like many of his generation, he also had no idea of what he did want to do—so he ended up dropping out for the next four years and traveling throughout India. There, he became a vegetarian and formulated his desire to construct a "right livelihood" where the Golden Rule could be applied to business. In his own words, this meant that

"Everyone who touches the stream of revenue must be doing good for society."

When he returned to the United States, Demos settled in Boulder, Colorado, and decided that the business of making healthy vegetarian foods, especially from soy products, had all the attributes to which he could apply his "right livelihood" philosophy.

Like many entrepreneurs, Demos tried various approaches before he hit on the one that would make him famous.

He started a natural nut butter company called Naturally Nuts. He ran a retail vegetarian delicatessen called The Cow of China. And he started White Wave Tofu, which today has become the largest soy foods and soymilk company in the world.

White Wave Tofu (now White Wave, Inc.) made its first sale of tofu on September 27, 1977, at 11:30 A.M. Tofu, also known as *bean curd*, is a soft, bland, custardlike food made from crushed soybeans. The tofu was made in Steve's apartment kitchen using $500 he borrowed from a neighbor to start the company. White Wave ran along for the next 20 years making various soy-based products, achieving sales of about $6 million in 1996. During those years, many products were tried and eventually dropped—like

Polar Bean (soy) ice cream and ToFruzen—products that Steve didn't realize until years later were viable but were then simply too far ahead of their time.

In 1996, after a successful "getting rich slowly" philosophy that had sustained White Wave for almost two decades, Steve realized that packaged soy foods like tofu and tempeh were probably never going to make the impact on society he had dreamed of when he started his company.

Soy seemed to be a very narrow niche market limited to those vegetarians who knew about it. The company had tried veggie burgers, tofu hot dogs, ice creams, and countless other ideas in attempting to entice the American consumer to embrace soy. Over those years, Steve realized that the product he was searching for would be one that required no customer education—it had to be a "nonthinking" product containing "freshness, familiarity, and convenience." Steve came up with Silk® soymilk later that year as the culmination of all of these insights.

Silk, a very fresh soymilk product made entirely from organically grown soybeans, is sold in freshness-dated, refrigerated cartons that look like quarts or half gallons of ordinary milk. It comes in plain, vanilla, chocolate, chai, and mocha flavors—and a companion Silk creamer product comes in Plain and French Vanilla. For the consumer, it is "fresh, familiar, and convenient," especially since it is now available in 91 percent of U.S. supermarkets.

In 1997, soon after launching Silk, White Wave sales rose 37 percent, from $6 to $8.2 million. Led by Silk, sales rose another 24 percent, to $10.2 million in 1998, and yet another 39 percent, to $14.2 million in 1999. Then the FDA and others began touting the benefits of soy products and sales more than doubled, to $29.6 million in 2000, and almost tripled in 2001, to $80.5 million. Company sales are expected to exceed $140 million in 2002—with some analysts predicting that the first $1 billion health-food company is only a few years away.[13] Silk today accounts for 92 percent of total company sales.

When I first phoned the main number for White Wave to set up an interview, Steve's voice greeted me on the company's voice mail: "Welcome to White Wave. This is Steve Demos, company president. The following menu will assist you." Since I had read about Steve before calling him for the interview and had seen tapes of his appearances on CNN and elsewhere, I was not surprised to hear him humbly attribute the enormous success of Silk to "the market was ripe, there was nobody present, and we had all the elements."

I was surprised to find this former society dropout highly versed in the vernacular of modern business—so much so that I could have been talking to any Fortune 500 CEO or professor at Wharton or NYU business school. When I complimented him on this he explained, "If you are really and passionately committed to what you want to accomplish, you adjust to the language spoken."

But Steve has done far more than simply learning the language of business in the twenty-first century. He practices it at the highest levels—levels not usually found in a food company or with a start-up entrepreneur.

According to Steve, "Most entrepreneurs are prepared for failure but not for success. Thus, when they succeed, they end up handing their business over to a competitor."

In 1998, Steve realized that he had a tiger by the tail and began to prepare for success. First, White Wave identified several strategic targets as investors—targets that could provide capital and operational support if Silk sales continued their meteoric rise. Then, after identifying the proper targets in its industry, White Wave hired an investment banker to execute the transaction and sold a minority interest in the company for $15 million to the second largest dairy in the United States. But White Wave never used the operational resources of their new dairy partner.

Instead, Steve retooled the Silk manufacturing process into a virtual process modeled on the best aspects of both the dairy industry and the much more profitable soft drink industry. Today, White Wave makes very high quality soymilk extract at three 20,000-square-foot, company-owned facilities that are strategically located in New Jersey, Colorado, and Utah. This highly valuable extract is then shipped in milk-type trucks to five major dairies that make and package the Silk—dairies carefully chosen to ensure that

White Wave is an important part of their overall volume and a profitable customer. These dairies not only guarantee Silk virtually unlimited manufacturing capacity, they already have the trucks and sales organizations to keep Silk in the dairy case at the local supermarkets. As Steve explains, White Wave now has a totally scalable model—"We draw a 500-mile radius around extraction, find facilities, and then expand."

Although most people today see Silk as an alternative to cow milk, Steve doesn't see the dairies as his competition. "We're not an alternative to milk," says Steve, "we're an option. I don't want to be dairy's nemesis—I want to be so superior that there is no comparison. I'm after Coca-Cola as much as I'm after milk." In this regard, White Wave's newest product is an 11-ounce plastic bottle of Silk soymilk packaged like a soft drink but with a 120-day nonrefrigerated shelf life. The average person in the United States consumes 24.2 gallons per year of cow milk, and that same average person also consumes 54.6 gallons per year of soft drinks.

The Vegetarian Burger Wonder: A Wellness Cautionary Tale

Steve Demos's concern about handing over your wellness business to a competitor after achieving success is well founded. Entrepreneurs must be prepared for success.

The story of Paul Wenner, the famous vegetarian chef, author, and founder of Gardenburger, Inc., contains an important lesson for wellness entrepreneurs. At the time of this writing, Wenner and his company appear to have lost out financially to competition after pioneering the market for vegetarian burgers. Nevertheless, Paul Wenner is a true wellness revolutionary who has made, and continues to make, a positive contribution to the lives of millions of people.

Paul Wenner didn't start out wanting to be a wellness revolutionary or even a great success. He thought that he had finally realized his lifelong dream in 1981 when he opened his gourmet vegetarian restaurant, The Gardenhouse Restaurant, in Gresham, Oregon. As he explains in his book, "Like all restaurateurs, I was soon faced with what to do with the leftovers. My solution was something I called the 'Gardenloaf Sandwich' made of leftover vegetables and rice pilaf.[14] Later I got the idea of slicing up the loaf into what

looked like patties—and suddenly the Gardenburger was born."
Soon, one out of every two lunches sold in his restaurant was a
Gardenburger.[15]

Then, in 1984, a recession hit Oregon and his restaurant folded.
Paul thought it was the end of the world, although, as he reflects
now, it was "the best thing that could have happened." Customers
started calling to ask where they could still get Gardenburgers, and
one day Paul's sister set up a meeting with the CEO of her company to see about financing a business to supply them. The CEO
tried the Gardenburger, offered Paul $60,000 to start the business,
and asked: "When will this company make money?" Paul had
absolutely no idea, so he replied, "In 13 months," based on the
notion that if it couldn't make money after a full year he wouldn't
be able to stick it out anyway.

**As Gardenburger grew, Paul learned to turn every nega-
tive experience into a positive one. When 9 out of 10
restaurant owners told him, "We don't get any vegetarians in here," his response was, "Maybe that's because
there's nothing vegetarian on your menu."**

The company went public in 1992, and Paul Wenner turned over
day-to-day management to food industry professionals in 1995,
retaining for himself a seat on the board and the title of chief creative officer. By 1998, Gardenburger, Inc.,[16] had sold hundreds of
millions of Gardenburgers and the company's products were distributed in tens of thousands of supermarkets and natural food
stores worldwide.

Unfortunately, as fast as Gardenburger grew, it wasn't fast enough
to satisfy the demand for what Wenner had started. In 1993 another
restaurateur, in Fort Lauderdale, Florida, decided he, too, could create a good-tasting vegetarian burger and started Boca Foods—which
by 1998 was making vegetarian substitutes for ground beef, chicken,
sausages, and other popular meat products. Another competitor,
Worthington Foods, also entered the "meatless meat" market with a
more complete line of soy-based products called Morningstar.

**Although Gardenburger achieved sales of $100.1 mil-
lion in 1998, this represented then only about one-fifth
of the market it had created for meatless vegetarian substitutes.**

The food industry professionals running Gardenburger were convinced that all they needed was more awareness and trial of their product before someone else acquired their future customers. In 1998, Gardenburger spent $1.5 million for an advertising spot on the last *Seinfield* episode. Although the ad was seen by a record 104 million viewers, critics claimed that the bulk of the benefit went to Gardenburger's competitors, who also reported increases in store sales the next day. To sustain its $100.1 million in sales in 1998, Gardenburger spent an incredibly high $15 million on advertising that year and was planning to continue such spending by raising more equity capital. The company sold $32.5 million in preferred stock in 1999—but that year its sales fell 12 percent to $88.8 million. Sales fell an additional 21 percent to $71 million in 2000, and the company recorded a loss of $32.7 million, or $3.67 per share.

To make matters even worse, in 1999, Kellogg, Inc. ($9 billion sales) purchased competitor Worthington Foods for $307 million, and in 2000, cigarette maker Philip Morris ($80 billion sales) purchased Boca Foods. Wall Street lost confidence that Gardenburger could ever recover against such strong competition, and its stock price crashed from $18 to less than 50 cents a share—causing Gardenburger to be delisted from the Nasdaq.[17] Hopefully, this delisting could be a blessing in disguise as its new CEO will be able to focus on restructuring the company into a profitable business rather than on its stock price.

Paul Wenner is now running a new vegetarian restaurant in Hawaii. He recently completed his book tour for *Garden Cuisine,* part autobiography, part how to start a business, part how to achieve a healthy body, part how to prevent cruelty to animals, and part how to protect our environment. Wenner still owns about 600,000 or so shares of Gardenburger, Inc., which insider trading reports showed him selling throughout 2001 for as little as $.47 per share.

Wenner's stake today is far less than the $10 to $15 million these shares might once have commanded, but this personal loss seems almost insignificant considering the billions of vegetarian burgers now sold and the positive impact Wenner has had on the lives of millions of people.

What Restaurant Entrepreneurs Need to Know

Restaurants like Wenner's have introduced more than just vegetarian burgers to society.

The restaurant industry is one of the most dynamic entrepreneurial components of the American economy—continually introducing new products and innovative concepts over the past four decades. How this industry grew over the past 40 years illustrates what is possible for the wellness industry over the next decade.

In 1961, few Americans ate their meals out of the home, and total U.S. restaurant sales were less than $20 billion. Today, about half of Americans eat meals out of the home each day, and total restaurant sales in 2001 were about $400 billion. If, back in 1961, someone were to have predicted this 20-fold increase in sales, you probably wouldn't have believed it for the following reasons.

First (you might have thought in 1961), only the very wealthy could afford to eat half of their meals out of the home. Yet advancing technology lowered production costs so much that by 2001 it was often less expensive to eat out than to dine at home.

Second (you might have thought in 1961), there weren't enough restaurants in America to seat that many people at mealtimes. Yet over the next 40 years tens of thousands of shopping centers were built to house the 844,000 U.S. dining establishments that now exist.

Third (you might have thought in 1961), people would be bored eating out so much, because, back then, only three basic types of cuisine were available (diner, cafeteria, and French). Yet hundreds of varieties of restaurants came to exist by 2001, many from places, like Thailand, that weren't even independently named countries in 1961.

Fourth (you might have thought in 1961), restaurants are labor-intensive and there simply aren't enough people in the United States to work in all those dining establishments. Yet advancing technology allowed manufacturers to lay off tens of millions of workers while still being able to serve their customers, and 11.3 million of these workers ended up in the restaurant industry by 2001. The restaurant industry today is the largest U.S. private sector employer.

Fifth, and finally, even if you were able to foresee these incredible changes in lower costs, increased number of dining establishments, unlimited varieties of cuisine, and available labor, you might have thought in 1961 that people just didn't have the time to eat out so often. In fact, a whole new category of restaurants emerged in the 1960s, defined not by their price, location, or country of origin, but by the speed of their service: fast-food restaurants.

Restaurant choice now is dominated by price, location, type of cuisine, and speed of service, but a new type of restaurant choice is emerging that will generate fortunes for the Ray Krocs and Dave Thomases of tomorrow who proactively jump in now and wait for the customer to come to them.

If you haven't guessed it already, it is exactly what Paul Wenner did in 1981 when he decided to open a restaurant focused on healthy food—although he was then too far ahead of his time to have it work out the way he originally thought it would.

The reason the time is ripe to open specialty restaurants focused on healthy cuisine has to do with the nature of who is spending the most profitable part of the $400 billion consumed at U.S. restaurants today.

The average American family spends 45.6 percent of their food budget on meals prepared outside of the home, but households with incomes of $50,000 or more spend *70 percent* of their food budget on meals prepared outside of the home. Those households with incomes above $100,000 spend even more than 70 percent of their food budget at restaurants. Although baby boomers comprise only 28 percent of the U.S. population, boomers account for more than 50 percent of households with incomes over $50,000 and 60 percent of the households with incomes over $100,000.[18] On a per-person basis, boomers today spend more than twice as much dining out as did the generation of their parents.[19]

As explained in Chapter 2, the single item that characterizes most boomer spending to date is the desire for products that remind them of their youth. In restaurants, they have not had much to choose from in this regard, other than a few establishments with themes or menus reminiscent of earlier times. But think for a moment what would happen if boomers could choose restaurants that served healthy cuisine that could actually make them younger or could slow down the effects of aging in the future—cuisine like Silk soymilk or Gardenburger meatless patties, or just ordinary cuisine prepared without the addition of heavy creams or saturated fats.

Boomers would flock to such restaurants, as evidenced by the fact that such health-food restaurants already exist in almost every city, and most regular upscale establishments have added one or two healthy or vegetarian entrées to their menu.

Instead of being considered fringe-type food or something grudgingly added to restaurants' menus, by 2010 healthy cuisine will be almost universal. Whereas today people choose restaurants mostly based on taste, price, and convenience, millions will soon choose restaurants based on the healthiness of the cuisine or how they will feel afterward.

Today, on hearing this prediction, you might think that consumers would never flock to healthy cuisine because it costs too much to prepare—yet history proves that advancing technology drives prices lower and lower in response to consumer demand, especially in the food service industry.

Second, you might think that there aren't enough locations left to open hundreds of thousands of healthy restaurants—yet most of the existing 844,000 U.S. restaurants will be forced to retool their menus or lose their leases to new owners who will. There will be widespread consumer rejection of restaurants perceived to serve unhealthy food. Additionally, today's upscale restaurant patrons limit going out when they are watching their weight—these profitable patrons will eat out even more often if they are given more healthy places to choose from.

Third, you might think that people will get bored eating only healthy food again and again—yet all types of restaurants, from French to Italian to Thai, will be embracing a healthy menu, and the term *health food* will soon become as meaningless in describing the type of food at an establishment as the word *restaurant* is today.

Fourth, you might think that healthy food simply doesn't taste good, yet once you get the toxins, high levels of sodium, and dangerous chemicals from processed foods out of your system, you won't believe what you have been missing. There is nothing more delicious than food in its natural state—from bananas to fresh grains to raw vegetables—but our taste buds have been chemically altered by processed food companies for so long that most of us have been unable to appreciate them.

And finally, even if you now accept my predictions on lower prices, locations, types of cuisine, and great taste, you might think that this type of change in the restaurant industry won't occur because people's dining habits are so well entrenched—yet something even more fundamental than all of these changes is about to happen to the dining habits of society, beginning in the United States.

Consumers everywhere will soon understand that there is a monumental connection between the food they consume today and the way their bodies will feel tonight, let alone tomorrow.

The "professionally beautiful," as explained in Chapter 1, already understand part of this relationship as they navigate through the menus at exclusive restaurants. As you look around, from your nightly newscast to the advertising and packaging that affect and shape our thoughts, you can see that everyone will soon embrace the age-old wisdom of Hippocrates: "Let food be your medicine and medicine be your food."

Before Proceeding to the Next Chapter

Action Plan for Entrepreneurs, Investors, and Distributors

1. Analyze how the coming changes in agriculture will impact each of your three current areas of potential wellness businesses.

2. How will each of your three current areas of potential wellness businesses rise or fall with a potential consumer flight away from dairy products?

3. How are your three current areas of potential wellness businesses positioned for the major changes coming in the American diet?

4. Steve Demos (Silk soymilk) spent 21 unsuccessful years trying to change American dietary habits (by getting people to eat tofu). He then succeeded in 1997 when he made a product (soymilk) that required no change in the dietary habits of consumers. Analyze the major changes in dietary habits that need to be overcome for each of your three current areas of potential wellness businesses to succeed. How would you plan to accomplish these necessary changes?

5. Steve Demos made his worst enemy (the dairies) his best ally—by making a healthy substitute milk product for the dairies to distribute. Analyze how you might be able to similarly induce an existing food company or industry to distribute your product(s) for each of your three current areas of potential wellness businesses. How are each of your three areas positioned to take on strategic partners to grow?

6. Paul Wenner's Gardenburger, Inc., eventually failed by not being able to supply its customers before competition took hold. How are each of your three areas positioned to succeed without being eaten alive by the competition?

7. In a similar vein, what products will be displaced by each of your three current areas of potential wellness businesses, and what action are their manufacturers or industries likely to take for or against you?

8. Analyze the impact of ubiquitous healthy food on each of your three areas for development or investment—particularly if one of your three areas is in the restaurant business.

Based on your answers to these questions, think about dropping and replacing any or all of your three individual areas of wellness business opportunity.

CHAPTER 5

Making Your Fortune in Medicine

Let thy food be thy medicine and thy medicine be thy food.
—HIPPOCRATES (460–377 B.C.)

Most of the fortunes in medical wellness will be made by people outside of the sickness industry. In this chapter, we will examine a salesperson who invented multivitamins, two unusual physicians who have branched out of traditional medicine, and an extraordinary female athlete who has built a $100 million health club business.

Many consumers mistakenly still think that their medical wellness should come from their traditional sickness providers—doctors, hospitals, and pharmaceutical companies. This is why it is critically important for every wellness entrepreneur to be able to explain the history of wellness medicine and the current state of scientific knowledge when it comes to keeping our bodies healthy, fit, and youthful.

The Search for What's Inside the Black Box

Throughout most of our history, the human body has been a black box. A black box is a device, like a computer or a car, that does something, but whose inner workings are mysterious—either because its inner workings cannot be seen or because they are incomprehensible.[1]

> The history of medicine is the search for what's inside
> the black box called the human body and how it func-
> tions.

In the Stone Age, most of humankind accepted debilitating illness as something that was caused by a higher being for no apparent rhyme or reason—people were not responsible for medicine
and thus could not affect it or change it. Those few cultures that
did practice medicine believed that cures lay in expelling the
disease-causing demon from the body—so-called medicine men
developed elaborate rituals and techniques, like trepanning (boring
a hole in the skull), as treatments.[2]

Later in antiquity, humankind developed the belief that sickness
was punishment from a supernatural being and that the cure for
sickness lay in prayer and repentance for the action (or inaction)
that had angered whichever god had caused the disease. The
thought that you, or someone you loved, were being punished for
your actions added even more trauma to the most painful of human
experiences.

Hippocrates:
The First Wellness Practitioner

One of the earliest people to refute both of these beliefs was the
Greek physician, Hippocrates (460–377 B.C.), the founder of modern medicine.[3] Hippocrates is best known today for the Hippo-
cratic Oath still recited by medical school graduates. Unfortunately,
medicine today has evolved far from the most important beliefs of
its most famous practitioner.

Hippocrates regarded the body as a "whole" being rather than
just the sum of operating parts—whereas today modern medicine
often treats each organ or illness in isolation. Hippocrates studied
each patient in his or her own environment, from their occupation
to their diet. In doing so, Hippocrates came to the conclusion that
health was the natural state, that disease was abnormal, and that
the role of the physician was to assist nature to regain its natural
(i.e., healthy) state. But most important,

> Hippocrates was the first physician focused on *prevent-
> ing* disease as well as treating disease. In all areas of
> medicine, he taught that the right types of nourishment
> and exercise were the key to both avoiding sickness and

regaining health. This is the key difference between wellness and sickness medicine: avoidance and prevention.

When we consider what we know today about human evolution, from Charles Darwin's *Theory of Natural Selection* to Michael Behe's *Theory of Intelligent Design*,[4] Hippocrates' teachings about diet and exercise make even more sense. Our bodies evolved on this planet to exist in their natural state (i.e., *good health*) based on a natural diet and a natural amount of exercise. For more than 99 percent of human evolution and existence, a natural diet consisted of eating the wide variety of carbohydrates, fats, proteins, vitamins, and minerals that were abundantly available by grazing a mostly vegetarian supply of food. A natural amount of exercise consisted of physically laboring throughout each day for food and shelter.

It is easy to see how far we are today from this natural ideal in terms of our health. Our Western diet is far from that of our biological ancestors—it contains much more fat and is low in essential vitamins and minerals. Similarly, few of us get the amount of exercise all day long that our biological ancestors got naturally in their daily search for food and shelter.

Our Limited Vision

In the parable *The Blind Men and the Elephant* by John Godfrey Saxe (1816–1887), six blind men encounter an elephant for the first time: The first, touching its side, exclaims, "The Elephant is very like a wall." The second, touching its tusk, exclaims, "The Elephant is very like a spear." The third, touching its trunk, exclaims, "The Elephant is very like a snake." The fourth, touching its leg, exclaims, "The Elephant is very like a tree." The fifth, touching its ear, exclaims, "The Elephant is very like a fan." And the sixth, touching its tail, exclaims, "The Elephant is very like a rope." Each blind man remains convinced that he alone knows the nature of the elephant.

Throughout history, medicine men and women in every civilization have thought that they could finally explain the human black box and how it functioned. In hindsight, we can see that they were as foolish as the six blind men because they were similarly blinded by the limited tools they had available for observation.

Moreover, each time a new tool allowed scientists to open what they thought was the final black box, scientists saw another, previously unknown black box inside that had to await further tools to be opened.[5]

Early scientists believed that all matter was made of four "elements"—earth, air, fire, and water—since that was all they could see with their eyes. Fledgling biologists believed that all living bodies were regulated by what they could see—the four humors of blood, yellow bile, black bile, and phlegm—and that all disease arose from an excess of one of these humors. Dissection was generally prohibited, and therefore the tools for observation were limited.

From the time of Hippocrates up to the nineteenth century, medicine didn't focus much on *why* something worked—medicine focused mostly on finding out *what* worked through trial-and-error treatment and observation.

When something worked, it was written down, and thus was medical knowledge accumulated over the centuries and occasionally passed between cultures.

The Scottish physician James Lind is credited with eliminating scurvy in the British navy by prescribing the mandatory consumption of citrus fruits among sailors. Yet Lind had no idea why citrus fruits eliminated scurvy and only came up with his "discovery" after reading that the Dutch navy had done this for hundreds of years. The Dutch probably picked up the practice from some other culture with abundant citrus during their great explorations in the fifteenth through seventeenth centuries.

The invention of the movable type printing press in the fifteenth century spread information to physicians worldwide about treatments that worked in alleviating specific ailments. This knowledge of so many treatments helped medicine establish itself as science (as opposed to religion or magic) by the eighteenth century. Of course, even though by then thousands of medicines or treatments were known to work, doctors were mostly at a total loss to explain *why* they worked.

The breakthroughs of Robert Hooke and others in the seventeenth and eighteenth centuries allowed the development of the inexpensive compound optical microscope. Using this new tool, scientists in the nineteenth century were able to see the previously invisible world of cells, which they then thought were the smallest and "final" building blocks of human matter.

The ability to watch cells function, especially in reaction to invading bacteria and medicines, led biologists and physicians to believe that they finally had the tool to discover why medicines worked. Doctors became international heroes as they eliminated major diseases (e.g., smallpox, tuberculosis, typhoid, polio) that had been the scourge of humankind.

Emboldened by this success, most Western medical practitioners and researchers also began arrogantly rejecting age-old treatments and cures that had accumulated over the millennia—simply because they could not scientifically explain their function.

Today we know how wrong they were in assuming that the individual cell was the smallest or final building block of human anatomy. An optical microscope cannot resolve two points that are closer together than approximately one-half of the wavelength of the illuminating light—and an individual bacterial cell, for example, is approximately one-tenth the wavelength of visible light.[6] Although it takes about 10,000 human cells to cover the head of a pin, each cell is composed of *trillions* of molecules that cannot be detected with even the best compound optical microscope. Most important,

---

Virtually everything we know today about the critical biochemical functions performed by proteins, vitamins, minerals, and nutritional supplements takes place on a molecular versus a cellular level.

Today we also know that it is the individual quality of each cell that matters most when it comes to human longevity, vitality, strength, and everything else we desire from medicine beyond the treatment of disease—in short, wellness.

Since our cells are constantly being replaced on an hourly to monthly basis, the quality of our cells is a function of the quality of the molecular reactions that constantly occur in manufacturing them.

> The quality of these molecular reactions is dependent
> on the quality of their components—the amino acids
> (proteins) and minerals that are the building blocks of
> cellular matter and the vitamins and minerals necessary
> as catalysts to combine molecules from raw materials.

Scientists generally agree on the daily components necessary to properly regenerate our cellular matter—13 essential vitamins, 14 essential minerals, and 20 basic amino acids (10 of which we must get from external sources). But scientists are far from agreeing on how these components combine in our bodies to form the complex proteins that make up our individual cells. Scientists have identified more than 100,000 different proteins in our bodies, manufactured from the same 20 basic amino acids, and are still identifying thousands more complex proteins faster than they are learning about specific protein deficiencies and how to treat them. We have just discovered that each cell contains its own time clock or biological programming for regenerating itself—DNA—but at this point in time we have a long way to go before we are able to read this programming.

The best we can do today when it comes to preventive or wellness medicine is to seek out the natural type of diet and natural program of exercise originally prescribed by Hippocrates. Today, this means the following:

1. Eating the proper amount (calories) and types of foods (e.g., unsaturated fats, soy, fibers) to maintain optimal health and avoid obesity
2. Avoiding harmful chemicals and hormones in our food—especially those contained in dairy and animal foods
3. Eating foods (including supplements) that yield a daily supply of our requisite vitamins, minerals, and basic amino acids (proteins)
4. Exercising throughout the day to yield the equivalent of a natural amount of exercise

This is much easier said than done in our modern society. Eating only the amount of calories you need requires a great deal of self-discipline—especially since your body is programmed to eat each meal as if it were going to be your last and to store fat for later consumption. Avoiding harmful hormones and chemicals is virtually impossible, as most of them aren't even disclosed—especially in meat or dairy products. Ensuring a minimum daily supply of vitamins and minerals is difficult because many are missing from our processed foods, and, as we discuss in a moment, many supplements do not currently contain the items stated on their labels. Finally, if you were to try to get the same "natural" exercise as our ancestors, you wouldn't have time during the day to do anything else.

Fortunately, a few wellness medical entrepreneurs already exist, but we need thousands more like them, dedicated to making wellness easier than ever before and using technology to solve many of the wellness problems that technology has created.

Multivitamins and Multilevel Marketing

While working in China as a salesperson for Colgate between 1915 and 1927, Carl F. Rehnborg observed that urban dwellers showed terrible signs of malnutrition, but that this malnutrition was not as widespread among the poorer citizens in rural areas. He began to study the relationship between health and nutrition and realized that there were many plant-based substances critical to the human diet. He thought about making a plant-based supplement for the human diet and, on returning to the United States in 1927, set up a laboratory on California's Balboa Island to study which such supplements were needed.

The more Rehnborg studied, the more he could see that the average person needed a single simple solution to the complex problem of dietary supplementation.

After years of research Rehnborg came up with the then-revolutionary idea of combining every needed mineral and vitamin into a single product. He called his company California Vitamins and produced the world's first multivitamin/multimineral food supplement in 1934. The name of the product and the company was changed to Nutrilite in 1939.

Back then, the concept of a single food supplement containing many different vitamins and minerals required a great amount of customer education—especially to a public just learning that vitamins existed. Moreover, since Nutrilite's new multivitamin/multimineral product was a hybrid between a food and a medicine, it wasn't carried by either traditional supermarkets or pharmacies.

In order to distribute his product, his wife suggested that Rehnborg set up his own sales force of people— people who were already zealous consumers of Nutrilite themselves. This strategy created a constant need for Nutrilite to recruit and train new salespeople as the company expanded.

In 1945, Rehnborg and his two main distributors came up with another idea that not only revolutionized the marketing of his nutritional supplements but also created a whole new multibillion-dollar distribution industry.[7]

Rehnborg's second revolutionary idea was a marketing plan that would allow salespeople both to sell the Nutrilite product and to recruit and train new salespeople—earning one line of income from their product sales and another line of income from the sales of the people they recruited and trained.

Each individual salesperson, now called a *distributor,* would be treated equally by the company based solely on their sales and the sales of the people they recruited. When the sales of an individual salesperson reached a certain level, they could break away from the person who recruited them and become direct distributors for the company themselves.

In 1949 two young entrepreneurs from Grand Rapids, Michigan, Jay Van Andel and Rich DeVos, purchased a Nutrilite sales kit and quickly rose to the highest sales levels in the company. Ten years later, while keeping their existing Nutrilite sales business, Jay and Rich started a new company to sell household products based on a similar marketing plan. They called their new company Amway, for "American Way." In 1972, Carl F. Rehnborg passed away at age 82, and Amway purchased Nutrilite Products, Inc. Today, Nutrilite is still maintained as a separate corporate entity and, with several billion dollars in annual sales, is one of the largest vitamin/mineral/supplement manufacturers in the world.

Nutrilite pioneered the use of technology to solve the problem of combining minimum daily requirements of vitamins and minerals into one convenient package. In a similar vein, the company is again pioneering the use of technology to solve the problem many Americans have today with being overweight and obese. In 2001, Nutrilite began marketing a new high-protein (versus high-carbohydrate) food bar—not as a food supplement but as a full meal replacement. This product, which contains large amounts of protein and a completely balanced meal in one convenient package, is a simple solution to a complex problem, as was Carl Rehnborg's original multivitamin/multimineral back in 1934.

Rehnborg successfully used technology to solve a problem with our food supply (lack of vitamins and minerals) that had been created by another technology (food processing). There are thousands of entrepreneurial opportunities today to solve similar problems created by our processed and fast-food industries.

ConsumerLab.com:
Sharing Knowledge Is Big Business

Despite the success of Nutrilite and several other quality manufacturers, the U.S. $70 billion dietary supplement industry has had a tainted reputation. Although hundreds of millions of people use their products every day and often swear by them, millions of people have had similarly negative experiences and call supplement products "expensive urine"—referring to the fact that some of these products just pass through the digestive system without having any effect. Additionally, some people have actually become ill after taking supplements and called for supplements to be banned from the marketplace. Recent evidence is yielding proof that some of these skeptics and harbingers of disaster may be correct—but not for the reasons they might have suspected.

Between one-quarter and one-third of the dietary supplements (vitamins, minerals, and herbals) sold in the United States today have one or both of the following problems: (1) The products do not contain what they say they do on the label. (2) The products contain undisclosed dangerous substances in addition to what appears on their labels.

> **No wonder about a third of the people who have tried dietary supplements have found them to be ineffective or even dangerous!**

The U.S. Food and Drug Administration (FDA) is supposed to monitor and regulate dietary supplements through the Dietary Supplement Health and Education Act (DHSEA) of 1994. Unfortunately, due to woefully inadequate personnel and a limited budget, FDA regulations are rarely enforced when it comes to dietary supplements. This has left the door open for unscrupulous or simply ineffective supplement manufacturers to get away with outright fraud. But it has also opened the door for dedicated medical entrepreneurs like Dr. Tod Cooperman, to make a significant contribution to wellness while striking out to make their own fortunes in the wellness industry.[8]

Tod Cooperman started his company, ConsumerLab.com, in 1999, and it is already the leading business in the world testing multivitamins, multiminerals, and herbals for consumers.

> **ConsumerLab.com independently purchases most major brands within each category of supplements and then scientifically tests them to ensure that they contain the ingredients, and only the ingredients, stated on their labels.**

Although ConsumerLab.com provides consumers a wealth of information about each category of supplements, Cooperman is careful not to express his own or any other opinion regarding the medical efficacy of a particular product category—the business of ConsumerLab.com is strictly limited to rating the manufacturing quality control of individual brands.

Tod Cooperman didn't start out to become the consumer watchdog for dietary supplements—or even a businessperson or an entrepreneur. He was born in Flushing, New York, and grew up on Long Island. On graduating from public high school he was accepted directly into the prestigious six-year BA/MD program at Boston University School of Medicine. By the time he received his M.D. at age 24, he found the practice of medicine to be somewhat "cookbookish" and hoped he could find a way to make a greater contribution to society.

While in medical school, he worked one summer at an investment bank in New York, evaluating start-up healthcare companies, where he watched stockbrokers hawk biotechnology stocks with no scientific basis to unsuspecting investors. He worked another summer in the Office of Technology Transfer at the University of Pennsylvania, bringing new medical technology from the laboratory to the marketplace, an experience that landed him his first job after graduation: working for the biotechnology division of medical giant Bristol-Myers. Between 1987 and 1993 he worked with Bristol-Myers and other new medical technology firms until he realized an important point:

What patients needed most wasn't more new technology, but the ability to make intelligent choices between the dizzying array of competing health plans and new medical technology that was already on the market.

In 1994 Cooperman started CareData Reports, which rated health plans and other HMOs solely on the basis of consumer satisfaction. CareData.com expanded into evaluating pharmacy benefits, dental benefits, and vision care. Cooperman found he liked being an entrepreneur and providing consumers with information that they could act on in managing their health—particularly on a preventive basis. In 1997 he sold CareData.com (now the healthcare division of J.D. Power and Associates) and remained with the company until 1999, when he realized that consumers had an even greater need for information about dietary supplements.

One of his first actions when starting ConsumerLab.com was to hire one of the world's leading experts on dietary supplements, Dr. William Obermeyer, who was then working for the FDA. Obermeyer had already made his mark in nine years at the FDA identifying severe contamination in supplements, and he was ready to bring his expertise to the aid of consumers—helping them make decisions about what to take and what *not* to take. In general, the FDA takes action only in cases where there is an extreme health problem, rarely commenting on manufacturing quality or labeling accuracy of products.

To date, ConsumerLab.com has tested 400 different products in 20 categories, representing about 90 percent of all supplements sold in the United States. According to Cooperman, "More than one-quarter of the products we have tested have failed, and this number has been as high as 60 percent for some categories." They also test popular fortified foods like Tropicana calcium-enriched orange juice.

> **Products are tested for the following criteria:**
>
> 1. *Identity and potency.* Does the product meet recognized standards of quality, and does the label accurately reflect what is in the product?
> 2. *Purity.* Is the product free of contaminants?
> 3. *Bioavailability.* Can the product be properly used by the body?
> 4. *Consistency.* Does the product have the same identity, potency, and purity from year to year?

Products that pass are posted on the company's web site—www.ConsumerLab.com. Consumers can read about selected products and supplement categories for free, and subscribers ($15.95 per year) can get complete listings of every product that passed (and the number of products that failed). ConsumerLab.com also sells technical reports on the laboratory tests used primarily by manufacturers.

ConsumerLab.com launched its $15.95 per year subscription program in February 2001 and had 11,000 paid subscribers by August of that year—plus more than 1 million site visits. But most gratifying to Cooperman are the thousands of e-mails he gets from consumers thanking him for helping them choose the right supplement. Although you may not have tremendous sympathy for a woman choosing a vitamin-enriched antiaging cream that turns out to be plain petroleum jelly, think about the following:

- The father who makes the informed decision to treat his enlarged prostate with saw palmetto only to find out too late that he was taking sugar pills

- The mother who conscientiously gives her four-year-old daughter a daily vitamin that contains more than twice the tolerable level of vitamins for her age

- The father who takes ginseng to boost his energy but chooses a brand that is contaminated with potentially carcinogenic pesticides

- The woman who takes valerian to help her sleep at night but is actually taking a brand that contains no valerian

- The mother whose depression affects her whole family who turns down Prozac in favor of Saint-John's-wort only to find out years later that she had purchased the wrong brand

To these, and hundreds of thousands of other wellness consumers, the importance of Cooperman's work in the wellness industry cannot be overstated. As Cooperman explained, "You wouldn't buy a car or a stock or bond without knowing how experts rate it. Why would you want to consume a supplement that has not been independently evaluated?"

The wellness industry is growing so fast that the government agencies that normally regulate medicines, food, and commerce cannot keep up. Private, dedicated entrepreneurs like Dr. Tod Cooperman, who are stepping in to serve the consumer's need for quality control, may eventually prove more effective for consumers than the traditional government agencies that currently regulate the sickness industry.

The Wellness Cardiologist: How People Are Transforming Traditional Roles

Dr. Frank Yanowitz tells the following story to his fourth-year medical students.

It was graduation day at Harvard Medical School, and the top student, Michael, was walking along the Charles River with his favorite professor. Suddenly, a drowning man crying for help came floating down the river. Michael jumped into the water, pulled the man above water after he had gone under for the third time, dragged him, unconscious, to the shore, and applied closed-chest cardiac massage and mouth-to-mouth resuscitation—until finally the victim regained consciousness. Michael was elated to have had this opportunity to shine in the eyes of his teacher, and the professor congratulated him on a job well done as the ambulance arrived to take away the victim.

Wet and exhausted, Michael continued walking with his teacher until a second victim crying for help came floating down the river. Again, Michael jumped in to the rescue and brought the victim back to consciousness on the shore. Incredibly, this happened again and again until, when the seventh victim came floating down the river, an exasperated Michael turned to his professor and said: "I know I'm a doctor dedicated to helping people, but I just can't keep this up anymore!"

"Then," replied his professor, "why don't you run ahead upstream and stop whoever is pushing these unfortunate people off the bridge?"

Cardiologist Frank Yanowitz is the medical director and cofounder of the Fitness Institute at LDS hospital, a high-technology medical center in Salt Lake City, Utah.

The Fitness Institute is run by some of the best physicians and therapists in the country, but they rarely see a patient with a disease. Instead, the Fitness Institute focuses on the prevention of disease among very healthy individuals—keeping wellness-oriented people from becoming customers of the sickness industry. Dr. Yanowitz's personal intrapreneurial[9] story and that of the Fitness Institute provide a glimpse into the future of medical wellness.

Frank Yanowitz was born in 1939 in Malone, New York, a small town at the northern tip of New York State near Montreal. In public high school he developed a love of music and studied classical piano and trumpet. In college at Cornell, he bounced between various engineering disciplines and became interested in medicine when he took a course in physiological psychology and comparative neurology.

In 1971 he entered the U.S. Air Force School of Aerospace Medicine in San Antonio, Texas, where he had his first encounter with wellness.

Unlike the patients of most cardiologists, the patients Yanowitz got to see in San Antonio were extremely well. As jet pilots, they were some of the healthiest and most fit individuals in the nation. They were required to see Yanowitz on a regular basis just to maintain their flying qualifications, and they were required to report even the slightest abnormality in their physical condition.

Moreover, Yanowitz was given virtually an unlimited budget to investigate the pilots' condition and to work with them to maintain their flying fitness. This gave him a unique preview of the a priori effects of diet and exercise on health.

"It was there," he reflects today, "that I began to see the very earliest stages of heart disease—long before I would normally encounter these patients in a typical hospital setting." This experience taught him a lot about the connection between diet, exercise, and disease.

After serving in the Air Force, Yanowitz accepted a position as a cardiologist at LDS Hospital in Salt Lake City and as an instructor at the University of Utah School of Medicine. The first thing he noticed when he came to Utah was the need for a specialized cardiac rehabilitation program to work with patients following heart surgery, but there was little support back then for such a program. The prevailing view was that a patient who had had heart surgery was "fixed" and that you shouldn't waste time and money on someone who was already fixed. Undeterred, Yanowitz and a physical therapist named Marlin Shields started a cardiac rehabilitation program, but they got very few patients. Although they received tremendous gratitude from the few patients they had, who were happy to be regaining their health and learning how to diet and exercise, "We got very few referrals from the medical community, who felt no need to send patients after they had been 'fixed.'"

In the late 1970s, Yanowitz began working with three colleagues: a student working on his Ph.D. dissertation in exercise physiology (Ted Adams), an orthopedic surgeon (Tom Rosenberg), and physical therapist Marlin Shields. The four of them formed the Fitness Institute in 1980 to focus on prevention and wellness, screening individuals at high risk for heart disease, cardiac rehabilitation, and sports medicine. But by the end of its first year, the Fitness Institute was almost entirely focused on prevention and wellness.

When they first opened, the expected referrals from other physicians never occurred, and their business lost money for its first 10 years. This forced them to learn how to market directly to their customers, and today they put fitness tips on the radio and meet directly with major employers and executives in the area.

I first became aware of their work when I was a 47-year-old patient completing my annual physical. After telling me I was in perfect health, my internist (Dr. Mary Parsons) asked me if there was anything I wished I could change about my body. Completely in jest, I said, "Sure, when I bike up to Jupiter Peak [10,300 vertical feet] I collapse on the dirt, as I have trouble breathing after riding for 10 miles uphill!" Dr. Parsons then referred me to the Fitness Institute for a VO2 Max test before recommending that I begin a strenuous bike training program. A VO2 Max calculates the maximum amount of oxygen that can be removed from circulating blood and used by working tissues during a specified period.

When I arrived at the Fitness Institute I thought I was walking into a very modern, high-technology fitness club—until I looked closer and saw that each of the machines for working out had a dizzying array of meters and probes attached to them.

As Dr. Yanowitz explained to me, "People don't come here to work out but to be evaluated." The institute offers a complete line of internal medical care, but it does not manage any chronic problems, catering mostly to a market for periodic checkups and to people dissatisfied with their HMOs or primary care physicians. Here's what a typical six-hour first visit to the Fitness Institute (which costs about $600) includes:[10]

- An analysis of all body systems, including cancer screening
- Blood and urine tests to assess your risk for heart disease, diabetes, infection, and anemia
- A maximal treadmill stress test by a cardiologist to screen for heart disease and assess your fitness level
- Written evaluations to assess medical history, personal stress factors, and nutritional adequacy
- Hydrostatic (underwater) weighing to determine your percent of body fat and ideal body weight (based on BMI)
- Pulmonary function tests to screen for obstructive lung disease
- Orthopedic evaluation by a physical therapist to assess your strength, flexibility, and risk for orthopedic problems
- One-on-one wellness counseling to review results and recommend necessary changes in diet, exercise, and stress management
- Screening test for colon and breast (women only) cancer
- A take-home copy of *Maintaining the Miracle: An Owner's Manual for the Human Body,*[11] a comprehensive personal wellness encyclopedia published by the Fitness Institute

Not surprisingly, Frank Yanowitz has had his own wellness transformation. In 1978, at age 37, while teaching some high school students how to use a sphygmomanometer, one of the students took his blood pressure, whereupon Yanowitz was shocked to see an unexpectedly high reading. He had the student repeat the test again and again, in front of the entire class, to confirm the results. That night he realized the irony of his developing interest in wellness when he himself was overweight, sedentary, out of shape, and now had dangerously high blood pressure. He began a regular program of watching his diet, taking medication to lower his blood pressure, and exercise. Within a year he was running 40 to 50 miles a week and doing 10K and half marathons.

Today, at age 62, although never athletic as a child or in college, Frank Yanowitz has completed four marathons, runs 10 to 15 miles each week, mountain-bikes, road-bikes, hikes, skis, and snowshoes.

His curriculum vitae includes 68 publications and 18 major research projects. He has written a full-length book titled *Coronary Heart Disease Prevention*. He was the first chairperson of the Utah Governor's Council on Physical Fitness. He has personally affected the lives of tens of thousands of patients. But Yanowitz lights up the most when he talks about the groups of medical students assigned for one-month tours of duty at the Fitness Institute—the cardiologists of tomorrow—who will hopefully go forth from his tutelage dedicated to *preventing* heart disease rather than just treating its symptoms.[12]

Physical Exercise: A Wellness Entrepreneurial Opportunity

The words *physician* and *physical,* as in physical exercise, come from the same Greek word, *physis,* which loosely translates as "nature." This connection is more than just etymological.

Many people today mistakenly think of physical exercise as something primarily for aesthetic rather than medical wellness benefits. This is far from the truth—a lack of regular physical exercise is attributed as the cause of approximately 12 percent of the 2.1 million deaths in the United States each year, about 250,000 people.[13]

Thousands of studies have shown direct relationships between a lack of physical activity and coronary heart disease, hypertension, cancer, diabetes, anxiety, and depression.

Yet amazingly, only 15 percent of U.S. adults engage in regular vigorous physical activity, and 60 percent report getting effectively no exercise at all from a regular or sustained leisure time activity.[14]

It is difficult today to get what Hippocrates might have prescribed as a "natural" amount of exercise.

Many of us have sedentary occupations, with little time for exercise outside of work. Most of us live in urban environments with inclement weather. Moreover, when it comes to exercise, our bodies require both generic aerobic exercise (running, biking) and specific exercises (weight training, flexibility) to keep us healthy and functional.

Fortunately, just as there are wellness entrepreneurs using technology to change our diets and to ensure we get the minimal daily building blocks of our cellular material, wellness entrepreneurs are also beginning to use technology to change how and where we get our exercise.

One who stands out in particular is fitness entrepreneur Jill Stevens Kinney—the woman *Club Insider News* called "America's #1 Female Club Entrepreneur."[15] Her story, and the rapid rise of her company Club One, Inc., illustrates some of the potential for the $24 billion fitness industry in the coming $1 trillion wellness economy.

America's #1 Female Club Entrepreneur

Jill Stevens Kinney has always been very healthy. She grew up in a family agribusiness in Fresno, California, eating lots of fresh fruits and vegetables. She started jogging regularly with her father at age 6. And she had a successful career as an athlete (as a downhill ski racer) before graduating from the University of California at Berkeley in 1979.

After graduation, Kinney met Dr. Jack Bagshaw, a successful cardiologist in wealthy Marin County, who was fed up with treating the symptoms of heart disease. Bagshaw wanted to open a holistic health center that would teach people how to avoid getting heart disease in the first place. He hired Kinney to be his business manager, and together they opened a facility called Physis, catering to senior executives in the San Francisco Bay Area. Physis charged $3,000 for a three-month program consisting of an initial assessment, three personalized 90-minute training sessions each week, educational workshops on topics from healthy cooking to stress management, and a final assessment of progress at completion.

Kinney was optimistic, but even she was truly amazed at the results. "People didn't just get more fit," she lights up as she reminisces, "marriages got better, careers improved, and in some cases whole lives were turned around—emotionally as well as physically. By the end of the three-month program I was positively hooked on what balanced exercise and a holistic professional approach to fitness can do for people!" Kinney feels very fortunate to have started out first in a wellness center, not a health club:

"The health club industry was launched by people out to make a buck versus people out to make a difference."

After the initial success of Physis and while still in her twenties, Kinney was hired by a national sports and fitness club chain, where she rose to become the chief operating officer with a staff of 800 people. In 1985, after getting calls from several real estate developers wanting to have sports and fitness facilities as part of their projects, she was hired to open one of the most prestigious clubs in the nation: the Sports Club LA in Los Angeles. The great success of this project—her staff presold the 5,000 memberships needed to break even before the club even opened—led to a series of similar entrepreneurial assignments throughout the United States. Kinney became *the* person to hire if you wanted to open the most prestigious sports and fitness club in your city.

During this time, Kinney, who was also chairperson of the market research committee for the International Health, Racquet & Sportsclub Association (IHRSA) from 1984 to 1989, began to notice a shift in the marketplace. Her prime clientele, the baby boomers, were moving past their twenties and becoming more concerned with wellness and aging issues than with sports and social activities. Most of the megasize sports and fitness clubs opened in the 1980s were inconveniently located for aging baby boomers, who now, with families and more intensive jobs, had less time for exercise. Kinney's research showed that these boomers now wanted a convenient location near home or work (as in choosing a dry cleaner) more than they wanted sports activities, social activities, and megasize physical facilities. But at the time, 98 percent of the local conveniently located fitness clubs were single-unit inexpensive mom-and-pop facilities with few amenities—not the kind of places that would appeal to baby boomers used to high-quality clubs like Sports Club LA. In 1989, Kinney began to work with businessman John Kinney on a business plan to serve this market for high-quality fitness facilities at convenient locations.

In 1990, she and John Kinney wrote the business plan for Club One and also got married that same year. On June 17, 1991, they opened their first Club One facility at Citicorp Center in San Francisco, followed by a second facility later that year at Embarcadero Center.

Originally, the Kinneys thought they might keep opening similar 12,000-square-foot facilities and become the "Starbucks of fitness clubs," but John Kinney quickly saw a greater financial opportunity in consolidation—purchasing existing single-unit clubs in good locations and updating their facilities. This strategy not only saved money in most cases, it attracted instant members while eliminating a local competitor.

In addition to focusing on convenient locations, one of Club One's unique approaches was to attract the best fitness professionals (trainers, nutritionists, yoga teachers, massage therapists, etc.) as dedicated professional employees rather than as independent contractors without benefits, continuing education, and defined career paths. Over her years in the fitness business Jill Kinney had seen some of the best of these professionals leave the industry when faced with the task of continually marketing themselves or trying to balance their need for continued professional education against their need for current income. Just as some of the best doctors and other professionals function better in salaried nonentrepreneurial environments, Jill Kinney felt that her customers and some fitness professionals themselves would benefit from a similar professional-employee approach. She says, "When you make the commitment to empower them to grow their career, everyone benefits."

Their plan worked. Club One quickly went from start-up to sales of $60 million per year and 71 locations—one of the fastest-growing businesses in the fitness club industry. The Kinneys are most proud of their fitness professionals, all of whom work as salaried professional employees, with Club One charging customers standard hourly rates for their services, depending on their education, experience, and expertise.

Fitness careers of the future include the following certified professionals:

Fitness trainer

Personal trainer

Specialty trainer/sports conditioning

Clinical exercise specialist

Chiropractor

Physical therapist

Nutritionist

Massage therapist

Seniors trainer

Youth trainer

Personal coach

Group exercise instructor

Yoga instructor

Pilates instructor

Performance training coach

Despite executing a well-thought-out business plan, most of the Club One success came from a surprise phone call Jill Kinney received in 1995. Autodesk, Inc., one of the leading software companies in the world and a prestigious employer in the Bay Area, called to ask if Club One would be willing to design, open, and manage a proprietary on-site fitness club solely for Autodesk employees. After determining that Autodesk was motivated by a real concern for the wellness of its employees and not just adding a perk to attract new hires, Club One took on the contract. A year later the company opened similar on-site corporate fitness facilities for The Gap and Electronic Arts. By 2000, the Kinneys had 50 such corporate facilities under management, with 500,000 corporate members—on-site corporate employees with free access to a private fitness club managed by Club One. The "convenience" objective of Club One had always been a five-minute desk-to-club experience. Having such a private facility located at the workplace more than met this objective.

Jill Kinney sees the corporate centers managed by Club One as the greatest challenge and training ground for her organization because her customers in these centers closely parallel the typical U.S. employee—not someone who walks into a private fitness facility ready to join with their own funds.

These corporate members need much more education and motivation. According to Jill Kinney, this "gives us the opportunity to serve people who really need us—people who are overweight, people with clinical issues and addictions, people with eating disorders—and we can use exercise as the medium to start helping them make the right changes in their life."

Club One has recently expanded its contract management program to a new location in Redwood City, California, where several corporations share the same private facility adjacent to their offices. Club One also has signed a contract with a group of Jewish community centers to manage fitness facilities at their locations. At these sites, the uniforms worn by fitness consultants, from personal trainers to nutritionists, may say "JCC," but they share the same certification, continued training, and professionalism as Club One professionals at all of their private and public locations.

The corporate customers of Club One are motivated by a sincere desire to help their employees achieve wellness. But irrespective of their altruistic motivations, a key advantage of such a program is that it enjoys a 2-to-1 financial advantage over employees purchasing Club One membership for themselves. As we see in the next chapter, the company receives a deduction from its state and federal income taxes for the cost of the Club One facility, and the employee does not have to pay state and federal income taxes on the monthly value of the membership.

Before Proceeding to the Next Chapter

Action Plan for Entrepreneurs, Investors, and Distributors

1. Analyze how a return of medicine to a whole-body approach (Hippocrates) would impact each of your three individual areas of wellness business opportunity.

2. Dr. Yanowitz and his M.D. colleagues (The Fitness Institute) run a completely wellness-focused business within the traditional medical arena. Analyze how a shift in medicine toward prevention would impact each of your three individual areas of wellness business opportunity.

3. Carl Rehnborg (Nutrilite) had to set up his own sales force of distributors because his product was neither a medicine nor a food that could be carried by pharmacies or grocery stores. Analyze the individual products of your three areas of wellness business opportunity from the standpoint of how they will be distributed, and by whom.

4. Rehnborg hit upon network marketing as the most cost-effective way to continually educate new distributors. How could network marketing impact your three individual areas of wellness business opportunity?

5. Analyze the products of your three individual areas of wellness business opportunity from the standpoint of manufacturing quality. If more businesses similar to ConsumerLab.com emerge, will this help or hurt each of your three areas?

6. Jill Kinney (Club One) has been able to build what was formerly a local mom-and-pop business into a $100 million national chain for the reasons listed here. Analyze how each of your three individual areas of wellness business opportunity could be similarly impacted by these reasons.

    a. Riding a quality-demand shift from sports fitness to convenience

    b. Riding a quality-demand shift from sports fitness to wellness

    c. Standardization of product quality

    d. Marketing directly to employers

    e. Tax advantages of having employers versus consumers pay for products or services

Based on your answers to these questions, think about dropping and replacing any or all of your three individual areas of wellness business opportunity.

CHAPTER 6

What You Must Know about Health Insurance

The opportunity to provide consumers with wellness-based financial services, like Wellness Insurance™,[1] is almost as great an entrepreneurial opportunity as is the entire wellness industry itself.

It is an opportunity every businessperson must understand—even businesspeople who don't want to become wellness entrepreneurs themselves. Businesspeople will want wellness financial services for their families, and they must be ready to offer Wellness Insurance to their employees in order to remain competitive.

For wellness entrepreneurs, understanding and being able to explain to others how wellness-based financial services work is crucial for success, because this will eventually be the primary payment mechanism for most of their businesses.

However, in order for you to become a wellness entrepreneur and in order to be able to understand wellness-based financial services, it is first necessary for you to understand the existing U.S. sickness-based health insurance system:

- Much of the current demand for wellness products and services in the United States comes from the failure of sickness-based health insurance.
- Our new system of wellness finance will be built on the rubble of the collapsing sickness insurance system.
- Would-be entrepreneurs have to deal with the nightmare of losing their family health insurance when they decide to start their own businesses.

Before we examine Wellness Insurance in Chapter 7, let's review and examine the existing U.S. sickness-based health insurance system.

In previous chapters explaining some of the problems with food or medical services, you were asked to consider solutions in light of a wellness business. As you now read what is wrong with our current healthcare system, stop each time a problem is noted and see if you can visualize how to solve it by creating a wellness-based entrepreneurial business.

The New Economic Slavery

Today millions of working Americans owe their soul to the company *doctor* versus the company *store* in the famous Merle Travis song "Sixteen Tons." Most employees cannot afford private health insurance, and even among those who can, many have a family member with a preexisting medical condition.

Like indentured servants in olden times, these Americans cannot change jobs or quit and strike out on their own because they cannot obtain affordable medical care for their families except from their current employer.

The U.S. federal government is primarily responsible for this new form of economic slavery. Income tax laws over the past 50 years have subsidized 50 percent or more of a family's medical costs *only* if they obtain their medical care from their employer. This massive federal tax subsidy has preempted the private sector from developing affordable direct-to-consumer health insurance plans that serve individual needs. It is also indirectly responsible for continuing to focus our current health insurance system on sickness rather than on wellness—paying for the treatment of symptoms of disease rather than for their prevention or their cure.

Escalating Medical Costs

Moreover, another by-product of this nineteenth-century servile system, escalating medical costs, threatens to bankrupt many companies and even the entire economy, given the fact that doctors and patients consume mostly *other people's money* when making their decisions. The $1.5 trillion Americans currently spend on sickness is growing much faster than the U.S. gross domestic product. It is expected to more than double by 2010 and, if current trends continue unchecked, will exceed the GDP itself by 2050. Its fallout could make the $200 billion savings and loan disaster of the 1980s pale by comparison. Tens of millions of Americans could lose their life savings to medical expenses. Despite a steadily rising economy in the past decade, U.S. personal bankruptcy filings doubled, from approximately 750,000 in 1990 to 1.5 million in 1999, with much of the increase resulting from family medical catastrophes.

Fortunately, change is under way. And there is great opportunity for wellness-oriented individuals to profit from the coming chaos. But in order to navigate through the icy waters ahead and to take advantage of these opportunities, it is first necessary to understand how company-paid medical care works and how it became so widespread in the first place.

How Employers Became the Providers of Medical Care

One of the last entities anyone should want to have involved in their family's medical care is their employer. That is because today people spend less than 25 percent of their time at work, about 40 hours out of a 168-hour week, and typically change jobs up to 10 times over their lives. One hundred years ago this was not the case. People worked from dawn to dusk, six days a week, and often for the same employer their entire life. This is when company-provided medical care began, at very large plants or mines, and care was administered by a single visiting or company doctor. Off-site medical coverage expanded in the 1930s—during a period of federal wage and price controls, unions bargained for company-paid medical care in lieu of prohibited cash raises.

As noted in Chapter 2, individual U.S. federal marginal income tax rates rose throughout the twentieth century, reaching peak rates of 92 to 94 percent by 1964 before stabilizing at 70 percent in the 1980s. In several states in the 1950s, some taxpayers actually experienced marginal income tax rates *above* 100 percent—that is, they had to pay more than $1 in income taxes for each additional

$1 earned.[2] Today in the United States, high-earning individuals pay about 50 percent of their income in federal and state income taxes (not including property taxes, sales taxes, gasoline taxes, etc.).

Because increased income to high-earning business executives would mostly have ended up in the pockets of the federal government, businesspeople lobbied Congress in the 1950s for the right to receive even more tax-free perks (e.g., medical care for their entire families) paid for by their employers. Congress obliged, and soon the concept of having employer-paid healthcare for your entire family, for both wage-earning employees and executives, was almost universal.

Originally, companies thought of this as a great way to compensate employees with the federal government paying about half the cost. However, it soon grew into the cost-escalating, out-of-control system we have today, where almost everyone (except the elderly and poor) receives their healthcare benefits from an employer—the last entity people would like to have involved in their personal medical care if they had a choice.

Today, under a qualified medical plan, employers are allowed a 100 percent corporate income tax deduction for medical insurance premiums, and employees do not report these medical benefits as income when they pay their income taxes. This system is terribly unfair.

Americans working for large corporations get up to 50 percent or more of their medical costs paid (indirectly) by the federal government, whereas the working poor, the self-employed, and the unemployed have to earn up to $2 before income taxes in order to have $1 (or less) to spend on medical care.[3] Either everyone should receive tax-deductible healthcare or no one should.

Moreover, because the subsidy is in the form of a tax deduction rather than a tax credit, wealthier individuals receive much higher subsidies than lower-income taxpayers. And because the subsidy comes in the form of a complex set of tax regulations, it is easily manipulated by large medical insurance and pharmaceutical companies seeking to protect their profits. When it comes to treating depression, some sections of the U.S. federal tax code allow a tax deduction for the purchase of expensive prescription drugs (like Prozac) but do not allow the same deduction if the consumer elects to treat his or her depression with a safer and cheaper nonprescription remedy like Saint-John's-wort.[4] The Internal Revenue Service should not be telling consumers what drugs to take or not to take for their ailments.*

How Employers Squeeze the Physicians in order to Reduce Costs

As medical costs have spiraled upward, corporations providing healthcare benefits have focused mostly on cutting costs for existing services rather than on providing innovative new products that consumers want, like wellness services and alternative medicine. The cost-cutting efforts of these large corporations have often directed their immense bargaining power *against* healthcare professionals. Today almost every physician, pharmacy, hospital, and healthcare provider operates under a labyrinthine payment system designed to extract the most out of the people who can often afford the least. Here's how this system works.

A physician might competitively set the price for an individual service or office visit at $75. A large employer or healthcare insurer, representing half of the physician's existing patients, negotiates a lower price for its employees of $55—typically a 15 to 35 percent discount off the standard rate. The physician has no choice but to oblige this request and seek to make up the losses by raising the $75 set price to $95 for other patients. Over time, as multiple large players (generally through preferred purchasing organizations, or PPOs) enter the marketplace, a multitiered system emerges with different patients being charged four to five different prices for the exact same item or service.

It is a credit to their profession that most medical professionals still seek to provide the same level of service to each patient regardless of how much they are being paid. But among some cost-strapped professionals, a new form of appointment rationing has begun, where the patient with the highest-paying PPO gets the first available appointment (encouraging the lesser-paying PPO patient to go elsewhere or forgo the service entirely).[5]

Besides being terribly unfair, this byzantine system creates irrational consumption decisions on the part of consumers and providers. As the price paid by the consumer and received by the

*On August 2, 2001, Senators Tom Harkin (D-IA) and Orrin Hatch (R-UT) introduced the "Dietary Supplement Tax Fairness Act of 2001." This bill, if passed, would give dietary supplements parity with prescription drugs under the U.S. tax code.

doctor bears less and less relation to actual cost, the free market is not allowed to work its economic magic. Doctors overutilize services for which they get higher reimbursement, and patients underutilize services priced artificially high, to the detriment of themselves and their children.

Treating Symptoms versus Curing or Preventing Illness

The biggest problem with our current medical care insurance system, where more than 90 percent of expenses are paid by someone *other than* the patient and the doctor deciding on the treatment, is that it is focused on paying for treating the symptoms of illness rather than on curing or preventing illness.

This is partly because it is much more profitable for medical companies to produce products that create customers for life—products that treat symptoms of disease rather than products focused on cures or prevention.

Suppose you were a member of the board of directors of a pharmaceutical or medical company—appointed to your position by a pension fund for the purpose of increasing the value of their investment. Would you direct your company to spend millions of dollars in R&D to make a one-time-use product costing $50 a pill that could cure or prevent a disease, or would you direct your company to spend millions of dollars in R&D to make a product costing only $1 a pill that consumers would take every day for the rest of their lives, 365 days a year.

It's easy to see why the overwhelming majority of new medical technology today is focused on treating the symptoms of disease rather than on cures or prevention, and why 90 percent of the pharmaceuticals sold today are maintenance drugs consumers take daily for the rest of their lives.

But the major reason that U.S. medicine is not focused on curing or preventing illness is because the insurance companies and ultimately the employers do not have a financial stake in the long-term health of their employees.

Employees used to stay with one company for 25 years or more. Today, the average employee is projected to change jobs more than 10 times over his or her 45-year working life. Most of the major illnesses on which you can spend $1 today to save $100 tomorrow (like heart disease from obesity or cancer from poor nutrition) will not show up until an employee is long gone or retired, at which time the $100 cost is picked up by another employer or by taxpayers through Medicare.

As medical costs have escalated, employers have, in effect, told their medical insurance companies to pay for only those expenses related to keeping or getting the insured back to work—and this does *not* include paying for the prevention of a disease that will not manifest itself during the expected tenure of the employee with the company.

Weight reduction, nutritional advice, vitamins, minerals, smoking cessation, and hundreds of other wellness-related or preventive-type treatments are excluded from almost all corporate- and government-sponsored medical plans. But not for long, as you'll see in the next chapter!

This causes even greater escalation in medical costs. Many physicians I interviewed believe that the majority of nongeriatric medical expenses are caused by poor diet and smoking, both of which they are effectively limited from treating in the current PPO or HMO[6] environment.

The Dirty Secret about Employer-Provided Health Care

Have you ever been in a work situation where a person got promoted in lieu of someone more deserving of the promotion? Or have you ever made a promotion recommendation only to have it overruled by the owner of the company where you worked? Here's what could have been going on behind the scene.

Assume a typical situation where a 100-employee U.S. company provides medical benefits at an annual group premium cost of $500,000 per annum ($5,000 per employee or family).

If employees were to purchase this same coverage themselves, even at the same direct cost of $5,000, it would cost the employer twice as much. Here's why: The employer would have to pay an additional $10,000 in wages and withholding taxes for the employee to have the same after-tax out-of-pocket $5,000 to buy medical insurance. In other words, the employer is saving $5,000 per employee, and the U.S. taxpayer is making up the $5,000 difference. It's easy to see why most working Americans today receive their medical insurance through their employers, and why employer-paid medical insurance premiums exceed $600 billion per annum—approximately $5,000 per year for 120 million workers, covering 187 million people, including dependents.

The concept of insurance works because of the mathematical law of large numbers. In order to provide insurance for a catastrophic medical occurrence, an insurance company relies on fact that there will be a large enough pool of people paying premiums so that the extraordinary costs of the unhealthy few can be borne by the healthy many. Each corporate group of employees is considered to be a separate pool for insurance underwriting purposes.

Assume that one of the employees, or one of their children, develops a chronic disease like diabetes or becomes permanently disabled in an automobile accident—a condition that allows the employee to continue working but ends up costing $75,000 in recurring annual medical expenses for drugs and treatment. Initially, the employer's insurance company bears this $75,000 expense, but next year it will raise the employer's $500,000 annual premium to $575,000 or more to cover this now-anticipated additional expense (as well to try and recoup its prior loss).[7] The employer, although free to shop around for a different insurance provider, is unlikely to find a better deal since the main criterion used to underwrite and price a group policy is the prior years' medical expenses of that group.

The employer and the employee are both trapped.

The employer needs to get rid of the employee to lower its total group medical insurance premium, but under federal law cannot fire someone for medical reasons if that person is still "doing their job." Fortunately for the employer, but unfortunately for the employee, a person with a chronic medical condition or a very sick child, is unlikely to be able to continue "doing their job."

In the event that the employee is still capable of doing his or her job, often by putting in extra hours, the employee cannot quit, as most new employers will not hire a "liability."

That is, such a person won't be hired unless the $75,000 in antici-
pated annual medical expenses for the preexisting condition are
excluded from their medical insurance coverage.[8] It is estimated
that of the 187 million Americans receiving healthcare benefits
from employers, approximately 22 percent, more than 41 million
people, have some preexisting health condition in their family limiting their ability to get healthcare coverage from a new employer or
insurance company.[9]

**This is the dirty secret of employer-provided healthcare.
Virtually every small business owner knows the name of
each employee who has a family member with such a
preexisting condition. While compassion suggests that
the owner try to ignore this fact in making decisions
regarding promotions and terminations, competition and
the need for economic survival often dictate otherwise.**

The Government "Solution"

To ease the short-term burden on terminated employees, and perhaps to ease the consciences of the employers who were forced to
terminate them, Congress passed the Consolidated Omnibus
Reconciliation Act (COBRA) in 1986. COBRA mandates that terminated employees must be allowed to purchase health insurance
from their former employer for up to 18 months after their
employment ends, at a premium not to exceed 102 percent of the
group rate. After 18 months, some states require that former
employees with COBRA become automatically eligible for individual policies. Although COBRA and such individual policies generally cover preexisting conditions, few terminated employees can
afford this insurance, especially without the income tax advantages
of employer-paid insurance. Only 21 percent (approximately) of
terminated eligible employees elect to purchase COBRA insurance.[10] Moreover, the COBRA program implicitly assumes that the
employee will find another job that provides health insurance
before the end of this 18-month period. Few with preexisting
chronic medical conditions probably do.

Similarly, the Health Insurance Portability and Accountability
Act of 1996 (HIPAA) was enacted by Congress to limit insurance
companies from excluding coverage for a preexisting condition to
new employees if the employee was covered for such a condition by
a prior employer. However, among other limitations, HIPAA does

not apply if the employee has had a lapse in coverage (e.g., he or she has been out of work without COBRA) for more than 63 days.

Employees Feeling the Safest Are the Most at Risk

One reason some would-be entrepreneurs decide not to go into business for themselves is because they feel safe with the health benefit package they are receiving from their long-term employer. These employees are in for a rude awakening.

As the company's pool of employees ages over time, more of them (or their dependents) will develop some chronic condition that will raise the cost of the group medical insurance premium and make them individually unemployable somewhere else. Moreover, the increased costs of these chronic conditions may eventually cause the employer to cut back on medical benefits or even go out of business entirely—as the company loses customers to competitors with younger, healthier, and thus less costly employees.

This is the most ironic part of the U.S. health insurance system today: Those who feel the safest—individuals receiving health insurance through their employers— are actually the most at risk. For many of them, it is only a question of time before they or one of their dependents develop a chronic condition. Even if this never occurs, it is only a question of time in our rapidly changing technological world before they find themselves out of work before age 65.[11]

When such people find themselves out of work before age 65, either through termination or early retirement, they often cannot obtain affordable individual medical insurance at any price—even if they don't have any preexisting conditions. There are several reasons this is so.

First, since the majority of Americans receive medical insurance or coverage from their employers, in many states there are simply not enough people left over to create a marketplace for affordable individual policies. Each individual health insurance policy type and rate must be separately approved by the insurance commissioner in each state. Even in larger states where there are enough potential applicants, insurance companies find it difficult to market profitably to, underwrite, and service individuals not connected to an employer (who typically has an on-site healthcare benefits administrator).

Second, employers naturally hire the most productive people and avoid or fire the ones who produce the least. In a nation with 61 percent of the population overweight and 27 percent clinically obese and unhealthy, those who don't get hired (or who do get fired) are often also the most unhealthy. Employers skim the cream off the top of the health insurance marketplace—leaving a disproportionate number of unhealthy people to the individual health insurance market. Insurers often automatically assume there is something wrong with anyone who doesn't already have health insurance, and they use much stricter standards to underwrite individual applicants who have no prior health insurance policy.

Third and most important, even when approved, individual applicants are sometimes charged more for the same benefits than applicants in a group policy. This occurs for several reasons—one of which is the number of laws that protect individual policyholders from having their premiums raised (or their policy dropped) in the event that they or a dependent develop a chronic condition.

In the preceding example, where the individual employee (or his or her child) develops a chronic condition costing $75,000 per annum on an ongoing basis, the insurance company is allowed to raise the employer group premium to cover this anticipated future expense.

If this same person had an individual versus a group health insurance policy, the insurance company would not be allowed to raise the premium or drop the insured from coverage.[12] In general, insurance companies may only raise premiums equally for all individuals in a defined class (typically individuals residing in that state). Legally, they cannot raise rates only for specific persons with high claims.

Note that although this legislated protection can limit a person's ability to obtain an individual health insurance policy, *it can be a great asset for a wellness-based entrepreneur in structuring a long-term wellness-oriented solution to the health insurance dilemma.* We discuss this in Chapter 7.

Several states have tried unsuccessfully to force insurers to offer individual health insurance policies. For example, insurance carriers offering group health insurance in the state of New York are required to offer guaranteed-issue community-rated individual health insurance to all applicants. *Guaranteed-issue* means that the carrier is not allowed to consider, or even ask about, the health of applicants or their dependents. Preexisting conditions must be covered after a maximum of six months, except for pregnancy and certain other conditions, which must be covered immediately. *Community-rated* means that the premium charged must be the same for all applicants, whether they are 18 years old and in perfect health or 60 years old with a terminal illness.

The effect of these onerous regulations in New York (and the few other guaranteed-issue states[13]) is that insurance companies offer individual policies there only at extremely high cost (typically $800 per month for a family of three) or not at all, and they discourage applications with practices such as refusing to pay outside agency commissions on individual policies. Savvy applicants and insurance agents play a cat-and-mouse game to get around some of these restrictions. For example, pregnant women buy policies in their eighth month of pregnancy and cancel them after childbirth. Insurance agents form private open-enrollment "associations" or "unions," which are really vehicles disguised to sell marked-up restrictive group coverage to individuals and create commissions for the agents, disguised as "dues."

The Coming Solution for Wellness-Oriented Entrepreneurs

For the past 20 years, I and several other economists have argued in the White House and in Congress about the unfairness of allowing only corporate employees tax-deductible health insurance. These policies have detrimental effects on our entire healthcare insurance and delivery system. Congress has begun to listen.

Thanks to recent legislation, beginning in 2001 self-employed individuals were allowed to deduct from their taxable income 60 percent of the amount they spent on health insurance premiums for themselves, their spouses, and their dependents.[14] This figure rises to 70 percent in 2002 and to 100 percent in 2003 and beyond.[15]

This, coupled with recent legislation allowing Medical Savings Accounts on an experimental basis until 2003 and other new medical income tax deductions, which we

examine in Chapter 7, is the crack in the wall of the corporate sickness insurance monopoly.

No one yet has any idea of how efficient, and even how enjoyable, shopping for wellness (and sickness) services might be if consumers were given the ability to choose freely among competitive,
cost-effective providers, but we are about to find out.

Approximately 50 million people in the United States
are either self-employed or have some part of their
income derived from self-employment. By 2003, many
of these individuals will be allowed to freely purchase
part or all of their medical care on almost economic
parity with large corporations.[16] These astute consumers
will comprise the first major group spending their own
versus someone else's money on healthcare.

Moreover, many of these individuals with self-employment income
live in households with traditional corporate- or government-
sponsored medical benefit plans.

Competitive forces will eventually force even traditional
providers to allow their customers to choose the wellness and sickness products that they desire versus the
products and services forced on them by cost-cutting
corporate employers and lobbyist-controlled government
medical plans.

No one knows how innovative and efficient we will become when
we get the federal government out of large segments of the healthcare business and apply good old Yankee ingenuity to the distribution side of our healthcare system. But when we look at the growth
of so many other industries (food service, transportation, consumer
electronics), we begin to get an idea of what might be possible.

Food service outside of the home used to mean either a dull
cafeteria or an expensive restaurant. Through innovative technology, the restaurant industry lowered its prices and increased its
product offerings so much that the demand for its product
increased 1,000 percent. From 1950 to 2000, Americans went
from spending 5 percent to 50 percent of their household food

budget on meals prepared outside of the home. Fifty years ago a child's "Can we go out to dinner?" was met with "What do you think we are—millionaires?" Today, such a request is usually met by "What kind of food do you want?" and dining out is an enjoyable and affordable experience for almost everyone.

Similar examples abound for air transportation, vacations, fashionable clothes, consumer electronics, and hundreds of other luxury services and products that people thought could never be made affordable to mass markets.

The 50 million Americans who are self-employed or who derive some part of their income from self-employment will be the first supercustomers of the greatest entrepreneurial opportunity of the twenty-first century—the wellness industry.

In the next chapter we examine this opportunity and see how entrepreneurs can financially provide themselves and their families with such efficacious wellness (and sickness) products and services.

Please note: For more information, see Appendix B, "The Impact of Healthcare Reform on the Wellness Industry."

Before Proceeding to the Next Chapter

Action Plan for Entrepreneurs, Investors, and Distributors

1. Analyze the impact of the current health insurance system on each of your three individual areas of wellness business opportunity. How would the collapse of the current health insurance system impact each of your three areas of interest?

2. Analyze the impact of physicians on each of your three individual areas of wellness business opportunity. How will continued cost-cutting efforts by medical providers impact each of your three areas of wellness opportunity?

3. Employers and employees play cat-and-mouse games to get around existing healthcare regulations and restrictions. Analyze how these games help or hinder your three areas of wellness business opportunity. If everyone were to receive free government-provided sickness care, how would it impact each of your three areas? Conversely, what would happen to each of your areas if existing employer-provided sickness coverage were greatly reduced?

4. Analyze how each of your three areas of wellness business opportunity will be affected by the legislation taking effect in 2003 allowing self-employed individuals to take a 100 percent tax deduction for health insurance premiums.

5. Analyze how each of your three areas of wellness business opportunity is affected by the 2001 extension of Medical Savings Accounts (MSAs) until 2003, and how each will be affected when Congress makes the MSA program permanent after 2003 or discontinues it.

6. Analyze how each of your three areas of wellness business opportunity could be affected by proposed legislation to make dietary supplements tax deductible.

7. Analyze how each of your three areas of wellness business opportunity would be affected if employers began giving each employee a wellness allowance or spending option.

Based on your answers to these questions, think about dropping and replacing any or all of your three individual areas of wellness business opportunity.

CHAPTER 7

The Gold Mine in Wellness Insurance

Wellness Insurance™ is health insurance that covers expenses to prevent disease (e.g., weight control, vitamins, supplements, and exercise), along with major medical expenses above an annual deductible amount.[1] Every wellness entrepreneur must understand Wellness Insurance for two reasons:

1. Most of the purchasing of wellness products and services will eventually be paid for by Wellness Insurance.

2. There is a great business opportunity in switching consumers from sickness insurance to Wellness Insurance.

Even ordinary businesspeople who may not want to become wellness entrepreneurs themselves must understand Wellness Insurance. Every businessperson will want Wellness Insurance for his or her own family, and employers will have to offer Wellness Insurance to their healthy employees in order to keep them from leaving for competitors who do.

Employers and health insurance companies will begin offering turnkey Wellness Insurance–type products within several years. But you can get Wellness Insurance today for your customers by teaching them how to combine a high-deductible health insurance policy (HDHP) with a Wellness Savings Account™ (WSA)[2] to pay for current and future wellness investments in their health.

In this chapter, you learn three things:
1. How individuals and employers will finance investments in their future wellness
2. How your customers can get Wellness Insurance today—saving up to $3,000 per year that they are wasting on sickness insurance

---

> 3. How you can channel all or part of this $3,000 in sickness insurance savings into purchases of your wellness products or services

This chapter is written for you, the wellness entrepreneur, rather than for your business associates or for consumers. However, in order to assist you in explaining Wellness Insurance, the back of this book has two appendixes directed toward your business associates and your customers:

1. Appendix C: Summary of Wellness Insurance (for your business associates)
2. Appendix D: Frequently Asked Questions about Wellness Insurance (for your customers)

Understanding Wellness Insurance is also very important for the wellness investor and for those investing in traditional health insurance companies. Some wellness companies may stumble simply because they fail to properly structure their products to be covered by Wellness Insurance. Some health insurance companies will benefit by being the first to offer Wellness Insurance products, and some health insurance companies will suffer great losses when their healthy customers switch to Wellness Insurance, leaving only unhealthy insureds in their risk pool.

Now, let's get started understanding the opportunity in Wellness Insurance, beginning with why such a large opportunity exists in the first place.

Most U.S. Consumers Waste Thousands of Dollars Each Year on Their Health Insurance

Most people have comprehensive insurance on their automobiles. Yet they don't file a claim with their car insurance company when they buy gasoline, have their car cleaned, replace the tires or brakes, or change the oil. Even if they have an accident they are typically 100 percent responsible for any costs below the deductible on their policy.

Most people have homeowner's insurance on their homes. Yet they don't file a claim with their property insurance company when they buy heating fuel, have their house painted, or install a new roof. And here, too, they typically have a deductible where the insured pays entirely any claim below $500 or $1,000 per event.

Any financial advisor will tell you that it is foolish to buy insurance covering an expense that you can afford to pay on your own. The cost of the paperwork involved on each transaction, plus the costs incurred by the insurance company in issuing and enforcing the policy, would cause the premiums to far exceed, over time, any potential benefits. Many consumers have discovered that they can save hundreds or thousands of dollars a year by raising the deductible on their automobile and homeowner policies.[3]

Homeowner's, automobile, life, and all other types of insurance *except one,* are used to cover only those catastrophic expenses that the insured cannot comfortably afford to pay on their own. In these cases, most of the premiums paid for insurance serve a valuable function for the insured and his or her family.

In health insurance, most of the premiums paid do not serve a valuable function for the insured or his or her family.

Most people have health insurance policies with coverage for incidental maintenance expenses that healthcare consumers don't really need to have covered. In addition to being economically foolish, this coverage supports a byzantine distribution system and payment mechanism that wastes hundreds of billions each year.[4] Consider how inefficient it would be if you had to file a claim with your automobile insurance company every time you bought gasoline or changed your oil—or if you could buy gas or have your car maintained only at a particular service station where your insurance company had negotiated a discount for such services.

Consider how difficult it would be if you had to get approval from your homeowner's insurance company to pay utility bills, change your carpets, or paint your house—and if you could purchase such items only from a store selected by your insurance company and could purchase only certain types of carpet or paint colors that your insurance company had preapproved.

Consider how much lower the prices are and how much better the selection is at the mass merchants and category busters ranging from Home Depot to PetsMart to Staples—and consider how none of these retailers would exist if the consumer were not free to shop competitively in each of these areas.

When you stop and think about it, it doesn't take long to see how inefficient we are in distributing medical products and services—

and what great opportunities are probably being missed. But our medical services distribution system actually looks efficient compared to our medical services insurance and payment system.

The $3,000 per Family High-Deductible Health Policy (HDHP) Opportunity

If you contacted your health insurance company today and told them that from now on you would like to pay directly the first $2,500 per year of your medical expenses, they would probably lower your annual premium by about $3,000. This puts you ahead by $500 per annum even if you had a medical catastrophe every year.

As illogical as it may sound, most health insurers would lower your annual premium by roughly 120 percent of the increase in your annual deductible, approximately $3,000 savings in annual premium for a $2,500 increase in your deductible—putting you ahead by at least $500 a year, even if you become very ill. Here's why.

When you incur a $50 expense at a doctor or other medical service provider, your insurance company incurs an expense of $75 or more—$50 to pay the doctor and at least $25 for the paperwork and overhead required by the transaction. This is one of the reasons insurance companies have been pushing their insured to enroll in health maintenance organizations (HMOs), which pay the provider a flat annual amount per patient (capitation) rather than paying for each service rendered.

On average, health insurance companies spend about 20 percent on overhead, but this average number masks the true picture of what is happening. To approve and pay a single $10,000 hospital bill might cost an insurance company only $500 (5 percent) in transaction costs—dealing with the hospital and cutting them a check. But to approve and pay a $50 medical bill from a single provider might cost the insurance company $25 (50 percent) or more in transaction costs—sometimes even more than the actual cost of the medical service itself.

The first $2,500 of a family's annual medical expenses are typically spent in $50 to $125 increments in 20 to 30 different transactions—which costs the insurance

company the $2,500 plus an additional $500 to $1,500
in transaction processing costs.

No wonder your insurance company might lower your annual
premium by $3,000 if you would agree to increase your annual
deductible by $2,500. Most, in fact, already have, by incorporating
such a 120 percent or greater reduction of premium into their published rates.

For example, in 2001, Blue Cross–Blue Shield of Utah offered a
zero-deductible individual health policy for $415 per month, or
$4,980 per year (two parents age 35 with three healthy children).
The premium for virtually the same policy (a high-deductible
health policy or HDHP) with a $2,500 deductible was $159 per
month, or $1,908 per annum—a $3,072 (123 percent) annual
reduction in premium for a $2,500 increase in the annual
deductible.

Blue Cross–Blue Shield Health Insurance Policy
Two parents (age 35) and three children

	Annual Deductible	Annual Premium
Traditional policy	$ 0	$4,980
HDHP policy	$2,500	$1,908
Annual savings		$3,072

Moreover, with this particular HDHP policy, as with most major
medical high-deductible policies nationwide, the insured still par-
ticipates in the insurance company's preferred provider organization (PPO) network for expenditures below the $2,500
deductible—getting the 15 to 35 percent negotiated discounts even
though the insured pay for these transactions themselves.[5]

However, 78 percent of people with traditional health
insurance do not spend anywhere near $2,500 per
annum on medical care—this 78 percent would simply
reduce their annual sickness insurance premium from
$4,980 to $1,908—a $3,072 annual savings (less a few
hundred dollars for annual checkups).

Overall, about 70 percent of the U.S. population spends $150 or
less per annum on medical expenses.[6]

Why the $3,000 per Family HDHP
Opportunity Still Exists

Why, then, if the insurance companies already offer such 120 percent or greater premium reductions for high-deductible health policies (HDHPs), do most people still have zero- or low-deductible
policies—policies for which the paperwork cost of the service provided sometimes exceeds the price of the actual service itself?

One reason is simply inertia on the part of employers and employees who purchase most private health insurance. Employers (wisely)
don't put the same time and talent into managing healthcare benefits that they do into managing their businesses. Moreover, since the
days when most laborers worked at a plant with a company doctor,
employees are used to getting a 100 percent medical benefit from
their employers. Changes in healthcare benefits, even changes that
benefit employees, are often met by employees with a don't-
confuse-me-with-the-facts attitude. This is particularly prevalent at
the lower end of the employment spectrum, where prospective hires
sometimes compare medical benefits between employers as much as
they compare the wages being offered.

Another reason that most people have such wasteful low- or no-
deductible medical insurance policies is the U.S. tax code. If an
employer raised the deductible in its group policy to $2,500 a year
per employee or family and agreed to pay employees any additional
amounts they spent toward meeting their $2,500 deductible, these
additional payments would not be tax deductible—the company
would have to pay employees about twice as much before state and
federal taxes to net each employee the same amount.[7]

> **But the major reason that employers are not yet offering
> higher-deductible health insurance policies for their
> employees is that they are locked into providing health
> insurance for their entire group—including the 22 per-
> cent of employees who consume far more than $5,000
> per year in annual medical expenses.**

About 22 percent of employees with employer-paid health insurance (or one of their dependents) have a preexisting medical condition. If they were to leave their current employer, this condition
would hinder their ability to obtain a private individual health
insurance policy or find employment (along with medical coverage) somewhere else. This unfortunate 22 percent utilize medical

services far in excess of the typical $5,000 annual premium paid by their employer—they average about four times this amount ($20,000) per annum on a recurring basis.

Insurance companies agree to cover this 22 percent of unhealthy employees costing $20,000 per annum only because they also receive the $5,000 per annum premium on the 78 percent of healthier employees who incur almost no annual medical expenses.

Health and life insurance originated with the eighteenth- and nineteenth-century "friendly societies" of the working classes—where the randomly fortunate many agreed to take care of the randomly unfortunate few. This system implies that any single unidentifiable member of the group has an equal chance of being struck by the insured catastrophe. In healthcare today this is no longer the case.

Today, with 27 percent of Americans obese and 61 percent overweight, the overwhelming majority of nongeriatric healthcare expenses are incurred by people easily identifiable by their diet, weight, or smoking habits.

Wellness-oriented employees might be eager to give up part of their income for the child of a coworker struck randomly by leukemia. But, if given a choice, those same employees might not be eager to give up part of their income to treat disease in a coworker caused by the coworker's poor diet, or hypertension in a coworker who is 100 pounds overweight due to gluttony, or lung disease in a coworker who refuses to quit smoking. However, until now, because of U.S. tax regulations, such a choice for wellness-oriented employees on how to spend their money has not been available.

Converting Your Customers from Sickness Insurance to Wellness Insurance

As explained in Chapter 6, U.S. legislation taking effect between 2001 and 2003 is leveling the health insurance playing field between corporate- and self-employed individuals—by making health insurance tax deductible for self-employeds. This is making such a choice (i.e., opting out of the "broken" system) available for healthy wellness-oriented individuals.

Individuals in the 78 percent group of healthy employees without preexisting medical conditions can now choose to drop the employer-based sickness insurance system before it drops them—opting out of the employer-paid health insurance monopoly.

This choice can save wellness-oriented individuals approximately $3,000 per year on their family's annual sickness insurance.

Yet these individuals will not simply pocket the savings—savings that they either receive directly themselves or indirectly by making a financial agreement with their employers.[8] Most of these individuals will choose to invest part of their $3,000 savings into what they hold dearest, their continued health and wellness, and to save the balance for future wellness investments.

Wellness-insured individuals will invest a portion of their $3,000 in annual savings in their continued wellness— vitamins, fitness clubs, minerals, weight control programs, and hundreds of other wellness-related or preventative treatments.

Wellness-insured individuals will save the remaining portion of their annual savings in specially earmarked Wellness Savings Accounts (WSAs)—monies they will have available to make future wellness investments and to meet the annual deductible on their HDHP in case of a family medical catastrophe.

The combination of these two phenomena will make hundreds of billions available each year for consumers to purchase wellness products and services—especially those wellness products and services tailored to meet the requirements of consumers with Wellness Savings Accounts.

Wellness Insurance: Combining an HDHP with a Wellness Savings Account (WSA)

Here's an actual example of how wellness-oriented individuals can redirect $3,000 per year of the $5,000 they (or their employers) pay for sickness insurance into current and future wellness products and services.

Consider the healthy family described earlier with the zero-deductible Blue Cross–Blue Shield policy costing $4,980 per annum. This family would switch their policy to the $2,500-deductible HDHP from Blue Cross–Blue Shield costing $1,908 per annum—a $3,072 reduction in their annual premium. They would then contribute this $3,072 in annual savings to a Wellness Savings Account (WSA) that they would open at a local financial institution.

Each month the family would draw on its WSA for sickness expenses incurred below the $2,500 annual deductible amount, as well as for wellness products and services typically not covered by sickness insurance plans. Since most of these wellness purchases would not count toward the deductible, the family should set up reserves of $2,500 as soon as possible. To facilitate withdrawals, the local financial institution would give them a Visa-type debit card and checkbook on the WSA account. The Visa debit card could also be the same PPO card they use to obtain discounted services in the Blue Cross–Blue Shield network.

During the first year with this program, they might spend $400 or so in medical expenses for annual physicals and $600 on wellness products and services, putting $2,072 reserves in their WSA to meet the annual deductible should a catastrophe arise.

Year 1: Wellness Savings Account (WSA)	
Beginning WSA account balance	$ 0
Interest earned*	$ 82
Annual WSA contribution	$3,072
Medical expenses	$(400)
Wellness expenses	$(600)
Ending WSA account balance	$2,154

*8% compounded monthly on average balance.

The next year they would begin with last year's $2,154 surplus ($2,072 contribution plus $82 interest). Thus in year 2 and beyond (holding constant their $400 per annum in medical expenses), they could spend up to $2,672 per year on wellness products and services—while still keeping a $2,500 minimum balance in their WSA to meet their annual deductible in the event of a medical emergency. However, let's assume for now that they continue to spend only $50 per month, or $600 per annum, on wellness—creating a $2,072 recurring annual surplus in their WSA that would soon accumulate to tens of thousands of dollars.

Year 2: Wellness Savings Account (WSA)	
Beginning initial WSA account balance	$2,154
Interest earned*	$ 260
Annual WSA contribution	$3,072
Actual medical expenses	$(400)
Actual wellness expenses	$(600)
Ending WSA account balance	$4,486

*8% compounded monthly on average balance.

If this money were invested at 8 percent, in just 10 years the accumulated surplus would exceed $31,000. The interest alone on this amount could fund the entire $1,908 annual sickness insurance premium—giving the family effectively free sickness insurance for the rest of their working lives. Or it could become a $31,000 nest egg to supplement Medicare or to leave to their children.

Year 10: Wellness Savings Account (WSA)	
Beginning initial WSA account balance	$27,235
Interest earned*	$ 2,343
Annual WSA contribution	$ 3,072
Actual medical expenses	$ (400)
Actual wellness expenses	$ (600)
Ending WSA account balance	$31,649

*8% compounded monthly on average balance.

A healthy couple in their twenties could accumulate more than a quarter million dollars for future wellness investments by their fifties.

Year 30: Wellness Savings Account (WSA)	
Beginning initial WSA account balance	$236,084
Interest earned*	$ 19,676
Annual WSA contribution	$ 3,072
Actual medical expenses	$ (400)
Actual wellness expenses	$ (600)
Ending WSA account balance	$257,832

*8% compounded monthly on average balance.

Over a healthy lifetime, this same couple could accumulate more than $1.3 million for future wellness investments in their seventies.

Year 50: Wellness Savings Account (WSA)	
Beginning initial WSA account balance	$1,262,600
Interest earned*	$ 104,873
Annual WSA contribution	$ 3,072
Actual medical expenses	$ (400)
Actual wellness expenses	$ (600)
Ending WSA account balance	$1,369,545

*8% compounded monthly on average balance.

This scenario for your customers, where they are allowed to accumulate tens of thousands of dollars for future wellness purchases, is today actually even better than these numbers show.

Thanks to legislation enacted in 2001, the first 750,000 American families who act before December 31, 2002, are allowed to take a full income tax deduction for up to $3,800 per annum that they invest each year until retirement in a special WSA-type account called a Medical Savings Account (MSA). This $3,800 per annum tax deduction is in addition to the amount they may deduct for the cost of their annual HDHP premium if they are self-employed.

Over the next 10 years, these 750,000 families could accumulate up to $58,000[9] each, tax free, in their Medical Savings Account (MSA)—more than $43 billion for future wellness expenses. When and if the MSA program is extended, up to 50 million U.S. families with some self-employed income could similarly accumulate up to $2.9 trillion in 10 years for future wellness expenses.

Wellness entrepreneurs are already discovering that consumers with MSAs are "supercustomers" for wellness products and services for the following reasons:
1. MSA consumers are required to have HDHPs— they are used to making their own intelligent health choices and investing in their future wellness.

2. MSA consumers reap the financial benefits of making efficacious wellness investments. They get to keep any unspent amounts in their MSA account, and even use these amounts for nonmedical purposes after age 65.
3. MSA consumers know that they will be paying the costs of their future sickness expenses, so they have an added incentive to invest in their wellness.

How Medical Savings Accounts (MSAs) Work

Congress has passed legislation authorizing up to 750,000 U.S. families to open Medical Savings Accounts on an experimental basis. The experiment is currently scheduled to expire on December 31, 2003.[10] But for families who take advantage of this legislation by opening an MSA before December 31, 2002, the benefits of their MSAs, and the right to make future contributions until age 65, are grandfathered for the rest of their lives.

An MSA is similar to the previously described WSA account, but with one additional important feature: 100 percent of the contributions made to the MSA are tax deductible. These contributions are deductible from adjusted gross income, meaning that self-employed individuals do not have to record a profit in order to get these tax benefits.[11]

To qualify to open an MSA account, an individual must be either self-employed with an HDHP or employed by a small employer that has established an HDHP for its employees.

Until they reach age 65, individuals who open MSAs before January 31, 2002, are allowed to make tax-deductible contributions to their MSAs of up to $3,800 each year (increased annually in $50 increments for inflation).[12] They can liberally make withdrawals to pay medical expenses from their MSA with a Visa-type debit card or checkbook—or they can just leave their money in their MSA to earn tax-free interest for future medical expenses. Coupled with the recent legislation allowing self-employed individuals tax deductions for health insurance premiums, beginning in 2003 these individuals will be allowed a 100 percent tax deduction for the annual premium of their HDHP. In cases of economic hardship, such as if they go on unemployment or COBRA, they are allowed to withdraw from their MSA tax-free funds to pay the premiums of their medical insurance policy.

And best of all, when they go on Medicare at age 65, the entire unspent amount in their MSA may be withdrawn for any purpose whatsoever with no penalties. As with an IRA, they pay income taxes on only the amount withdrawn, at their then-lower retirement tax rate. But even better than an IRA, they pay no income taxes on amounts withdrawn to pay for medical expenses not covered by Medicare or other health insurance.

During the first year after my wife and I opened our family MSA account, we deposited the maximum allowable amount, but foolishly made withdrawals of approximately $1,000 throughout the year to pay for medical expenses. This was foolish because, although we received the full tax deduction for putting in the maximum $3,800 amount, we received no additional tax deductions for taking out the $1,000 for medical expenses that we could have afforded to pay with other funds. This lowered the balance in our MSA account by $1,000, and, assuming 8 percent tax-free interest, this additional $1,000 would have grown to $11,000 in 30 years. Since the MSA carries all the advantages of an IRA and then some, consumers who can afford to should put the maximum allowable amount in their MSA each year, then leave it alone to earn tax-free interest as the ultimate family savings vehicle.

Consumers using their MSAs in this manner, as a tax-free family savings vehicle, receive the financial equivalent of a $3,800 per annum wellness tax deduction.

The MSA is the ultimate vehicle when it comes to allowing individuals to make the right choices for themselves and their families. Individuals are allowed a tax deduction for almost all of their medical expenditures, just as though they worked for a large corporation. Individuals themselves decide where to spend their money and are free to negotiate their own deals in the marketplace. Individuals get to keep any money they don't spend today to pay for medical expenses tomorrow, to fund their retirement, or to leave to their children.

But most of all, individuals with MSAs can make intelligent wellness investment decisions for their own continued wellness—weighing choices like the cost of vitamins and better nutrition today versus the cost of treating a chronic disease later on.

> Individuals with MSAs (accompanied by the required
> HDHPs) are, in effect, your wellness supercustomers—
> which is why teaching consumers how to open MSAs
> and HDHPs should be a key component of any wellness
> business!

Why Congress Will Have to Expand Medical Savings Accounts

When considering making an investment of money or time in your
business, a potential investor might be concerned that Congress
could end the MSA program or that it might be too late to get in on
the MSA experiment before 2003 (or when 750,000 MSA accounts
have been opened). Here's how to dispel these concerns.

First, while the current MSA experiment is scheduled to end on
December 31, 2002, individuals who open an MSA before then are
allowed to enjoy the benefits of their MSA account, including the
right to make additional contributions each year until they reach
age 65.

Second, I strongly believe that Congress will soon make the MSA
opportunity permanently available to all. Congress really has no
choice, because the public already has spoken.

Between 1931 and 1976, federal law prohibited banks from paying interest on checking accounts. In 1976, a small savings bank in
New England began offering interest on its checking accounts
(calling it a savings account with checks versus a checking account
with interest). The competition cried foul and demanded federal
action. By the time the federal government got around to taking
action, so many people had opened such accounts that the action
Congress was forced to take was to pass laws allowing interest on
all checking accounts.[13]

Similarly, for almost 50 years, federal law prohibited retailers
from selling certain name-brand items below the manufacturer's
list price. When Wal-Mart and other expanding retailers started
ignoring these laws and discounting name-brand items, the public
response was so favorable that Congress was forced to abolish so-
called fair trade laws in 1975.

A hunting dog proudly marches in front of the hunters, keeping a
watchful eye behind to make sure that it is being followed. If the
hunters decide to go in the opposite direction, the dog sprints to a
new place in front of them, again proudly proclaiming its place as

their leader. Politicians today are like hunting dogs—carefully watching the latest poll to see in which direction the public wants to go, then adopting this position as "leader."

Today, one of the things people want most is more choices in how they spend their money on the sickness and wellness of their families.

Regardless of what Congress does in the near future to make the MSA option permanently available for self-employed individuals, there is no stopping MSA or equivalent WSA accounts. The laws and regulations prohibiting them are so vague and so contrary to the public interest that self-employed individuals and perspicacious entrepreneurs are now structuring WSA-type vehicles for themselves and for general public consumption.

As we now examine, Wellness Insurance products are becoming available for self-employed individuals and for the employees of large corporations irrespective of whether or not Congress sanctions them through new legislation.

Structuring Opportunities for Wellness Insurance

Wellness entrepreneurs must understand the existing laws and regulations limiting Wellness Insurance, and some of the legal loopholes around them, for two important reasons:

1. Wellness entrepreneurs will want to structure proprietary Wellness Insurance vehicles for their customers to finance the purchase of their products.
2. Wellness entrepreneurs will want their wellness products and services to qualify for purchase by consumers with third-party Wellness Insurance.

Approximately 50 million people in the United States derive part or all of their income from self-employment. Here are three examples of opportunities you can take advantage of today in structuring tax-advantaged Wellness Insurance for these 50 million potential customers and in making sure that your products qualify for Wellness Insurance these customers obtain from third-party suppliers.

These examples also apply to organizations and associations seeking to structure tax-deductible Wellness Insurance products for members with self-employed income.

Structuring Opportunity #1: Increasing Tax Deductions for HDHPs

Section 162 of the Internal Revenue Code says that a self-employed individual can take a tax deduction only for medical insurance *premiums* for themselves, their spouse, or their dependents.[14] This excludes amounts spent for medical expenses other than insurance premiums—such as amounts incurred for direct medical expenses below the annual deductible or outside the coverage of a health insurance policy.

Thus, a self-employed person in 2003 paying a $5,000 ordinary health insurance premium gets a full tax deduction for the $5,000 premium amount, but if this self-employed person switched to an HDHP with a $2,000 premium and a $2,500 annual deductible and incurred $2,500 in additional medical expenses, only the $2,000 premium portion of the $4,500 in total medical expenses would be tax deductible.

Fortunately, the IRS code does not specifically define what *insurance* or a *premium* is or limit the amount of medical reimbursements provided by an insurer receiving the tax-deductible premium.

The insurance company or organization offering the HDHP could simply increase the annual premium from $2,000 to $4,500 and give the insured a Visa-type debit card and checkbook good for up to $2,500 in sickness or wellness expenses—with any unspent amounts each year accruing to the future benefit of the insured (similar to the cash-value increase portion of a whole life insurance policy).

The insured would have all the benefits of a WSA or an MSA account in a single financial vehicle—and with the addition of a minor life insurance component might even be able to take advantage of extremely favorable tax regulations governing whole life policies and annuities. Moreover, the sponsoring insurance company or organization could expand their PPO discounting group to include wellness as well as sickness expenses—giving their customers additional purchasing power and earning themselves an additional source of revenue from wellness providers joining the PPO.

To ensure the full tax deductibility of the higher $4,500 premium, the insurance company and the insured would be responsible to see that their $2,500 wellness allowance went only toward purchasing IRS-approved tax-deductible medical expenses.

Structuring Opportunity #2: Making Wellness Investments Tax Deductible

Despite many attempts by the IRS to stop them, the tax courts have ruled that any medical expense legitimately prescribed by a licensed physician is tax deductible. Even luxury cruises qualify as tax-deductible medical expenses when prescribed by a doctor, and the IRS now allows a tax deduction for the expenses of an accompanying spouse if considered medically necessary (e.g., if the patient is in a wheelchair).

Most doctors would gladly issue "prescriptions" for weight-loss programs, fitness training, special vitamins and minerals, and all wellness-based products and services—especially if supplied with documentation demonstrating the medical efficacy of the requested product or service.

The only reason many doctors haven't issued such prescriptions up until now is that they haven't been asked, nor have they been supplied with scientific data documenting the efficacy of many wellness products and services. This hasn't occurred because in the past most wellness items wouldn't be covered for reimbursement by traditional company-sponsored sickness insurance plans.

Wellness entrepreneurs should consult with licensed physicians and make medical prescriptions easily available for their products and services.

Despite the fact that the courts have ruled that virtually anything legitimately prescribed by a physician is tax deductible, there is a conflicting IRS revenue ruling saying that only prescription (versus over-the-counter) drugs qualify as tax-deductible medical expenses.[15] This ruling has been used (and abused) for years by large pharmaceutical firms who make more expensive prescription versions of their over-the-counter products—both to satisfy the IRS and to get employer-based sickness insurance policies to pay for them. Wellness entrepreneurs could take similar advantage of this same ruling.

Wellness entrepreneurs should make special versions of their products and services that would be available only with a doctor's prescription—to take advantage of existing tax laws and to help their customers obtain reimbursement for their products from traditional sickness insurance providers.

If you are considering making a prescription-only version of a dietary supplement, check first to see what has happened to the Dietary Supplement Tax Fairness Act of 2001 introduced by Senators Tom Harkin (Democrat, Iowa) and Orrin Hatch (Republican, Utah). This bill, if passed, would give dietary supplements parity with prescription drugs under the U.S. tax code and limit some of the opportunity to make prescription-only versions of dietary supplements. But even if it passes, wellness providers might still want to offer prescription-only versions of their products so that their customers can get reimbursement from traditional sickness insurance providers (who typically cover only prescription drugs).

Structuring Opportunity #3: Wellness Insurance Covering Only Your Products and Services

In many cases, Wellness Insurance will be sponsored by organizations who are themselves wellness providers. For example, a network marketing company that manufactures vitamins might sponsor Wellness Insurance for its distributors. In such cases, it would be foolish to offer insurance covering vitamins and other products made by the competition.

Just as traditional health insurance companies limit consumer choice in picking medical providers and pharmaceuticals, innovative Wellness Insurance sponsors

> could offer Wellness Insurance that covers only their particular brand of wellness product or service.

Such a limitation need not be a negative for consumers. In cases where the wellness provider combined this limitation with making their product tax deductible (as described previously in Structuring Opportunity #2), the wellness company would be making their wellness products uniquely tax deductible for its distributors. Or the wellness company could offer discounts to members using Wellness Insurance to purchase its own or an affiliate's proprietary products.

A fitness organization like Jill Kinney's Club One might sponsor Wellness Insurance that automatically includes its monthly membership dues, making such dues tax deductible by bundling them with the Wellness Insurance HDHP premium. The fitness organization might also offer discounts for a privately labeled line of dietary supplements.

A network marketing company might sponsor Wellness Insurance that includes a $200 per month allowance for purchase of its dietary supplements, bundled with a monthly membership and training credits at a local or national fitness club.

These are just three examples of structuring opportunities that you and your wellness company can use to take advantage of existing tax regulations to better serve your customers. Keep in mind that these examples don't apply only to large wellness entrepreneurs. An individual wellness distributor could create prescription-only packages of his or her regular products. A lawyer wellness entrepreneur could create and market his or her own Wellness Insurance product (e.g., combining a simple trust agreement with an off-the-shelf HDHP product and depository account).

Obtaining Wellness Insurance for Dependents of Corporate Employees

Many of your potential customers will be corporate employees who are automatically covered by their employer's group medical insurance policy. While the 78 percent of these who are healthy would probably prefer to drop out of their group plan and purchase their own Wellness Insurance, they will not be able to do so: They would probably not receive any extra compensation for dropping out, and their eligibility for such a group medical plan could limit their ability to obtain efficacious Wellness Insurance. One of the primary qualifications for opening an MSA account and taking advantage of the new self-employed health insurance tax deductions is that the applicant not be currently eligible for group medical insurance.

This could limit many working people with part-time self-employment income from opening MSAs and from being able to obtain HDHPs.

> **However, because most corporate policies no longer freely cover spouses and dependents, even individuals working for major corporations can now structure tax-advantaged Wellness Insurance policies for their spouses and their children.**

Employers used to pay the full health insurance premium for their employees *and* for their spouses and dependents. However, most private employers have recently changed to paying the full premium *only* for their employees. Spouses and dependents are typically allowed to participate in the company group policy only if part or all of the additional premium is paid by the employee.

> **Since most employer group health insurance policies are of the low-deductible type, switching a spouse or dependent to an HDHP will often save the employee money while guaranteeing the spouse or dependent renewable, affordable health insurance for life.**

As explained in Chapter 6, by law, insurance companies must raise premiums on individual policies *equally* for all individuals in a defined class rather than only for specific persons who have filed large claims for medical care.

> **It is less expensive to switch a healthy spouse or child from an employer's group policy to an individual HDHP because about 22 percent of the employees (or their dependents) in any group typically have expensive preexisting medical conditions.**

Of course, your customer's dependents may be in the unfortunate 22 percent group, but if their spouse or child is in the healthy seventy-eighth percentile today, you should help them obtain an individual HDHP as soon as possible. You will help the family save money while creating a supercustomer for your wellness products and services. But much more important, one of their dependents could develop a condition that could limit their future eligibility for an individual HDHP, and thus their options for future employment.

If you use the services of an insurance agent to price HDHP or any health insurance policies, keep in mind that the commission on a low- or no-deductible policy is several times larger than the commission on an HDHP—even though the agent often has to perform the same amount of work.

One of the main reasons MSA accounts and HDHPs have not yet sold as well as expected is a reluctance by some insurance brokers to switch their customers to high-deductible policies that pay much lower commissions.[16]

Keep in mind that most U.S. insurance is *sold* versus *bought*. Customers are typically sold the best policy as presented by a given agent rather than the best policy available in the marketplace for their specific needs. Few agents carry policies from more than a few companies, and sometimes the policies paying the highest commissions to the agent are the ones offering the least value to the consumer.

If you are a licensed insurance agent, combining a Wellness Insurance business with a wellness distribution business is a great opportunity: The money you help your healthy customers save on health insurance can be channeled into investments in your wellness products and services.

It is estimated that 67 million Americans currently obtain health insurance from the employer of their spouse or parent. Thus, approximately 52 million spouses and dependents (the healthy 78 percent of this 67 million) could save money by switching to HDHPs and using some of their savings for wellness products and services. In cases where breadwinners receive free group health insurance for themselves from an employer but also have part-time income from a family business, shifting this part-time income to the name of a spouse could allow families to maximize the value of the new self-employment health insurance tax deductions and potentially qualify to open an MSA account.

Why Large Employers Will Eventually Offer Wellness Insurance and What This Means for Wellness Entrepreneurs

Eventually, employers will be restructuring their health insurance offerings to allow employees to choose where to spend the employer health insurance contribution—and most employees will choose HDHPs with wellness allowances for themselves and their dependents. This restructuring is being accelerated by litigation, and it has dire consequences for the 22 percent of employees who cannot obtain health insurance elsewhere because of a preexisting condition.

Medical costs and sickness insurance premiums have skyrocketed, increasing 12 percent in 2001 alone. In response, employers have cut back on the number of medical services covered by their group insurance policies, services that used to include more expensive diagnostics as well as early-intervention treatments. Lawsuits have succeeded in holding employers liable in cases where an employee incurred greater injury by not getting such a diagnostic test or early-intervention treatment. Ironically, employers who once thought they were benevolently paying for most sickness expenses are now being sued for billions of dollars because of the few sickness expenses that they can no longer afford to pay.

The result of this litigation is that employers are demanding to be removed from making the decisions on what is and is not covered by their corporate medical insurance. The only solution, as many employers have already discovered, is a cafeteria-type plan, whereby employers contribute a fixed and equal amount for medical insurance for each employee and give the employee a list of options on how to spend it. Today these new employee spending options are somewhat limited and mostly come from within single insurance companies—because the insurer can afford to cover the unfortunate 22 percent only if it's allowed to keep the unused premium from the healthy 78 percent. However, this is rapidly changing in favor of the healthy 78 percent in response to the increasing demand for wellness products and services.

Entrepreneurs setting up new businesses are already offering Wellness Insurance cafeteria options—HDHPs with a $2,000 per year wellness spending allowance. With proper structuring, as previously described, this tax-free wellness allowance can be spent on fitness club memberships, nutritional supplements, or wellness counseling. Employers offering this type of Wellness Insurance receive applications mostly from healthy, wellness-oriented individuals—because these potential hires view the $2,000 annual wellness benefit as worth up to $4,000 in pretax wages. Less healthy individuals (or those with dependents who have preexisting conditions) are turned off by the company's typically $2,500 or higher annual deductible for sickness expenses.

Eventually, most employees will receive a tax-free $2,000 annual wellness spending allowance for efficacious wellness products and services. This will be the largest single financial factor taking the wellness industry from approximately $200 billion today to $1 trillion or more by 2010.

The cafeteria option plan is now sweeping through most major corporations. It is the beginning of the breakdown of the employer group health insurance system in which the healthy 78 percent of employees pay for the unhealthy 22 percent. Congress will soon have no choice but to face the cold, hard facts of reforming healthcare:

- Healthy Americans want more wellness options on a tax-deductible basis, and they want economic credit for making wellness decisions today that will save everyone money tomorrow.

- Private employers cannot be expected to pay (and pay and pay) for the unlimited sickness expenses of a minority of their employees—especially when this situation was created in part by government policies subsidizing sickness instead of wellness.

Congress already considered some of these issues when it established the Medical Savings Account (MSA) experiment.

Small businesses (i.e., generally less than 50 employees but in some cases up to 200 employees) are now allowed to set up company-sponsored MSAs whereby

> **the employer makes tax-deductible contributions to each employee's individual MSA account. Employees are allowed to keep their MSAs, or transfer them to another company, if their employment is terminated.**

This type of plan is exactly what union workers and employees of large companies will demand—especially once they learn that employees of smaller companies have already been granted this savings option through employer-sponsored MSAs. As noted earlier, individuals and corporations opening MSA accounts before December 31, 2003, are allowed to continue to make MSA contributions for the rest of their working lives.

CHAPTER 8

Making Your Fortune in Wellness Distribution

Throughout history, there have been fortunes made and fortunes lost in manufacturing or controlling some particular commodity. However, consistent success has come only from distributing the ever expanding production of cutting-edge technology.

> **This is especially true today because distribution costs now represent approximately 70 percent of the retail price for most products and services. More significantly, distribution costs will represent approximately 80 percent of the retail price for most wellness products.**

However, before we examine some of the opportunities in wellness distribution, it is important for wellness entrepreneurs to first understand the biological concept of *unlimited wealth,* which has created most of these opportunities.

Unlimited Wealth: The Biological Principle behind Modern Economics

Here's an exercise I use to teach the concept of unlimited wealth to my students. I have the members of the class pretend they are shipwrecked on a desert island with no provisions. In order to survive, they must organize a society and divide the work according to specific chores—gathering food, building shelters, collecting firewood, and so on.

At first, the students want to democratically rotate various chores in their new island society. However, as we role-play the various chores, they soon learn that it is much better for each person to specialize.

The person who goes out to find apples on Monday not only returns with apples, she knows exactly where to get the apples on Tuesday. By Wednesday, she not only knows where to find the apples, she has made tools like a sack or a wheelbarrow to carry them all back to the camp in one trip. By Thursday, she has made a tool to pick the ripe apples from the higher branches before they fall to the ground. By Friday, she is able to accomplish a former day's work in less than an hour, so she starts learning how to make apple cider and apple preserves.

Eventually, all of the chores necessary for survival (obtaining food, shelter, fuel, etc.) are performed in a fraction of the time and by a fraction of the people originally required to complete them. This frees some members of the society to explore new pursuits—producing new products, more tools, and even providing entertainment.

As the society grows, so much quantity and variety of goods are being produced that a new need arises—distributing all these goods and services. Before long, some people are engaged full-time in distribution, which mostly entails educating everyone about what the others are doing and what is available. These distributors, or merchants, end up being the wealthiest members of the island society because they add the most value—especially when the island society encounters another island society and the merchants begin trading more produce and more tools.

In this lesson, my students learn the two main principles of unlimited wealth underlying our modern economy.

First, over time, individuals can produce an unlimited amount of a single good or service (i.e., *unlimited wealth*) by making use of the advancing technology that automatically results from specialization.

Second, the total overall wealth of a society is thus limited only by distribution: the number of individuals available to consume and trade their specialized produce and tools.[1]

The economic power of the United States is based, in part, on distribution laws that initially made it the world's largest open marketplace for goods and services. The U.S. Constitution generally allowed each state to rule itself, with one very powerful exception: No state was allowed to make any law or rule that infringed on the rights of its citizens to freely trade with the citizens of any other state.

Similarly, the economic power of the developed nations today— Western Europe, North America, Japan, and the other Asian tigers (Taiwan, South Korea, Singapore, etc.)—is based on effectively free trade between their 1 billion or so citizens.

This trading block of 1 billion citizens—Western Europe, North America, Japan, and the other Asian tigers—comprises the international wellness marketplace of the immediate future.

From a political standpoint, the challenge for the less developed nations is how to allow their 5 billion people to join the free traders while fighting the political instability at home that often results from rapid economic change.

How Distribution Opportunities Surpassed Manufacturing Opportunities

In the 1967 movie *The Graduate,* actor Dustin Hoffman was offered a confident, one-word solution to the quest for economic success: "Plastics." Back then, due to a short-term shortage of raw materials that peaked in the 1970s, economic success for many did lie in finding less expensive ways to make things.

Today, however, thanks to plastics and so many other better ways of making things, economic success for most people no longer lies in manufacturing. Today the greatest opportunities lie in the distribution sector of our economy.

Back in 1967, a manufactured product that sold for $300, for example, such as a camera or a fashionable dress, typically had a manufacturing cost of approximately $150 and a distribution cost of approximately $150. Manufacturing costs accounted for approximately 50 percent of retail prices, so it was possible to make a great deal of money by lowering the costs of production. Back then, even a 10 or 20 percent reduction in manufacturing costs could lower your retail price by $15 or $30.

> In the 1960s, entrepreneurial fortunes were made by those who found ways to lower manufacturing costs significantly (e.g., from $150 to $30 or less), often by using plastics or relocating production facilities overseas.

Today, 35 years later, the same product of similar quality typically retails for approximately $100 (although people sometimes don't realize this because they have shifted to purchasing higher-quality products). This two-thirds price reduction for similar-quality items has occurred primarily because technology has lowered production costs from $150 down to approximately $30 or less.

> Distribution costs on that same product have also fallen, from $150 to approximately $70, to where they now account for approximately 70 percent of the price for a typical $100 retail product.

Typical Retail Product Cost Breakdown				
	1967		2002	
Manufacturing costs	$150	50%	$ 30	30%
Distribution costs	$150	50%	$ 70	70%
Total retail price	$300	100%	$100	100%

Relative distribution costs have not fallen as much as relative manufacturing costs because we have not yet applied to distribution many of the innovative methods that we have applied to manufacturing.[2]

Today, manufacturing costs represent only about $30 of a typical $100 retail price, so a 10 or 20 percent reduction in manufacturing costs might represent only a $3 to $6 retail price reduction on a $100 item.

But today, distribution costs represent about $70 of a typical $100 retail price, so a 10 or 20 percent reduction in distribution costs might represent a $7 to $14 retail price reduction on a $100 item. A 50 percent or greater reduction in distribution costs— sometimes feasible by eliminating a single link in the distribution chain between the factory and the consumer—might represent a $35 or even greater retail price reduction on a $100 item.

Due primarily to this increased percentage of distribution cost in retail prices, many of the production facilities that moved overseas in previous years have moved back to the United States. The majority of the foreign cars sold in the United States are now made in the United States. The largest auto plant in the world is the Honda Accord plant in Marysville, Ohio, which exports much of its production to Japan, and the hottest new line of Mercedes SUVs is made in Alabama.

The increasing percentage of distribution cost is why, over the past three decades, the majority of great personal fortunes have been made by people who found better ways of distributing things rather than better ways of making things.

In 1992, Sam Walton of Wal-Mart, who first became an entrepreneur at age 44, became the richest man in the world. Sam never manufactured anything during his life, and under his rule, Wal-Mart simply distributed name-brand merchandise made by other companies. In the 1980s, Ross Perot of EDS became a billionaire by discovering better ways of distributing other companies' hardware and software. In the 1970s, Fred Smith of Federal Express became a billionaire by building an entire airline for distributing products rather than transporting people. The list goes on and on.

More recent examples can be found in the megafortunes of Internet billionaires like Jeff Bezos of Amazon.com, who was chosen as *Time* magazine's Man of the Year in 1999. These cyberspace entrepreneurs found ways to use a new tool (the Internet) to distribute things more efficiently.

How Distribution Has Changed in the Twenty-first Century

When we look closer, especially at the fortunes that have been made most recently, we see that the nature of the distribution opportunity has changed.

Distribution is really two processes:
1. **Educating consumers about products and services that will improve their lives**
2. **Physically distributing products and services to consumers**

Sam Walton, Fred Smith, and most of the distribution billionaires of the twentieth century made their fortunes by finding better and cheaper ways to physically distribute products to consumers *that consumers already knew they wanted.*

On the other hand, Jeff Bezos and the distribution billionaires of the twenty-first century are making their distribution fortunes mostly by educating consumers about new products and services—typically products and services *that consumers don't even know are available.*

It is important for wellness entrepreneurs and investors to understand that this flip-flop in the nature of the distribution opportunity has occurred at least once before.

Prior to the nineteenth century, the work of distribution (of finished goods) mostly entailed educating consumers about products and services that would improve their lives. The peddler and the Main Street merchant alike prided themselves on the knowledge of what they sold, and explaining their products to customers took up the bulk of their time.

In the nineteenth century, these peddlers and merchants evolved into the department stores that characterized most of twentieth-century distribution, from Marshall Field in Chicago (1865) to Filene's in Boston (1881). Technological advances (e.g., centralization of credit, real estate, and buying functions) allowed department stores to quickly replace the peddlers and individual Main Street merchants from whom they themselves had sprung.

These department stores did a lot more than just use technology to lower the cost of selling merchandise. They prided themselves on the customer service of small retailers. This fueled the never-ending cycle of consumer demand that defied conventional economic logic. Instead of going to the department store to purchase something you wanted, you went to the department store to find out about something you didn't know existed but that you couldn't live without once you learned about it (electric lamps, dishwashers, icemakers, and self-cleaning ovens).

Looking back on those days before the advent of television and mass media, the department store best served the two distinct functions of distribution today. The department store first *educated* its customers about new products that would improve their lives. Then, once it had taught customers what was available and assisted them in choosing the right product for their needs, it *physically distributed* the product from the factory to the consumer.

From this point forward we use the following terms: *intellectual distribution* and *physical distribution.*

Intellectual Distribution versus Physical Distribution

Intellectual distribution is the process of educating customers about products and services, typically items that they either don't know exist or don't know are now affordable.

Physical distribution is the process of helping customers physically obtain products and services that they already know they want.

The wellness entrepreneur, like every other business today, must perform these two distribution functions in serving their customers.

From 1950 to 2000, the traditional department stores declined partly because advancing technology, such as universal credit cards and shopping malls, made most of their original innovations (like charge accounts) obsolete.

But department stores declined mostly because they failed to keep their physical distribution service at the same level as their intellectual distribution service.

As the consumer retail dollar shifted from traditional durables (major appliances, furniture) to more consumables (cleaners, paper towels, batteries), consumers desired to quickly obtain these items—items that they already knew they wanted—in as short a time as possible and on a regular basis. The physical layout of the typical multistory department store was ill suited to this task, and the department stores were slow to retool their layout. Many of us can remember running into a department store to buy a roll of film, only to have to wait while the same clerk who operated the cash register took 20 minutes to explain a new camera to a potential customer.

This led entrepreneurs like Sam Walton to open mass-merchandise stores dedicated almost entirely to physical versus intellectual distribution. These stores sold the customer exactly, and only, what they knew they wanted before they entered the store—in the shortest time possible and at the lowest possible price. The mass merchandisers decimated the traditional department stores.[3]

The mass merchandisers also benefited from the development of radio and television. Mass media allowed manufacturers of wide-appeal products to bypass the traditional department stores in communicating directly with their customers. Today most manufacturers "handshake" with their customers through the mass media, and the surviving retailers for most products are the lowest-cost, most efficient, physical distributors of merchandise—like Wal-Mart, Kmart, and Target stores. Customer loyalty has shifted from individual retailers (Sears, Macy's, J.W. Robinson's) to individual manufacturers (Sony, Levi's, Procter & Gamble).

When this trend began 30 years ago, a commonly heard shopping complaint was that the customers knew more than the clerks about what they were selling. Today, most retail store shoppers just assume that *they* are more educated about their purchases than the people who sell them.

This story about how the mighty department stores declined contains an important lesson for wellness entrepreneurs:

You must maintain your physical distribution service at the same level as your intellectual distribution service, and vice versa, constantly riding the flip-flop that occurs in the nature of the distribution opportunity.

Applying the Lessons of Business History

Business history, such as this story of the department stores and the mass merchants, contains many important lessons for the wellness entrepreneur. However, when you study these stories and then seek to apply them to the distribution of wellness products and services, you must do so with one very important caveat:

Changes that used to take place in 50 to 100 years or more now take place in 5 to 10 years or less.

Starting in 1981, it took only seven years for the 70-year-old carburetor industry to be displaced by electronic fuel injection. Starting in 1985, it took only five years for the 50-year-old phonograph record to be displaced by the compact disc. Starting in 1995, it took only three years for the 30-year-old fax machine to be largely displaced by e-mail.

In studying the past, you must condense time when considering solutions applicable to your wellness business of the future—as changes that now take place in five years may soon take place in five months, or even less.

The Category Busters: A Supersized Wellness Opportunity

Recently, a new retailing trend has emerged, *category busting,* which preserves the physical distribution benefits of the mass merchandisers while exceeding the intellectual distribution services of traditional department stores.

These category busters, which include stores like Home Depot, PetsMart, CompUSA, Toys "R" Us, and Babies "R" Us, are effectively mass merchants in just one category—carrying the largest array of merchandise in their category at the lowest prices. This makes consumers willing to travel greater distances to reach them and thus allows the category busters to continue to open even larger stores with greater selection at lower prices.

Since they are focused on only one type of merchandise, they attract employees who are interested in the product category itself. Plus, most category busters hold on-site classes for employees and for customers interested in learning more about their products. Category busters often know more than manufacturers about their products and how consumers use them.

> **This knowledge, coupled with the extremely favorable buying and marketing power of the category busters, has led to a new phenomenon in retailing: custom-packaged, brand-name merchandise that is retail-priced below the average single-unit manufacturing cost. In effect, retail goods that are priced below wholesale.**

Here's one example of how this arrangement works.

In 1992, a particular company sold a tool air compressor for $300 wholesale (200,000 units per annum) that retailed for $600 at high-end hardware and tool shops. The company manufactured this item for $200 per unit—$50 in variable labor and material costs and $150 in five-year-amortized design, tool, and die costs. To make a five-year production run of 1 million units, the company had to spend $150 million up front ($150 per unit) on the plant, research, tool dies, engineering design, and so forth.

In 1993, Home Depot hypothesized that at a much lower retail price than $600, say $200 retail, it could sell 500,000 units of this product. Home Depot offered to purchase 500,000 units—for $100 each. At first the company scoffed, stating that it cost them twice this price just to make them. After reflection, however, the company realized that the offer would technically be profitable on a marginal basis, and, if they didn't accept the offer, Home Depot would go to a competitor who could build a higher-volume plant and put them out of business. They accepted, and Home Depot actually ended up selling 800,000 units. Subsequently, the manufacturer used the higher volume to retool and lower their fixed costs to less than $50 per unit—far below the initial $150 per unit.

The ultimate beneficiary of this story was the consumer, who was and still is able to purchase a formerly $600 product for $200—50 percent below the original wholesale price of $300.[4]

Similar innovations (e.g., purchasing during slow periods or downtimes of manufacturers) are allowing both category busters and innovative mass merchants to continually sell top-quality goods below actual wholesale.

For example, certain stores, like Costco, don't carry any specific items on a continual basis. Costco gives open orders to name-brand manufacturers that are typically filled when their manufacturing plants have idle time. Since the manufacturer has to pay for labor and overhead anyway during these time periods, it accepts these orders at far less than normal wholesale cost. Moreover, Costco suppliers are typically required to take back (including freight) any items not sold in a short time period, so Costco is assured that it gets only the most fashionable, top-quality merchandise.

Category busters currently represent the state of the art in retailing technology, combining the best customer education and physical distribution services with the ability to continually sell first-quality merchandise at below-wholesale prices. Yet at this time no significant category buster has emerged in the wellness industry.

This is one of the greatest opportunities in wellness: creating a one-stop supersized shop, or perhaps a mall, for many wellness products and services that combines the best intellectual and physical distribution services.

Moreover, as we now examine, the category-buster opportunity can be especially lucrative for the wellness entrepreneur because of the unique nature of many wellness products.

The New Era of
Zero Marginal Product Cost

Category busters can profitably sell top-quality goods below whole-sale because of a profound change taking place on the economic landscape:

We are entering the era of effectively *zero* marginal production and physical distribution costs.

This statement has enormous implications for suppliers and retailers in every industry, but especially in wellness, because of the low or zero marginal cost of most wellness products and services (e.g., vitamins, supplements, and fitness club memberships).

The per-unit price of raw materials and automated labor has fallen so low that the amortized per-unit research and development (R&D) cost and the amortized per-unit marketing cost are almost all that matters for many types of goods.

The pipeline from raw materials to finished products travels through four stages:

1. Research and development (R&D)
2. Physical manufacturing or production
3. Intellectual distribution
4. Physical distribution

Traditionally, the largest component costs in products and services were in variable per-unit physical manufacturing costs (item 2) and physical distribution costs (item 4). Expensive raw materials and hand labor made up the bulk of manufacturing expenses and went up or down almost directly with each unit (or 1,000 units) produced. Similarly, the physical distribution costs of storing, transferring, and delivering the finished product made up the bulk of distribution expenses and also went up or down almost directly with each unit (or 1,000 units) distributed.

But today, most of the expense in making products and services are in research and development costs (item 1) and intellectual distribution costs (item 3). This applies almost 100 percent to new products and services like software, entertainment, communications, and especially wellness—products whose costs are composed almost entirely of R&D and marketing expenses. It even applies to traditional physical products and services like cameras, clothes, and other consumer items.

Thus, the nature of the opportunity in manufacturing and in distribution is changing—especially for products with low marginal manufacturing or physical distribution cost, like wellness products and services.

> **The opportunity in manufacturing is now in the design or invention of the product rather than in finding a way to simply lower the per-unit cost of physical production. And the opportunity in distribution is now in intellectual distribution versus physical distribution.**

Mass merchants are the first retailers to feel this change. Millions of consumers are discovering how much more efficient it is to purchase their household consumables online or via some type of automatic, direct, factory-to-home replenishment system. In addition to lower prices resulting from bulk buying and from direct shipment from the manufacturer, the cost of physical delivery from UPS is often lower than the time and mileage cost for consumers to lug these items home from retail stores.

And these initial savings are just the beginning. As millions more consumers embrace direct delivery of household consumables, manufacturers will eventually ship the bulk of their products directly to homes rather than stocking items at intermediate waypoints like mass merchants. Increased volume will drive prices down even further.

Anticipating this trend, we built our family residence with an enclosed glass-door front porch so delivery people can leave items when no one is home—it has a refrigerator, heater, a hanging rod for dry cleaning, and an electronic camera that takes a picture when someone is present. Such electronic butler areas, perhaps with magnetic card access, should eventually become standard household fixtures.

At the beginning of the twentieth century, railroads dominated the national physical distribution of manufactured goods and raw materials. The railroads diminished in importance because of an us-versus-them mentality (i.e., the railroads versus the transportation industry)—and thus they failed to capitalize on customer relationships and make the transition from railcars to trucks. Several mass merchants are determined not to make this same mistake.

Wal-Mart, Costco, and other merchants that specialize in physical distribution are rapidly building cyberstores like Wal-mart.com and Costco.com, hoping to beat the technological clock that threatens to put them out of business. But they are fighting an uphill battle because they are collectively still focused on a shrinking component of overall cost: physical distribution. For now and for the foreseeable future, the greatest retailing opportunities will be in intellectual distribution.

Within intellectual distribution, the greatest entrepreneurial opportunities exist with wellness products and services—because consumers don't know many of these products exist and because many wellness products and services have low or effectively zero marginal-unit product cost.

The Importance of Combining High Touch with High Tech

New products and services have always required one-on-one customer education that only a trained user of the product can provide—"high touch" combined with "high tech." Some of these items were VCRs in the 1970s, discounted long-distance service and telephone answering machines in the 1980s, and, of course, better vitamins and nutritional foods in the 1990s.

Every year for the past few decades, more and more of the consumer dollar has been spent on such new products and services. Yet even with the recent growth of the category busters, there are still far too few places for the consumer to learn that such products exist, let alone how to use them.

This required combination of high touch and high tech in new products accounts for much of the growth of person-to-person direct selling companies—particularly in areas of new technology, and especially in wellness.

In the 1980s, Amway distributors launched consumer discount long-distance telephone service through an arrangement with MCI, as well as home-based electronic voice messaging through Amway's proprietary Amvox service.

In the 1990s, the most successful vitamin and nutritional supplement products were launched through direct marketing companies. Many of the most popular categories of supplement products, like ephedra (weight loss), pycnogenol (antioxidant), and echinacea (colds and flu), were available only through direct selling companies before they became off-the-shelf store products.

Led by wellness products and new technology, sales of direct selling companies in the United States alone recently rose 50 percent, from approximately $17 billion in 1995 to $26 billion in 2000. This was almost twice the sales growth rate of traditional retail stores during a similar period.[5]

Despite this 50 percent increase, direct selling companies have a long growth curve ahead of them before they reach the saturation now being experienced by their competition.

Annual U.S. direct selling sales of approximately $30 billion today amount to less than 1 percent of the more than $3 trillion ($3,000 billion) in sales at traditional U.S. retail stores. The sales of just one mass merchant, Wal-Mart, exceeded $165 billion in 2000.

Despite the growth of both direct selling companies and category busters, each year the backlog of unused but more efficacious consumer products continues to grow. For every household that starts using a better consumer product, from the latest digital camera to educational software to healthier foods and nutritional supplements, there seem to be dozens more new products and services that consumers haven't yet learned exist.

Thus, teaching consumers about such products and services, intellectual distribution, is the greatest entrepreneurial opportunity now and for the foreseeable future.

Some direct selling companies themselves don't fully understand their own business. They still refer to end users of their product as *customers* to whom they sell versus *clients* whom they educate.

Direct selling distributors need to understand the differences between selling and education, and between physical and intellectual distribution, in order to fully exploit the high-touch advantage they have over traditional retailers.

The Impact of the Internet and Dot-Com Companies

Every businessperson today must consider the impact of the Internet—how their business will use the Internet and how Internet-based companies will compete with their business.

Wellness entrepreneurs in particular must understand the history of the Internet and its function in distribution— to incorporate the Internet into their business plans and to be able to answer questions about the Internet from their investors and business associates.

The Internet of today was started in the 1960s by Pentagon weapons researchers who sought to develop a system of communication that could survive the most catastrophic nuclear holocaust. This system was designed to connect disparate locations in a manner such that there was no one central processing location. Thus the surviving systems could continue indefinitely regardless of how many others were destroyed.[6]

It is this distinct feature, treating every sender and every receiver as a unique client/server or mainframe unto itself, that has allowed the Internet to evolve into the incredible democratizer it is today—changing the focus of world and economic power from the organization to the individual.

The first node on the Internet was installed in 1969 at University of California at Los Angeles, connecting computers on a network at UCLA with another computer at Stanford Research Institute. Two more nodes were soon added at University of California at Santa Barbara and University of Utah. This original Pentagon-funded net, called ARPANET, quickly grew to connect thousands of scientists and universities around the globe. A new standard for communication, called TCP/IP for short, was implemented in 1983.

Although funded by various government agencies originally to connect only defense-related scientists, in 1985 a decision was made to give access to all qualified users on campus access regardless of their academic discipline. This led to a nine-year program to privatize the backbone communication lines of the Internet—the

backbone being the high-speed communication lines that connected one university's network to another's. By the time this pri-
vatization was accomplished, the Internet had grown to over
50,000 networks on all seven continents and outer space—even so,
the Internet as we know it today had not yet begun.

In 1995 the historic decision was made to allow individual users
to obtain their own Internet accounts, accounts independent of
their university affiliation or the organization to which they
belonged.

We noted earlier that distribution costs as a relative percent of
retail prices rose over the past three decades, from about 50 percent at the end of the 1960s to about 70 percent today, and that
thus the greatest fortunes during this period were made by pioneers who found better ways of distributing things versus better
ways of making things. These distribution pioneers succeeded by
using electronic real-time communication to connect retailers and
producers with their suppliers. For example, Wal-Mart, whose
computer database is now second only to that of the Pentagon,[7]
was able to greatly reduce distribution costs while actually improving customer service—delivering just what their customers wanted,
when and where they wanted it.

At the beginning of the 1990s this just-in-time technology was
generally limited to large companies that could afford to establish
proprietary communication links between themselves and the
mainframe computers of their suppliers. This real-time high-speed
communication ignited the fire of economic expansion that characterized the decade of the 1990s. The historic decision that was
made in 1995, allowing individual users to obtain their own
Internet accounts, had the effect of pouring gasoline on this fire.

Overnight, the economic and lifestyle benefits of instant real-
time communication became available to everyone—leveling the
playing field from the smallest entrepreneur to the largest Fortune
500 company. Companies that had already built their own proprietary communication systems now found themselves having to start
over, since consumers (their ultimate customers), as well as thousands of smaller suppliers, were all going to be on the Internet
themselves.

The results of this decision are just beginning to be felt on Main
Street, from the act of waiting for a bus to the task of shopping for
food. Bus stop shelters will be electronically connected so that driv-
ers pull off the road only when passengers are waiting. Shoppers
with electronically connected pantry closets will find their basket of

replenishables (paper towels, milk, eggs) already pulled, loaded, and waiting for them when they arrive at the supermarket; or groceries may be automatically delivered to their homes.

But the results of this decision have already been felt on Wall Street, where the smart money has already anticipated what is about to occur on Main Street.

Today the majority of the companies with the largest market capitalizations (i.e., net worth) on any Top 10 or Top 100 Wall Street list are the high-technology "toolmakers." Toolmaker companies don't produce a single product that can feed, house, clothe, transport, heal, teach, inform, or do anything else that a consumer might ultimately want.

Instead, toolmakers make products that help *other* companies produce these ultimate consumer products even better—so much better that the toolmaker companies have become worth more than their customers (because of their value-added ability).[8] Five of the ten highest-valued companies in the U.S. stock market today (Cisco, Microsoft, Intel, Oracle, and Vodaphone) are companies that effectively didn't exist 20 years ago but whose combined net worth today exceeds $1 trillion.

This is the most misunderstood part of Internet dot-com companies today: These and thousands of other technology-based companies are toolmakers. They do not produce end-use products desired by consumers—instead, they help *other* companies that *do* produce and distribute end-use products to lower their costs and better serve their customers.

Eventually, the companies that produce and distribute end-use products or services and who have the relationship with the ultimate consumer will have the final say. At the beginning of 2001, Wal-Mart became the largest company in the United States, in both sales and number of employees,[9] because, as John Maynard Keynes once said, "Consumption is the sole end of all economic activity."

Many entrepreneurs and investors have made the unfortunate mistake of seeing the Internet as a business unto itself. The Internet is a powerful tool that can be used to leverage the opportunities in another business.

The success or failure of any Internet-based business, and particularly Internet-based wellness businesses, will depend mostly on the products and customers of the business itself.

Before Proceeding to the Next Chapter

Action Plan for Entrepreneurs, Investors, and Distributors

1. Changes that used to take place over centuries now take place over decades, and changes that now take place over years will soon take place over months. Analyze how this accelerating pace of change will impact each of your three individual areas of wellness business opportunity.

2. How do you plan to educate potential customers for each of your three individual areas of wellness business opportunity? Analyze the cost of doing so. Do you receive revenue for performing such education, or is such education a cost of doing business? If it is a cost of doing business, are the costs of such education affordable for your business?

3. *Intellectual distribution* is the process of educating customers about products and services that they either don't know exist or don't know are now affordable. *Physical distribution* is the process of helping customers physically obtain products and services that they already know they want. Analyze the type of distribution opportunity for each of your three individual areas of wellness business opportunity. Keep in mind that the greatest distribution opportunities for entrepreneurs are now in intellectual versus physical distribution.

4. Assume that category busters like Home Depot or PetsMart emerged in the wellness industry. Analyze how this would impact each of your three individual areas of wellness business opportunity. Could you survive such competition? Could you become a provider to wellness category busters?

5. What is the marginal cost of each product for each of your three individual areas of wellness business opportunity? Will it approach zero? Why or why not? Could another supplier provide the same products or services at much lower cost? If so, how can you become this type of supplier first?

6. What role would the Internet play with respect to each of your three individual areas of wellness business opportunity? Analyze how you could utilize this powerful tool for each area. Is there another type of business or individual who could better use the Internet in supplying your customers? If so, what can you do to become this type of individual or business?

Based on your answers to these questions, think about dropping and replacing any or all of your three individual areas of wellness business opportunity. Look back at your notes, and the Action Plan at the end of the previous seven chapters, and reconsider all of the potential business areas you have thought about.

Before proceeding to Chapter 9, pick the single best of your three potential areas of wellness business opportunity. Proceed through the next chapter, pausing to think about how each example and opportunity applies solely to this wellness business area. If you still desire to consider one of the other two areas of wellness business opportunity, do so by beginning Chapter 9 afresh with only this other area in mind.

Staking Your Claim

In narrowing down your possibilities for entering this trillion dollar industry you are probably continually asking yourself: Where is the best place for me to stake my claim in this emerging $1 trillion industry that does incredible good?

Should you become a manufacturer of wellness products like Steve Demos (Silk soymilk) or Paul Wenner (Gardenburger)? Should you become a provider of wellness services like Jill Kinney (Club One) or Dr. Frank Yanowitz (The Fitness Institute)? Should you become a specialized wellness consultant distributing the best wellness products to your friends and associates—focusing on intellectual versus physical distribution? Should you become an investor, or even an investment banker, specializing in this emerging dynamic industry? Or should you become a tool provider for others who enter these and other wellness professions, like Dr. Tod Cooperman (ConsumerLab.com)? What about pursuing more than one of these opportunities simultaneously?

On an individual level, I cannot answer these questions for you any more than a surgeon could tell you what type of operation you should have without first doing his or her own individual diagnosis. But I can lay out some general parameters to help you assess your prior experience and answer these questions for yourself.

It is first important to understand that the wellness industry will encompass parts of virtually every sector of our economy—from the food we eat and the medical care we desire to the air we breathe and the bedding we sleep on at night. You need not necessarily be in the wellness industry directly (i.e., food or medicine) to join the wellness gold rush.

> Many of the wellness fortunes will be made by bankers, lawyers, accountants, marketing executives, distributors, insurance brokers, and thousands of other professionals who provide tools and services to the wellness industry.

Providing Tools and Services to the Wellness Industry

Since 1876, the term *gold rush* has been a euphemism for staking your claim to "sudden wealth in a new or lucrative field."[1] But many of the fortunes made during the California gold rush weren't made mining gold—they were made by businesspeople providing services to the gold rush industry. The names Henry Wells and Daniel Fargo are synonymous with the California gold rush industry, yet neither of them ever mined an ounce of gold. Both were freight-forwarding agents in western New York before cofounding the American Express Company in 1850 to handle freight west of Buffalo.[2] In 1852 they decided to focus their shipping expertise on the needs of a group of their customers, the California miners, and formed Wells Fargo & Company. Over the years, their connections with stagecoaches, transporting gold, and financing miners led them to become leaders in general banking, travel, and insurance— they (and their successors) introduced the American Express Money Order in 1882, the American Express Travelers Cheque in 1891, and the American Express Travel Department in 1915. American Express actually remained in the freight-forwarding business until 1970.

In extending credit to miners, shipping their produce, and providing banking services, Wells and Fargo ended up knowing more about the gold mining industry than most of their successful gold miner customers.

> In a similar vein, certain providers of services to the wellness industry today have already emerged as wellness professionals, even though they do not manufacture or distribute wellness products themselves.

One such famous wellness professional is Stuart Johnson of VideoPlus, Inc. Johnson had his first exposure to wellness and personal development at age 15 in Fairhope, Alabama. He was recruited to become a distributor for Olde Worlde, Inc., a manufacturer of vitamins, supplements, and other home-care products. This was the first time he had ever been told that "you can be anything you want to be" and that "you and your choices, not your background, control your destiny." Johnson signed up, and by the time he turned 16 he was moving $5,000 of product a month—clearing more than $1,000 a month in part-time income. He especially loved the challenge and rewards of teaching others what he had just learned about his own potential.

At age 21 he was approached by some friends who were distributors for another wellness company, United Sciences of America. They had created various tools, audiotapes and brochures explaining different aspects of their products and their business, to hand out to prospective distributors.

Johnson saw immediately that these tools could be packaged together into what he termed a "long-distance sponsoring kit"—a cohesive package that a network marketer could use to sponsor others, across town or across the nation, without having to work with them in person. Once they were sponsored as a new distributor, they would need more training—which meant more tools—to develop their business.

Johnson left network marketing and formed VideoPlus, Inc., in 1987. VideoPlus created sponsoring kits and provided turnkey fulfillment on products for direct selling and network marketing companies, most of whom were in the wellness industry. VideoPlus manufactured customized sponsoring kits, answered the telephone with the name of the network marketing company, and shipped the actual kits direct to a company's prospects—faster and at less cost than the company or individual distributor could do it themselves. Having VideoPlus perform this back-office function also freed up more time for its client companies to recruit and train more distributors. Soon, VideoPlus was not just manufacturing and shipping tools produced by networking marketing companies, it was producing some of the best original generic motivation and educational tools in the wellness and direct selling businesses.

Today VideoPlus is the largest tool provider to the network marketing and wellness industries, annually duplicating 12 million video- and audiotapes and shipping over 1 million distributor long-distance sponsoring kits. Even though he is not a network marketer himself, in August 2000, Johnson appeared on the cover of *Network Marketing Lifestyles* magazine. The article called Johnson the "E.F. Hutton of network marketing" and stated, "when Stuart talks, industry leaders listen." VideoPlus's clients, with collective sales of over $12 billion a year, include most of the leading direct selling wellness companies in the world, including Avon, Freelife, Mannatech, New Image, Nikken, NSA, Nutrition for Life, Shaklee, and most of the larger Access Business Groups (formerly Amway).

Today, at age 37, Stuart is successful beyond any of his dreams. He serves on the board of the Direct Selling Association; he is the youngest founding board member of the Young Entrepreneurs Organization (YEO); and he lives on the ocean in Sarasota, Florida, with his wife and two children. But he feels he is just getting started and that his real purpose in life is to bring the personal-development message to every 15-year-old teenager who has never been told that "you can be anything you want to be" and that "you and your choices, not your background, control your destiny." To this end, he has cofounded The Right Stuff Foundation, which produces contemporary music with a positive personal-development message for today's youth.

As you begin your wellness business, whether in network marketing or wellness manufacturing, take note of your challenges and ask yourself if you think others pursuing the same path are having similar challenges. If the answer is yes, make a list of tools you could develop to help yourself and others on their way to success.

You may find out, as Stuart Johnson did, that you'd be more successful in helping others start a certain type of wellness business than in actually running the same type of business yourself.

Staking Your Claim in Wellness Finance

For financially oriented individuals, the entrepreneurial opportunity to convert households from sickness to Wellness Insurance is as great an opportunity as is the entire wellness business itself. This opportunity today parallels the opportunity seized 20 years ago by Art L. Williams, an ordinary person who changed the face of

the life insurance industry and is now worth an estimated $400 million.[3]

The son of a high school football coach, Art L. Williams was born in Waycross, Georgia, and grew up following in his father's footsteps. Tragically, when Art was in college studying to be a football coach, his father died of a heart attack, leaving his family penniless and with very little life insurance. Later on, after marrying his high school sweetheart and starting his own family, Williams was determined not to make the same mistake.

When he went out as an ordinary customer to purchase life insurance, Art Williams was surprised to find how much the consumer was then being taken advantage of by the life insurance industry.

Between 1950 and 1980, major life insurance companies sold mostly whole life policies, primarily to working class men and women. In those days, life insurance companies recruited individuals to sell their product in each local or ethnic community to their friends and neighbors. Rather then selling their whole life product on its financial merits, agents were taught to go for the emotional sale—which meant sitting down at the prospect's kitchen table and telling the spouse: "If he loves you, he'll sign right here to protect you and the children if something were to happen to him." What the agent didn't tell the prospect was that the same or better coverage could be had for a fraction of the cost elsewhere and that the agent was earning a commission equal to or greater than the first full year of payments.

A whole life insurance policy is, in effect, an ordinary term insurance policy with a mandatory low-interest savings account. For example, a $100,000 death-benefit term or ordinary life insurance policy for a healthy male, age 30, might cost about $1,400 per year. A whole life policy for this same amount ($100,000) typically costs about $5,000 per year—$1,400 for the term or death-benefit portion and $3,600 for the "whole" portion, which partially accrued in the cash value of the policy. Theoretically, the insured would pay $5,000 per year and receive the $1,400 per annum worth of term insurance ($100,000 death benefit) on dying, plus a "cash value increase" each year on the $3,600 extra payment for each year they lived. Eventually, after 25 years, the cash value amount of the policy would accrue to $100,000 and the policy would self-fund—meaning that the insured would not have to pay any further annual premiums and would simply receive their own $100,000 in cash value when they died.

That's the theory. In reality, (1) there was typically no cash value increase the first one or two years since the insurance company would pay $3,600 to $7,200 in commission to the salesperson; (2) only a percentage of the $3,600 would be applied to the cash value increase each year after that; and (3) a very low amount of interest would be paid on the accruing cash value (typically 2 to 3 percent). What the insurance salespeople never told the unsuspecting prospect (and may not have known themselves) is that the prospect could purchase the same amount of term or straight life insurance from the same company for $1,400 per year and deposit the same $3,600 in an federally insured bank account—and that by doing this, the same $5,000 per year would have grown to almost $200,000 in 25 years, guaranteed by the U.S. federal government, versus only $100,000 in 25 years guaranteed by a private insurance company.[4]

When a cousin explained this to Art L. Williams, he not only became a smart customer by purchasing a term policy and investing the difference, he started selling term insurance part-time to his friends and neighbors.

Williams developed a straight-talking "buy term and invest the difference" approach to educate his customers. It worked so well that soon he quit his job as a high school football coach and became a full-time insurance salesperson.

In 1977, along with 85 like-minded insurance agents, he started A.L. Williams & Associates to promote his "buy term and invest the difference" philosophy. They quickly recruited thousands of accountants, lawyers, and financial planners as their agents.

By 1990, Williams & Associates had a sales force of 225,000 and was the largest seller of individual life insurance in the United States—more than twice the size of his two nearest competitors (New York Life and Prudential) combined.

Eventually, all of the major life insurance companies were forced to end their misleading sales practices and offer products financially competitive to those of A.L. Williams. With more than $300 billion of life insurance in force, Williams sold his company to Primerica in 1990.[5]

A.L. Williams was successful because the numbers clearly demonstrated the superiority of the "buy term and invest the difference" approach—even in cases where the prospect had to pay penalties or lose cash value by terminating an existing whole life insurance policy. Another reason A.L. Williams agents were successful is that after their clients saw how much money they could save each year, this money was typically invested in annuities and other products sold by Williams & Associates—products that often paid much higher commissions than ordinary term life insurance.

> **As illustrated in Chapter 7, because most people don't need anywhere near the amount of sickness insurance they have today, the same opportunity exists in health insurance to "buy HDHP and invest the difference."**

Today, however, when consumers save up to $3,000 per year on their HDHP, they get to invest the $3,000 difference in something much more important to their family than just money—their continued wellness. Wellness product distributors can introduce HDHP to their healthy clients and then explain how they can invest all or part of the annual savings in wellness products and services to stay well.

> **The opportunity in wellness finance to "buy HDHP and invest the difference" will probably not be seized at first by the existing insurance brokerage community. Rather, a new insurance distribution mechanism or company will probably emerge to distribute this product.**

The reason for this is that in most cases, when a new technology comes along, it is often resisted by status quo companies with much to lose—in an often-futile attempt to stop their losses, they bury their heads in the sand until it's too late. Many insurance agents selling $5,000 premium, no-deductible health insurance policies that pay a $1,000 commission will try to avoid switching clients to $2,000 premium HDHPs that pay only a $400 commission. Eventually, they will pay the price for their shortsightedness when their misled customers take all their insurance business—health, life, auto, and homeowner's—elsewhere.

This opportunity to "buy HDHP and invest the difference" may be seized by a wellness product company outside of the insurance industry that doesn't even get paid for their efforts, because only licensed insurance agents are allowed to receive or share commissions.

Wellness distributors can profit simply by teaching their customers about Wellness Insurance—because the customer switching to HDHP has up to $3,000 per annum more disposable income with which to purchase other wellness products and services.

Getting Started

By now you may have noticed a pattern in the career of each wellness entrepreneur mentioned thus far. Each had different educational backgrounds, work experiences, and personal encounters before everything in their lives came together and launched their wellness careers. However, and more important,

---

Most wellness entrepreneurs started their businesses after first being a customer and finding that their wellness needs were not being met.

Steve Demos couldn't find good-tasting vegetarian protein products, so he started to make tofu and run a vegetarian delicatessen before discovering his fortune making Silk soymilk from the same raw material. Paul Wenner's vegetarian restaurant flopped, and he founded Gardenburger, Inc., only when his former customers could no longer get their vegetarian burgers at his restaurant. Dr. Tod Cooperman founded a company to evaluate consumer healthcare plans, which led him to founding ConsumerLab.com to evaluate nutritional supplements. Dr. Frank Yanowitz had his own personal wellness crisis before committing himself to The Fitness Institute. As a top athlete, Jill Kinney knew what she wanted in a fitness club *before* she began opening individual public fitness clubs and then stumbled into the fortune in managing private fitness clubs for large employers.

In the software industry during the past two decades, many of the fortunes were made by businesspeople who originally started out to create a computerized operating system for their own companies and then found out they could make more money selling operating systems to their competitors than they could running their original business. Similarly, many of the fortunes in wellness will be made by wellness customers who, on finding that their particular wellness need is not being met by the marketplace, start a company to serve that need for others with the same problem—just as A.L. Williams did for cost-effective life insurance.

The important thing is to get started now in almost any area of the wellness industry and see where your past experiences and knowledge take you.

It may actually be easier than you think since you already have a head start based on what you've been doing up until today, as wellness opportunities permeate almost every profession from A to Z.

Where All Professions and the Wellness Revolution Meet

An *accountant* or a *banker* could combine a wellness distribution business with the opportunity to convert customers to HDHP and Wellness Insurance.

A *cook* might learn how to make healthy versions of popular foods and then open a wellness restaurant, start a wellness catering company, or become a wellness food manufacturer.

Dentists could focus on wellness opportunities to sell more services within their own profession—dentists are already ahead of the medical industry because much of their practice is already focused on prevention.

An *economist*, like me, might focus on identifying trends in the emerging $1 trillion wellness industry, and then market this knowledge to other wellness professionals.

Farmers, or even home *gardeners*, as noted in Chapter 4, should start growing healthier foods like edamame and teaching their customers how to use them.

Hairdressers could start using healthier products in their practice, then start a wellness distribution business to sell these products to their customers.

Insurance agents could follow the example of Art Williams by leading their customers to Wellness Insurance and then market other, more-profitable insurance products (e.g., auto, home, life) once they've earned the trust of their customers.

A *journalist* could focus on wellness products or wellness companies, becoming known for expert reporting on the industry that people will want to hear about the most in the coming decade.

Lawyers might similarly focus on any one of hundreds of separate aspects of the wellness or wellness finance industries, developing expertise that will bring them new clients.

Massage therapists are in the ideal position to teach wellness and to begin distributing wellness products to their customers.

Nurses could reorient their practice toward preventing disease instead of treating the symptoms of disease and combine their reoriented practice with a wellness distribution or wellness consulting business.

An *optician* could similarly focus more on treating the effects of aging and failing eyesight before they occur and use this new focus to obtain new customers or start a related wellness distribution business.

Physicians are obviously in an excellent position to retool themselves for almost any area of the wellness industry—starting with proactively seeking healthy people and teaching them how to avoid becoming patients.

Salespeople can either distribute wellness products themselves or just become versed in the latest wellness technology since that's what will be of most interest to their clients—successful selling in every field starts with building credibility in the eyes of the client.

Teachers similarly need to know what is of most importance to their students—and, as explained in Chapter 8, because of the recent shift from physical distribution to intellectual distribution, teachers may be especially qualified for careers in wellness distribution.

Finally, *veterinarians* are in a unique position to promote human wellness to their customers and animal wellness to their patients. In fact, veterinarians are often more qualified than physicians when it comes to nutrition and supplementation. Unlike medical schools, veterinary schools of medicine have always taught the importance of nutrition, and veterinary schools pioneered the research in many of the human supplements we use today (e.g., glucosamine and major minerals).

Become an Investor in Wellness

The best advice I can give you about becoming an investor in wellness is to first become a customer of any company in which you are considering making an investment.

There is simply no substitute for using the products yourself when it comes to evaluating the long-term potential for a company. Once you have made an investment in a company whose products you like, you should also inspect competitive products on a periodic basis. Technology changes so fast that today's Wal-Mart is often tomorrow's W.T. Grant.[6]

If you are a physician, a wellness distributor, an insurance agent, or involved in any aspect of the wellness industry, you should continuously underwrite and evaluate the products of the companies within your specific industry. Based on what you actually do within the wellness industry, you will often be the first to know when a company is about to get into trouble and the first to know when a company has an important new product.

Suppose you are an ophthalmologist performing LASIK eye surgery for your patients. Not only should you always be in the market for better lasers for your patients, you should keep an active file on every laser made and what you think about the company that makes it—from the quality of their products to their sales performance and service. In doing so, you will be the first to know which companies in your field are poised for growth and which ones will fail, either because of poor management or new competition. If you are not capable of underwriting these companies yourself, you should team up with an investment professional more capable of using your firsthand customer experience to evaluate the stock value of the company. Keep in mind that the fact that you like a product is not by itself enough reason to invest in the company that makes it. The product you enjoy may be only a small percentage of the company's sales and thus have little bearing on the overall performance of the company.

One of my hobbies is personal computer software and hardware—I love to tinker with my computers and purchase a new PC or peripheral accessory almost weekly. I especially enjoy researching the "latest and greatest" new PC gadget and then finding it at the best available price. In the 1990s, one venture capital firm regularly invited me to speak to their investment professionals about what new PC toys I had purchased that month, why I bought each particular item or brand, and where I had purchased it. They told me that my firsthand product and purchasing experiences were more valuable to them than research done by hundreds of analysts.

As an economist, it is always amazing to me how hard lawyers, doctors, dentists, engineers, scientists, and other professionals work to make money in their chosen profession—only to see much of it lost when they blindly turn it over to an "investment professional" who claims to "know" which stocks are going to increase in price. If there were such a person who actually knew which stocks to purchase, why wouldn't that person be investing solely for themselves, and why would they dilute their efforts by sharing their information with you?

The Wharton Secret

However, I didn't have this belief back in 1973 when, as an undergraduate physics student, I decided to study business in order to become rich. Upon graduation, I entered the prestigious Wharton Graduate School of Business to get my MBA. When I arrived at Wharton, I heard that a course called Speculative Markets was the place to learn about the stock market and a surefire scientific method for getting rich very quickly. It was such a popular course that you had to wait until your last semester before graduation to get into the class.

On my first day of class in Speculative Markets, the professor asked us not to tell anyone what I am about to tell you—a secret I have kept to myself for 26 years. First, he explained that there was absolutely no way to get rich very quickly by picking stocks unless you were willing to violate criminal-penalty insider trading laws. But, he continued, when we graduated from Wharton, many wealthy people outside of Wall Street would wrongly believe that people like us with a Wharton degree did know which stocks to purchase to quickly get rich. He then explained how we could individually take advantage of this situation to get rich as new stockbrokers on Wall Street.

On your first day of work as a stockbroker, you purchase a list of 10,000 wealthy people along with their fax numbers. You send 5,000 people a fax stating: "I'm John Doe, and I know that General Motors (GM) stock is going *up* tomorrow, so I recommend you take $1,000 and purchase the following option."

Simultaneously, you send the other 5,000 people a fax stating that the opposite will occur: "I'm John Doe, and I know that GM is going *down* tomorrow, so I recommend you take $1,000 and purchase the following option." At the end of the next day, depending on which direction GM went, you rip up the list of the 5,000 people who got the wrong advice.

Then you send 2,500 people on your remaining list of 5,000 the following fax: "I'm John Doe. If you took my advice yesterday regarding GM your $1,000 investment would now be worth $2,000. I know that Ford is going *up* tomorrow, so I recommend you take your $2,000 and purchase the following option." You send the other 2,500 people a fax stating that Ford is going *down*. Again, the next day, you send 1,250 of the 2,500 people who received the correct advice a fax stating: "I'm John Doe. If you took my advice yesterday regarding Ford, your $2,000 investment would now be worth $4,000. I know that Chrysler is going *up* tomorrow, so I recommend you take your $4,000 and purchase the following option." The other 1,250 people get a fax stating that Chrysler is going *down*. And so on, and so on, until you have remaining 78 individuals who have irrefutable proof that you "know" which stocks to purchase. Then you start making appointments for lunch and figure out what you want to do with 78 high-net-worth people who think you are the smartest person on Wall Street that ever lived—and who are probably willing to mortgage their homes and give you their life savings on almost any basis if you will agree to invest it for them.

Days at work	Number of potential clients	Value of their $1,000 investment if they had followed your advice
1	10,000	$ 1,000
2	5,000	$ 2,000
3	2,500	$ 4,000
4	1,250	$ 8,000
5	625	$ 16,000
6	312	$ 32,000
7	156	$ 64,000
8	78	$128,000

The moral of this story, as my professor explained, is that when you meet someone who can demonstrate to you that he or she knows which stocks to pick to quickly get rich, you are merely one of the 78 out of 10,000 people (less than 1 percent) at the end of a similar chain of events. To make money on Wall Street, there is simply no substitute for taking a long-term position based on good research about a company—its management team, its capitalization structure, and, most important, its products. And the best way to know about those products is to invest within a field in which you already have great product knowledge—your own chosen profession.

Staking Your Claim through Your Religion

Some readers may desire to stake their claim outside of the business arena. Perhaps they wish to spread wellness through their church, mosque, or synagogue. These readers need to understand that wellness has always been part of our great religions and how wellness is already being embraced by some congregations. Readers, clergypersons, and church officers need to understand the connection between wellness and religion.

All wellness entrepreneurs need to understand the connection between wellness and religion in order to better motivate their customers to choose and stick to a wellness lifestyle. Additionally, some wellness entrepreneurs may want to combine spreading wellness through their church with their profit-making wellness business enterprise.

The great religions of the world became great partly by addressing the secular needs of their congregants. Today, although living a wellness lifestyle of diet and exercise is a great secular need, it is ignored by most religions and religious organizations. This is because the concept of becoming closer to God by having a fit and healthy body fell out of favor in the Middle Ages as a reaction to the emphasis placed on physical appearance and beauty by Greek and Roman persecutors. Yet the founding documents of most religions demonstrate that God wants us to be well.

The story of the Bible most common to all religions, the Garden of Eden, speaks of how God made "every tree that is pleasant to the sight, and good for food."[7] This reference goes beyond just aesthetic significance—the kinds and variety of foods prescribed in the Bible contain all the vitamins, minerals, and proteins necessary for wellness.

In our time, we keep discovering "new" age-old natural remedies—from gingko to improve our memories to Saint-John's-wort to alleviate depression. These discoveries continually illuminate the famous cabalistic statement: "God creates the cure before he sends the malady."[8]

Moses Maimonides, a twelfth-century rabbi and physician in Moorish Spain, is esteemed by Jews, Christians, and Muslims alike as one of the greatest theologians of all time. Maimonides reconciled Greek philosophy with the Old and New Testaments and concluded that our obligation to be healthy was a religious obligation, a first order of priority we must undertake before we begin to know our Creator.[9]

Some religious institutions teach congregants how to control their diet. The most successful program, the Weigh Down Diet, is based on the philosophy that overeating and gluttony are sins. Today there are nearly 30,000 Weigh Down workshops, mostly in U.S. churches, making a real difference in the lives of millions of participants.[10]

The Weigh Down Diet and similar programs stress the negative or sinful aspects of overeating. Although these programs have achieved good results, I believe the wellness answer for the majority of Americans will lie in a more positive approach.

I was raised in a Jewish family that observed religious dietary laws. We did not eat unkosher foods such as lobster, shrimp, or pork—rules I quickly abandoned when I left home for college. It wasn't until years later, when I started spending time in Israel, that I came to understand what I had missed growing up. To my observant Israeli relatives, the requirement to eat only the foods prescribed by biblical law is not seen as deprivation, but as one of God's greatest gifts. They thank God for this knowledge in prayers before and after every meal. For them, eating kosher food is one of life's greatest *mitzvahs* (good deeds).

Just as I in my youth misunderstood the purpose of keeping kosher, many people today wrongly imagine that a wellness lifestyle involves constantly saying no to things they enjoy. But wellness-oriented individuals have learned to cherish and appreciate God for their knowledge of how to take care of themselves. Through the small and reasonable disciplines of daily eating, a wellness-oriented individual, an orthodox Jew, and a practicing Muslim all experience a sense of distinction, specialness, and closeness to God.

Religious faith is the highest motivating force in the world. Wellness entrepreneurs can combine their religion with their wellness business—motivating their customers through faith to adopt and stick to a wellness lifestyle of eating healthy foods and performing regular exercise.

CHAPTER 10

Epilogue: Unlimited Wellness

"How sad it is!" murmured Dorian Gray with his eyes still fixed upon his own portrait. "How sad it is! I shall grow old, and horrible, and dreadful. But this picture will remain always young. If it were only the other way! If it were I who was to be always young, and the picture that was to grow old! For that—for that—I would give everything! Yes, there is nothing in the whole world I would not give! I would give my soul for that!"

—OSCAR WILDE, *THE PICTURE OF DORIAN GRAY* (1891)

Why Wellness Is Unlimited

The individual cells in our body are constantly dying and replacing themselves.[1] On a cellular level, the biochemical objective of most wellness activity is to ensure that these individual cells receive the raw materials—proteins, vitamins, and minerals—necessary to remanufacture themselves at the optimal level.

But at some point in a person's life, "something" tells each cell in each bodily organ to stop reproducing itself. This causes normal aging, illness, and eventually death. Sometimes, even when a cell or organ does not suffer from a biochemical deficiency, "something" tells abnormal cells in an organ to uncontrollably multiply until they impair the function of that organ (e.g., cancer). Today we know that this "something" is one of the many and complex instructions in the genetic code for life, commonly referred to as DNA, or deoxyribonucleic acid. DNA is an organic compound found in all cells that contains the genetic code for inherited characteristics and replication.

Our genetic code is a human "textbook" with over 3 billion different letters—written entirely in four characters (A, T, C and G) with no spaces or punctuation. While the actual substance we now call DNA was discovered in 1869, its role in inheritance was demonstrated only in the latter half of the twentieth century, and the complete mapping of the human genome was not completed until the beginning of this century.[2]

> **Our demand for wellness-based products and services is primarily driven by one function of the genetic code, the one that causes aging—from the wrinkles that appear in our skin to the ultimate breakdown of our bodily organs.**

Over the long term, the understanding and eventual manipulation of this genetic code holds the greatest promise for the wellness industry.

By examining a person's DNA, which can be taken from the mouth with just a small swab or scraping device, it is already possible to predict the probability that a person will develop certain diseases.

> **Soon, based on the recently completed mapping of the human genome, it should be possible to predict every forthcoming disease or condition not caused by external (e.g., diet and exercise) factors.**

Scientists expect this type of genetic testing to become widespread by 2010.[3] In just the next few years, by using this information to predict the probability of developing a certain condition, a wellness distributor could suggest a vitamin- or supplement-based therapy.

For example, a person with a genetic propensity to develop osteoporosis would be directed to take calcium supplements while they were still young, or a person with a genetic propensity for developing prostate problems would be an early candidate to take saw palmetto.

> **Wellness entrepreneurs who embrace this emerging DNA-based technology first, particularly those in the healthy food and dietary supplement areas, will see their businesses explode with new customers.**

Eventually, as technology progresses, vitamins and supplements used in this manner will probably be supplanted by genetic intervention—the actual modification or repair of the problematic gene containing the propensity to develop the disease. Scientists do not expect this type of intervention to become effective in treating the full spectrum of genetically determined diseases for several decades.[4]

For now and in the foreseeable next few decades, our genetic code and the aging it produces will continue to drive the unlimited demand for wellness products and services we experience today. Each breakthrough in genetically based wellness products and services that slows the aging process will simply increase the demand for more wellness, as satisfied customers seek to look and feel even healthier and existing customers live longer to consume more wellness products and services.

The Opportunity to Do Incredible Good

A few wellness entrepreneurs, like Steve Demos or Jill Kinney, will emerge as the billionaires and media darlings of our new century. Hundreds of thousands more wellness entrepreneurs will become millionaires— approximately 2.5 million new U.S. millionaires will be created in the next five years, many of whom will be making their fortunes in wellness.[5]

This book has focused on the strategies some of these wellness entrepreneurs are using to become rich and how you can duplicate their success. But as you become rich, something more important to our society than just your bank account will be improving.

Economically, we measure our lack of wellness in dollars and population. We spend $1.5 trillion in the United States each year on sickness, about one-seventh of every dollar we earn. Approximately 77 million Americans, or 27 percent of our population, are clinically obese. And 184 million Americans, 61 percent, are overweight and unhealthy. These numbers have doubled over the last few decades and risen 10 percent in just the last five years.

The true cost of our need for wellness cannot be measured in trillions of dollars or in millions of people.

Many of the 77 million individuals who are obese represent a life misspent. These individuals don't have the energy to fully enjoy their lives, their work, and their families. They spend a significant portion of their lives on a medical merry-go-round that treats a minimal amount of their symptoms—just enough to keep them working and consuming more unhealthy food and more sickness products and services.

The 107 million overweight, but not obese, individuals in the United States are often malnourished to the point of fatigue, nervousness, headaches, confusion, and muscle weakness. When they turn to their medical community for help, they are told that these issues are normal symptoms of advancing age.

Until, of course, these unfortunate individuals meet up with you and your wellness business.

As you go out each day to market your wellness products and services, you carry a message more important than the actual product or service you are trying to sell. Underlying the pitch for each wellness product is the notion that your customers can take control of their lives and begin a road to wellness.

Typically, before consumers purchase a new product or try a new service, they have made the decision to buy it twice before and then forgotten to do so. It typically takes several exposures to the product message to get to each of the three affirmative decisions that lead to eventual purchase. This is why, when launching a new product, advertising agencies tell clients not to expect actual sales until the consumer has had many exposures to the message.

Each time your wellness message reaches a potential wellness consumer, you bring the consumer one step closer to making one of these three affirmative decisions to do something about his or her wellness, even if the consumer does not favorably respond to your individual product or service. In this regard, all wellness entrepreneurs are colleagues, because even when you seemingly fail, you succeed in bringing the potential wellness consumer one step closer to making the decision that could change his or her life.

As we saw in Chapter 2, when you do succeed in getting consumers to try your wellness product and they have a positive wellness experience, they typically become voracious consumers of more wellness products and services—products and services produced or distributed by both you and by your wellness competitors:

- The single mother who lost 35 pounds now wants to join a fitness club for even more energy.
- The boy with more energy from a new vitamin regimen now wants to learn about better nutrition and change his diet.
- The father who eliminated pain with magnetic therapy now wants to learn about better vitamins.
- The parents of a girl who eliminated colds by taking echinacea now want to learn what's available for their other children.
- The former athlete using glucosamine who has returned to bicycling now wants something to improve his memory.
- The prostate patient who was cured with saw palmetto now wants to spread his message about naturopathic experiences.

The Importance of Sticking to Your Plan

It is my hope that you will embark on your particular wellness business today and become one of the leaders in this incredible industry. The sooner you begin, the greater will be your potential reward. But the sooner you begin, the higher the possibility that you might become discouraged if you don't succeed fast enough. Most consumers have yet to have their first positive wellness experience—the one that makes them consumers of more wellness products and services—and thus the universe of wellness customers is just beginning to grow. You might develop a successful product or service, but give up before you realize it because you don't get enough customers right away.

> Once you have found some initial success with your product or service, it is important that you have the intestinal fortitude and financial resources to keep marketing it to more and more potential customers until you accumulate enough statistics to be able to stand back objectively and make a worthwhile analysis of your results.

The mathematical concept of *frequency,* that individual events don't follow a set pattern but that many events collectively over time *do* follow a set pattern, is sometimes difficult to understand, particularly for new entrepreneurs. Here's an experiment you can use to better understand frequency or to teach the concept of frequency to your associates.

Flip a coin 10 times and record the result. You may be astonished to find that heads (or tails) appears 80 to 90 percent of the time instead of the expected 50 percent. Then flip the same coin 100 times—when you do this you will almost always record heads or tails appearing 47 to 53 percent of the time. This is why you should never become discouraged with the outcome of a few events. Analyzing *many* events, or *frequency,* is always a better predictor.

You might develop a particular strategy for selling your wellness product or service that would eventually succeed with 50 percent of your prospects, but fails with the first 8 or 9 of your 10 initial prospects. Conversely, you might find success on the first few sales calls and then expand too fast, before you understand how you need to refine your strategy.

Don't be discouraged if you sometimes have trouble explaining frequency to one of your associates who wants to give up. No less a genius than Albert Einstein had the same problem understanding this concept.

Why God Created Frequency

My father was a religious man. He firmly believed in a true and just God who had a reason for everything. Even while he was dying of cancer, he never wavered in his belief that his own medical situation and society's economic problems were both the result of our failure to utilize the tools that God has given us. He firmly believed, to quote Albert Einstein, that "God does not play dice with the universe."

Although my father cherished this quotation, Einstein actually made a great mistake when he said it.[6,7] Einstein was searching for what came to be known as a unified field theory, a theory that would explain the behavior of everything in the universe from the smallest electron to the largest planet. In conducting this search, Einstein could not accept that individual atomic particles appeared to move at random, like dice, but that when observed with enough frequency, the actions of the particles followed established laws of probability.

Today, the science of quantum mechanics, which is based on this probabilistic behavior of elementary particles, explains everything from nuclear energy to personal computers. What Einstein failed to take into account is that God invented dice, and God gave us the concept of frequency to understand how dice work and to make decisions based on the outcome.[8]

As a manager, a teacher, a parent, and a lay rabbi, I am often asked by young people "how come" such and such an effort didn't lead to the expected reward. While I try to console them, I, too, am frustrated that although God created a world with rules and order, God also made a world in which those rules are not absolute (i.e., frequency). I believe the reason God did this was to create a world that would constantly challenge, and thus strengthen, our faith. A world where everything doesn't work out *each* time, but a world where everything does work out *over* time—especially for those of us, like Job, with enough faith to follow our plan regardless of how much adversity we experience.

> So the LORD blessed the latter end of Job more than his begin-ning: for he had fourteen thousand sheep, and six thousand camels, and a thousand yoke of oxen, and a thousand she asses. . . . After this lived Job a hundred and forty years, and saw his sons, and his sons' sons, even four generations. So Job died, being old and full of days.[9]

The "Invisible Hand" behind Wellness

In 1996, when I began the research for this book, I was not opti-mistic that a solution could be found to our need for wellness. Although in my lifetime I had seen the virtual demise of Communism and significant improvements in combating world hunger and racial discrimination, I felt we could not overcome our entrapment in the "sickness" reactionary approach to health.

The reason for my pessimism was that the ill health in our nation is caused by the most powerful force in our society: economics.

John Maynard Keynes once said,

> The ideas of economists . . . are more powerful than is commonly understood. Indeed, the world is ruled by little else. Practical men, who believe themselves to be quite exempt from any intellectual influ-ences, are usually the slaves of some defunct economist.[10]

Our obese, overweight, and unhealthy citizens have become slaves to the combined economic interests of the $1 trillion food industry and the $1.5 trillion sickness industry.

In 2001, when I learned that the wellness industry had already reached $200 billion and was headed to $1 trillion by 2010, I could see that the wellness industry was the economic solution to the problem of sickness that economics had largely created.

In 1776, Adam Smith's *The Wealth of Nations* described how the unfettered pursuit by individuals of their own selfish interests leads directly to the increased well-being of society as a whole. The deeper Smith delved into the workings of the economy, the more fascinated he became by what he called "the invisible hand" that guided the actions of individuals toward increased societal wealth. Although Smith, as a progressive scientist in a secular and enlightened era, avoided using the term *God,* it is clear upon reading the original work that Adam Smith knew whose Invisible Hand was at work.

Today, there is no better example of God's hand at work than in the emerging wellness industry and in the positive economic forces behind the wellness revolution that is about to take place.

Fat: What Is It, How Do We Get It, and How Do We Define It?

Suggestion: Read this appendix once as a consumer; then go back and read it again as a wellness entrepreneur—marking the suggestions that you might want to further analyze as potential wellness business opportunities.

What Is Fat?

In the Bible the word *fat* is used to describe the most prized parts of the animal—so valuable that they were originally reserved to be burnt at the altar in a sacrifice to God himself. Historically, fat has been used in a figurative sense to describe abundance, exuberance, robustness, fertility, or outward success.

In our time the word *fat* has become almost exclusively pejorative—associated with laziness, disgust, slovenliness, greed, and gluttony.

But what exactly is fat, and why has it come to have such a negative connotation?

Biologically speaking, fats are a subgroup of a category of nutrients called *lipids,* the chemical name for a group of compounds that include fats, oils, and cholesterol. A lipid is generally referred to as a *fat* if it remains solid at room temperature and as an *oil* if it is liquid at room temperature. Fats and oils come from plant and animal products, whereas cholesterol comes *only* from animal products (e.g., meat, poultry, milk, and cheese).

Cholesterol

Cholesterol is an odorless, white, waxy, powdery substance that is found in every cell of our bodies. It is an important building block for cell membranes, hormones, and vitamin D. It also aids in the digestion of fat into caloric energy. When doctors talk about "good" and "bad" cholesterol they are actually speaking about lipoproteins.

A lipoprotein is a combination of fat and protein (lipid plus protein) that wraps around the individual fat and cholesterol molecules in our bodies, transporting them throughout our bodies and aiding the digestion of fat. Two major types of lipoproteins are low-density (LDL) lipoproteins and high-density (HDL) lipoproteins. LDL particles, which carry about 70 percent of the cholesterol in our bodies, are known as "bad" cholesterol because they stick to the walls of our arteries, which can lead to blockages, strokes, and heart attacks. HDL particles are known as "good" cholesterol because they travel throughout the body picking up cholesterol from dying cells and other sources.

The amount of cholesterol in your system is determined by many factors, ranging from your genes to your age to your level of physical activity. For example, smokers have higher cholesterol because smoking weakens the arterial walls and makes the surface membranes more receptive to fat and cholesterol deposits.

But the major determinant of how much bad cholesterol you have is your weight, or more specifically, how much excess fat you have in your system.

Saturated and Unsaturated Fats

There are three major types of fats: *polyunsaturated fat, monounsaturated fat,* and *saturated fat.* For purposes of simplification, we will refer to the first two types collectively as *unsaturated fats.*

Basically, saturated fats (e.g., shortening, lard, butter, meat fats) are the chief culprits in raising blood cholesterol—they are naturally saturated with hydrogen molecules. Saturated fats are typically solid at room temperature, and foods containing saturated fats have a longer shelf life than foods with unsaturated fats.

Unsaturated fats, like olive oil and canola oil, actually lower blood cholesterol. Unsaturated fats are typically liquid at room temperature, but start to solidify when cold, which is why an olive-oil-based salad dressing gets cloudy in the refrigerator. Fish contain more unsaturated and less saturated fat than meat, which keeps their bodies from starting to solidify in cold water.

Food manufacturers typically extend the economic shelf life of their products by adding hydrogen to unsaturated fats—a process called *hydrogenation*—which effectively turns unsaturated fats into saturated fats, or good fats into bad fats called *trans-fatty acids*. This is why it is important to avoid hydrogenated oils if you are trying to lower your cholesterol.

There is an immediate business opportunity today in providing foods without hydrogenated oils—particularly to consumers worried about heart disease. These products will have shorter shelf lives, but they could eventually become products of choice for all as consumers learn the difference between saturated and unsaturated fats.

Why We Crave Fats

Fat was prized in biblical times for many reasons. Back then, most humans suffered from a deficiency of fat, and basic calories were scarce. Being plump was often a sign of great wealth. Fat contains the most energy (9 calories per gram) of any of the six nutrient categories—an important consideration for people choosing to store food, either for traveling or for survival between harvests. But probably the main reason fats were so prized then (and still are) is because they taste so good.

We are biologically programmed to love the taste of fat; this programming is now killing us in our world of agricultural abundance.

In contrast to times when fat was prized and scarce, today calling someone "fat" is considered a great insult.

But eating fat does not directly cause you to become fat. Eating more calories than you burn makes you fat—or more correctly, makes you overweight. Eating fat indirectly causes you to become overweight because fat contains more than twice as many calories per gram as proteins or carbohydrates. Aside from containing potentially unnecessary calories, eating too much fat is bad because fats contain artery-clogging cholesterol.

Defining Overweight and Obese

When a person becomes overweight, his or her excess fat, as noted earlier, often appears first in the stomach and upper body on a man and on the thighs and lower body in a woman. Upper-body obesity (*android obesity*) is a male pattern characteristic strongly related to heart disease, hypertension, and diabetes. It is more dangerous than lower-body obesity (*gynecoid obesity*), which is a female characteristic and also dangerous to your health.

How much fat is too much? To answer this question it is first necessary to define the terms *overweight* and *obese*. Although they are often used interchangeably, *overweight* refers to an excess of total body weight (including all bodily tissues), whereas *obese* refers to an excess of body fat only. It is possible to be overweight without being obese, as in the case of a bodybuilder with great muscle mass. It is also possible to be obese without being overweight as in the case of a sedentary person with an excess of body fat and low muscle mass.

Four main concepts are used today to define being overweight or obese: percentage body fat, waist-to-hip ratio, Body Mass Index (BMI), and height-weight tables.

The first and most accurate method is to measure the percentage of your body that is fat. Men should have a percentage body fat between 13 and 25 percent and women should have a percentage body fat between 17 and 29 percent. Anything above these numbers is considered obese and is very dangerous.

Percentage body fat is best measured by comparing a person's weight to his or her weight underwater—this works because fat floats and is less dense than body tissue. Unfortunately, this method is too expensive and complicated and is considered primarily a tool for research.[1] Another method is to use special calipers to measure the skinfold thickness of the triceps and other parts of the body—this can be quite accurate when done by a trained professional because half of a person's fat is stored just under their skin. Bioelectrical impedance (resistance) can also be used to measure percentage body fat.

Another way to measure being overweight and/or obese is by using waist-to-hip ratio, calculated by dividing the number of inches around the waistline by the circumference around the hips. For example, a person with a 30-inch waist and 40-inch hip circumference would have a waist-to-hip ratio of 0.75. Obesity is defined as anything over 0.8 for a woman and 1.0 for a man. This method is obviously good for diagnosing upper body (android) obesity, but can be woefully inaccurate in many cases, particularly for someone with lower body (gynecoid) obesity.

The third method used to measure being overweight and/or obese, the Body Mass Index (BMI), was developed in 1835 by the French mathematician Adolphe Quetelet. Using a statistical model to develop the concept of the *homme moyen,* or average man, he developed the Quetelet Index, which today is better known as the BMI:

$$BMI = \frac{\text{(weight in kilograms)}}{\text{(height in meters)}^2}$$

For example, a person with a weight of 170 pounds and a height of 5 feet 9 inches would have a BMI of about 25, calculated as follows.

First convert 170 pounds into kilograms (2.2 pounds equals 1 kilogram):

$$\frac{170 \text{ lb}}{2.2} = 77.27 \text{ kg}$$

Next convert 5 feet 9 inches (5.75 feet) into meters (3.28 feet equals 1 meter):

$$\frac{5.75}{3.28} = 1.75 \text{ meters}$$

Finally, plug your conversions into the BMI equation:

$$BMI = \frac{77.27 \text{ kg}}{1.75^2} = 25.2$$

Now here's a shortcut you can use. Simply multiply your weight in pounds by 704.5, then divide the result by your height in inches, then divide that result by your height in inches again:

$$BMI = \frac{170 \times {}^{704.5}\!/_{69}}{69} = 25.2$$

Most countries and public authorities today use BMI as their measurement tool of choice. According to the National Institutes of Health in 2000, 61 percent of the U.S. population is overweight (defined as having a BMI of 25 or greater), and almost 27 percent of the U.S. population is obese (defined as having a BMI of 30 or greater).

While these numbers may be collectively accurate (just walk out-side to a public place and count the percent of people who appear to be overweight and obese), they are woefully inaccurate when applied to specific individuals. The BMI formula is the same for both sexes: a 5-foot 9-inch woman weighing 170 pounds is obviously different than a 5-foot 9-inch man weighing the same amount, yet both are considered overweight. The BMI formula is also not adjusted for individual variations. For example, weightlifters have more muscle, which weighs more than fat, and elderly people have lower muscle mass.

Finally, the fourth method, using a height-weight table, is what people are most familiar with since it has been used by the U.S. medical profession for decades. The popular "Desirable Height-Weight Table" was developed by the Metropolitan Life Insurance Company in 1959 and represents the weight and height statistically associated with the lowest incidence of mortality among their insured population (made up mostly of upper- and middle-class white males). The term *desirable* refers to having the lowest incidence of mortality, not the lowest incidence of disease, and was removed from the name of the table in 1983. Although the Height-Weight Table is potentially more accurate than BMI because it is broken down by sex, it has most of the same limitations and should not be considered definitive for any individual circumstance. Additionally, much of the data contained on the current Metropolitan Life Height-Weight Table is arbitrary—the concept of frame size (determined by elbow width) was added with no empirical data to support it.

Regardless of which method we choose to determine the percent of our population that is overweight or obese, it is clear that we have a problem of epidemic proportions.

The Impact of U.S. Healthcare Reform on the Wellness Industry

Some readers, especially those in the 22 percent group with preexisting medical conditions in their family, may find these concepts upsetting—they may find callous my frank explanation of this problem. If you are one of these readers, I ask your indulgence; I am simply passing on the bad news, not advocating it. I will share with you in this appendix how I believe our government must and will take care of the 22 percent of our population, both children and adults, with preexisting medical conditions.

Wellness for Children Will Be Financed by Government

One of the best things about life in the United States today is Medicare—the federal program that pays most medical expenses for the 40 million U.S. citizens over age 65. Since it began in 1965, Medicare has bestowed enormous social benefits on seniors and their families. Prior to Medicare and Social Security, retirement often led to outright poverty.

One of the worst things about life in the United States today is the absence of a federal program that pays most medical expenses for the 70 million U.S. citizens under age 18.

Economically speaking, it is incredible that our society pays hundreds of billions for the medical costs of seniors, and it pays virtually nothing for the medical costs of most children.[1]

Each time a senior incurs a medical expense, his or her life is prolonged, and the government is assured of many more such expenses in the future.[2] When children incur medical expenses for prevention or the treatment of illness, their future economic productivity is improved, and our society receives back many times the cost of the expense.

This is especially true because pediatrics is one area of U.S. medicine that has proven itself on disease prevention and wellness. Pennies spent on child inoculations and early disease detection routinely save hundreds of dollars in future medical costs, and potentially add thousands of dollars to our economy and to the government coffers by making the patient a productive, taxpaying adult.

> **I believe that Congress will soon recognize these facts and enact a Medicare-type program covering sickness, and eventually wellness, for every U.S. citizen under age 18.**

Such a program will pay for itself over one to two decades by helping children become more productive taxpaying adults. A child wellness program is the next natural step after the proven successes of similar sow-now-reap-later child development programs like Head Start and federally funded school breakfast programs.

> **Eventually, when the federal government realizes the financial benefit of financing wellness for children, an entire specialized pediatric wellness industry will emerge, with incredible opportunities for entrepreneurs who provide specialized wellness products and services.**

How the U.S. Healthcare System Distorts the Labor Supply

The average U.S. household earns about $40,000 in after-tax annual income and spends (directly or indirectly through an employer) about one-seventh ($5,500) of this amount on medical expenses. Sadly, U.S. households with annual incomes all the way down to $17,050 spend the same $5,500 on medical costs. When a family's income falls below the poverty line (currently about $17,050 for a family of four[3]), all of their medical expenses are paid for by the government Medicaid insurance program.

Seniors and families just above the poverty line often resent their poorer neighbors' health insurance benefits—particularly Medicaid's 100 percent coverage for prescription drugs. Even seniors on Medicare have to pay for prescription drugs, which is often the largest single monthly expense in the household of a retired couple.

Approximately 22 percent of doctors' prescriptions are not filled because of cost, and millions of (mostly) seniors make the daily choice between purchasing their food or their medicine.

The solution here is not to cut Medicaid benefits, but to extend the same benefits, including generic prescription drug coverage, to seniors and middle-class Americans with family incomes below the $40,000 national average.

Some families with chronically ill members are forced to stay deliberately unemployed just to qualify for Medicaid health insurance, especially prescription drug coverage. Some employees with preexisting medical conditions are forced to remain with their current employer rather than looking elsewhere for jobs that would pay them more and better use their services, which would benefit everyone.

These and other workplace inefficiencies are disrupting the U.S. labor supply, which ultimately generates the $10 trillion economy that pays for our $1.5 trillion in medical expenses.

Universal Basic Sickness Insurance Will Expand Wellness

I believe that Congress will eventually enact a basic sickness, hospitalization, and prescription drug insurance program unrelated to employment—first for seniors, then for children, and then for all U.S. citizens.

If properly enacted, such a national sickness insurance program could actually save U.S. taxpayers money and provide a boom to the emerging wellness industry.

The government cannot universally pay *all* medical expenses. Medical costs become unlimited if left unchecked. Almost every prematurely born infant or terminally ill patient could be kept alive by technology—especially if no regard is given to the quality of that life. Even healthy people could consume unlimited amounts of emerging new treatments, from Viagra for sexual impotence to Rogaine for thinning hair.

Instead, a properly enacted national sickness insurance program would cover all sickness and wellness expenses for children (if not already covered by prior child wellness legislation), and it would cover only certain sickness expenses for adults. A fixed amount would be payable for each treatment, just as Medicare and private insurance programs today cover procedures at "usual and customary" levels of payment. This basic program would also have limits for certain procedures determined by the age of the patient (e.g., heart surgery would not be covered for persons over 90 years of age).

Such universal basic sickness coverage should be economically neutral to the total U.S. economy. Americans without health insurance are already receiving basic sickness benefits today—although to receive them many have to go on welfare or take off work to use inefficient hospital emergency rooms for treatment. For Americans with health insurance, such a program would be a transfer of basic sickness insurance responsibility from employers to government, the costs of which could also be transferred over time. On the provider side, universal basic sickness coverage would spawn the entry of highly efficient providers into the marketplace—companies as efficient as Wal-Mart or McDonald's would line up to offer specialized sickness industry procedures at convenient locations.

This will help most employees in the unfortunate 22 percent group with preexisting conditions in their families, and it will finally relieve employers of maintaining the sickness safety net that has been unjustly thrust upon them.

But the real benefit for most Americans would be the supplemental premium sickness and Wellness Insurance programs that would emerge from the private sector.

Most working Americans would not be satisfied with a basic capitated government sickness insurance program that limited the amount spent on each sickness treatment. They would purchase supplemental insurance to cover a premium level of sickness industry services—from private rooms at hospitals to better providers to more diagnostic tests. And, most important, such premium supplemental insurance programs would also cover wellness industry products and services.

This would lead to a restructuring of the health insurance industry—from the adversarial relationship that exists today between the insured and their insurers to one of mutual benefit.

Once relieved of covering unlimited catastrophic sickness and preexisting medical conditions, insurance companies could focus their energies proactively on wellness—because, as supplemental sickness insurers, they would share in the benefits of efficacious wellness decisions. Just as accident insurers routinely inspect the plants of their insured and make suggestions on how to increase safety, Wellness Insurance companies would take active roles in keeping their policyholders aware of the latest developments in wellness technology and services.

Most employers today would relish the opportunity to increase wages and opt out of providing health insurance benefits to their employees. When the government gets around to providing basic sickness coverage for all, employers will be able to get out of the medical business and focus fully on what they do best: running their own businesses.

Summary of Wellness Insurance

Note: *This appendix is designed to assist you in explaining Wellness Insurance to your business associates.*

Wellness Insurance is a new health insurance program that covers expenses incurred to prevent disease (e.g., weight control, vitamins, supplements, and exercise) along with major medical expenses above an annual deductible. Traditional health or "sickness" insurance pays only for medical expenses when you are sick, and it pays mostly for treating the symptoms of disease rather than for the prevention of disease. Individuals can obtain Wellness Insurance today by combining a high-deductible health policy (HDHP) with a savings account to invest in their wellness, such as a Medical Savings Account (MSA) or a Wellness Savings Account (WSA). Here's a brief summary of why every eligible healthy individual should switch to Wellness Insurance.

1. *Cost savings.* The typical family no- or low-deductible health insurance policy costs about $5,000 per year. A family HDHP with a $2,500 annual deductible costs about $2,000 per year, a $3,000 annual savings. Even if the insured gets very sick and has to spend the full $2,500 deductible, he or she is still ahead $500 per year after switching to an HDHP.

2. *Wellness investment.* Since the people accepted for HDHPs are healthy, switching a family to an HDHP typically saves them up to $3,000 per year ($250 per month), which provides additional cash they can spend on wellness (vitamins, supple-

ments, exercise). Only approximately 78 percent of U.S. citizens with private health insurance today are healthy enough to qualify for an HDHP.

3. *Guaranteed coverage for life.* Once someone has an individual (versus a group) HDHP, no matter how sick they or a dependent become or what conditions they develop, their policy cannot be dropped, nor can premiums be increased for this reason.[1] This allows HDHP insureds to change jobs or go into business for themselves without being limited by preexisting medical conditions in their family (provided such conditions develop after they first obtain an individual HDHP policy).

4. *HDHP income tax advantages.* Beginning in 2002, self-employed individuals can deduct from their taxable income 70 percent of their health insurance premiums. The deduction goes up to 100 percent in 2003 and thereafter.

5. *MSA income tax advantages.* Individuals with Medical Savings Accounts (MSAs) may take a tax deduction for up to $3,800 per year (increasing annually, in $50 increments, with inflation) that they put into their MSA until age 65, with the investment returns accumulating tax-free. This money can be taken out tax-free anytime for medical expenses or, as with an IRA, for any purpose after age 65. While Congress has extended MSAs only until 2003, anyone opening an MSA before then receives these benefits for life—including the right to make future contributions until age 65 even if Congress terminates the program in 2003 (which it is not expected to do).

6. *Supercustomers.* A wellness provider can combine a subscription wellness product with the WSA component of Wellness Insurance to create a class of supercustomers who have funds available to invest in their wellness, often on a tax-advantaged basis.

7. *Dependent coverage.* Most employees receiving group health insurance from their employer today reimburse their employer separately for dependent coverage. Switching their dependents to an individual HDHP will typically save them up to 60 percent in premiums for their dependents *and* guarantee their family members affordable coverage for life—regardless of what happens to their job or what medical conditions their dependents may develop in the future.

Frequently Asked Questions about Wellness Insurance

Note: *This appendix is written for* **potential consumers of Wellness Insurance.**

1. **What is Wellness Insurance?** Wellness Insurance[1] is health insurance that covers expenses incurred to prevent disease—like weight control, vitamins, supplements, and exercise—along with major medical expenses above an annual deductible. Traditional health or "sickness" insurance pays only for medical expenses when you are sick, and pays mostly for treating the symptoms of disease rather than for the prevention of disease.

2. **How can I get Wellness Insurance today?** Employers and health insurance companies will begin offering Wellness Insurance in several years. But you can get Wellness Insurance today by combining your own high-deductible health insurance policy (HDHP) with a Wellness Savings Account (WSA). A WSA, as further explained herein, is an account used to pay for wellness expenses. The WSA could be established with a wellness provider or a third-party financial institution.

3. **What is a high-deductible health insurance policy (HDHP)?** An HDHP is a traditional health insurance policy with a higher than usual annual deductible—you are reimbursed only for medical expenses incurred above a cumulative annual amount, typically $2,000 to $4,500 per year, but you generally save this amount or more in your annual health insurance premium.

4. **Why would I want an HDHP?**   With an HDHP you decide how to spend the first few thousand dollars for your family's medical care without having to ask anyone's permission or argue later on for reimbursement. You can join your own health maintenance organization (HMO) or preferred provider organization (PPO)—although most HDHP providers include PPO membership at no additional charge. You can select your own discount pharmacy plan, eyeglass plan, vitamins and supplements plan, fitness club membership, or any other customized wellness or sickness services. If you are healthy, you will save thousands of dollars that you can invest today in your continued wellness.

5. **How much can I save with an HDHP?**   The annual premium savings with an HDHP are usually equal to or less than the annual deductible amount. For example, a typical low- or no-deductible health insurance family policy may cost $5,000 per year, whereas the same policy from the same insurance company with a $2,500 per person annual deductible may cost only $2,000 per year—a $3,000 reduction in the annual premium. With this HDHP, even if a member of your family becomes very sick and you have to pay for the first $2,500 of medical expenses, you are still ahead $500 per year. And if you all remain well, you have up to $3,000 per year extra cash to invest in your continued wellness and save for future health expenses.

6. **Why is such an HDHP up to $3,000 less expensive?**   Two reasons: (1) The first $2,500 per year of a family's medical care is typically spent in $100 increments in 25 transactions— and it costs the insurance company $30 or more to process the paperwork for each transaction ($2,500 medical cost + $750 processing costs = $3,350). (2) Only healthy people without preexisting medical conditions qualify for HDHP— insurance companies generally reject about 22 percent of HDHP applicants because they or someone in their family has a preexisting medical condition.

7. **How come I've never heard about HDHPs before?**   Three reasons:

   (a) If you have a group health insurance policy, your employer doesn't want you to leave the group since your typical $5,000 annual premium goes to support less-healthy group members.

(b) Insurance brokers do not actively promote HDHPs for individuals since the commission is about one-third to two-fifths of the commission on a non-HDHP policy.

(c) If an insurance company tried to advertise HDHPs, applications would come mostly from unhealthy people, and these applications are expensive to process and cause regulatory problems for the insurance company because many are rejected.

8. **What if a member of my family becomes chronically ill?** This is the best part about an HDHP. Once someone has an individual HDHP, no matter how sick they or a dependent become, no matter what conditions they develop, their policy cannot be dropped, nor can premiums be increased for this reason.[2] This allows people with an HDHP (versus employer-provided group health insurance) to change jobs or go into business for themselves without being limited by preexisting medical conditions of themselves or a dependent.

9. **What if I receive free health insurance from my employer?** Even if you receive free health insurance from your employer, you should consider getting an HDHP for your dependents and possibly for yourself. Most private employers charge employees for dependents who participate in the company's group policy—and if your family is healthy it could be much less expensive to buy them an individual HDHP. This will guarantee your family coverage if anyone develops a medical condition and you have to change jobs or your company plan is terminated. Additionally, ask your employer about restructuring your job (e.g., to be categorized as an independent contractor who would be paid more if you drop out of the company's group policy).

10. **What are the tax implications of paying for my own health insurance?**   Thanks to recent federal legislation, beginning in 2001 self-employed individuals may deduct 60 percent of the amount they spend for health insurance—this figure rises to 70 percent in 2002 and to 100 percent in 2003 and thereafter. Prior to this legislation, it was often not advantageous to obtain your own health insurance since employer-provided health insurance enjoyed up to a 2-to-1 income tax advantage over purchasing health insurance yourself with after-tax dollars.

11. **What is a Wellness Savings Account (WSA)?**   A Wellness Savings Account (WSA)[3] is a deposit account you open with a wellness provider or a third-party financial institution to invest the money you save by having an HDHP—this money is used to pay for current wellness expenses and the deductible amount on your HDHP should you become ill. Anyone with an HDHP should have readily available savings of at least the annual deductible amount (e.g., $2,500) in case they or a family member become seriously ill.

12. **What is a Medical Savings Account (MSA)?**   A Medical Savings Account is a special type of WSA authorized by Congress on an experimental basis until 2003. It is similar to an IRA in that you receive a deduction from your income taxes for up to $3,800 per year for funds deposited in an MSA, interest and dividends accrue tax-free, and after age 65 you may withdraw your money without penalties, even for nonmedical purposes. But even better than an IRA, you may withdraw money anytime, tax-free, to pay medical expenses before or after age 65.

13. **How do I quality to open an MSA account?**   In order to qualify to open an MSA, you must first obtain a special type of MSA-approved HDHP with a $3,050 to $4,600 annual cumulative family deductible. Then you are allowed to invest in your MSA up to 75 percent ($2,300 to $3,800) of this deductible amount each year. These figures are all increased annually with inflation in $50 increments. Single (nonfamily) individuals are permitted roughly half these amounts. To qualify for an MSA you are not allowed to be covered under any other major medical plan.[4]

14. **What happens to my MSA after 2003?**   Congress is allowing only 750,000 individuals to open MSAs until 2003—at which time the program expires unless it is renewed by new legislation. However, even if the program is terminated, anyone opening an MSA before December 31, 2002, receives these benefits for the rest of their lives—including the right to make continued annual contributions of $3,800 or more until age 65. Most political analysts today expect the MSA program to be extended and expanded before 2003.

15. **What is a Super-MSA™?**   A Super-MSA[5] is an MSA designed for higher-income taxpayers with family income in excess of $75,000 per annum. You contribute the maximum each year to your MSA, but do not plan to make annual with-

drawals except for emergencies. The money in your Super-MSA is invested for the highest long-term return and accumulates interest and dividends tax-free. Since taxpayers today receive all their income tax deductions when they put money into their MSAs (versus taking it out for medical expenditures), there is no financial incentive to remove it before retirement—provided they have other funds available to pay medical expenses below their HDHP deductible. MSA funds accumulate interest tax-free, and MSAs have all the advantages of an IRA and then some—thus the first savings account any taxpaying family should have should be their Super-MSA.

16. **Can employers offer MSAs and HDHPs to their employees?** Yes. Employers with up to 50 employees may offer MSAs with HDHPs to their employees. If the employer grows beyond 50 employees, it is allowed to continue to offer MSAs to all employees provided its average number of employees since 1996 remains below 200. The employer obtains a group HDHP for all employees and makes equal contributions to each employee's MSA—tax-deductible to the employer and tax-free to the employee. An employer-sponsored MSA program saves employers money over group health insurance while offering healthy employees up to a $3,800 after-tax bonus (worth up to $7,600 in pretax wages) to spend on wellness today or save for future medical expenses.

Introduction: The Next Big Thing

1. *Merriam-Webster's Collegiate Dictionary.* Springfield, MA: Zane Publishing, Inc., and Merriam-Webster, Inc., 1996.
2. Ibid.
3. Ford, like most entrepreneurs, at first did not succeed. He founded his first motor company in 1899—it flopped. He founded a second one in 1901, which also failed. And the firm we know today as Ford Motor Company, which he started in 1903, almost failed in 1906 because he went too far upscale before deciding to make the affordable Model T.
4. "Putting America on Wheels," *The Economist,* 31 December 1999.

Chapter 1: Why We Need a Revolution

1. *Merriam-Webster's Collegiate Dictionary,* 10th ed. Springfield, MA: Zane Publishing, Inc., and Merriam-Webster, Inc., 1996.
2. *Encyclopaedia Britannica,* www.Britannica.com.
3. Ibid.
4. Ibid.
5. In 1971, when I began college, half the world lived under Communism, and world leaders freely debated the merits of capitalist versus communist systems. In the United States, people were divided over whether the government or the private sector should be the exclusive provider of services, from mail delivery to phone service to train travel.
6. In 1845, Benjamin Disraeli, the future prime minister of England, warned of the danger of his country disintegrating into "two nations," as though they were dwellers in different zones or inhabitants of different planets.
7. *Prevalence of Overweight and Obesity Among Adults: United States, 1999,* National Center for Health Statistics, Centers for Disease Control (CDC).
8. Hostess Twinkies, Oreo, and McDonald's Happy Meals are registered trademarks, respectively, of the Interstate Bakeries Corporation, Nabisco, Inc., and McDonald's Corporation.
9. In photos, our one-year-old daughter, Miriam, always seems to have a vegetable or fruit in her hand. In reality every few minutes she has a different item of food in her hand as her taste buds (and attention) quickly tire of whatever she has just received.

10. The term *vitamin* was coined in 1912 by biochemist Casimir Funk. Funk discovered that these substances were vital for life, and he originally thought that they were all ammonia-based products—hence the term *vital amine* or *vitamin*. Later, as scientists identified the critical 13 vitamins required for human life, they discovered they were not all ammonia-based substances.

11. Another reason for these deficiencies is that the more we process foods from their natural state—mostly to differentiate them as distinct brands and to retard spoilage—the less efficacious their vitamins become. In addition, some vitamins should be taken with certain foods in order to be digested properly.

12. Oreo, Ritz, and Life Savers are trademarks of Nabisco Holdings, Inc.

13. Oscar Mayer bacon and Philadelphia brand cream cheese are trademarks of Kraft Foods, Inc.

14. Approximately 34 million of 39 million patients on Medicare do not receive prescription drug coverage. Generally, the 5 million Medicare recipients receiving prescription drug coverage do so because they elected to receive a lower standard of managed care in return for such prescription coverage.

15. Diller, Lawrence H., M.D., "Just Say Yes to Ritalin! Parents Are Being Pressured by Schools to Medicate Their Kids—or Else," *New York Times,* September 24, 2000.

16. There is so much overlap between the different categories that I have deliberately not listed current sales figures for each. For example, the vitamin industry claims current sales of $70 billion—although a close examination of this number yields the fact that it includes vitamins and supplements added to ordinary foods. Similarly, the $12 billion in fitness club revenues does not isolate amounts paid to the clubs themselves for the use of their trainers.

17. Witkower Press, Inc., of Hartford, Connecticut, had published *Arthritis and Common Sense* and claimed in their advertisements that it would help arthritic and rheumatoid sufferers. In 1954 the FTC ordered the Witkower Press to "forthwith cease and desist from representing, directly or indirectly, that their book was adequate, effective, and reliable in giving relief to arthritic and rheumatoid sufferers." Witkower Press accepted the ruling and did not appeal the case. In a similar case against Prentice Hall, the large publisher agreed to the FTC action because they did not want to enter into costly litigation with the federal government. (Pilzer, Paul Zane, "Rodale Press versus the Federal Trade Commission: A Comprehensive Analysis," senior thesis, Lehigh University, Bethlehem, PA, May 21, 1974.)

18. At the original hearing on this case before the FTC examiner, dissenting FTC commissioner Philip Elman foreshadowed the path that the FTC was about to take when he wrote: "Congress did not create

this Commission to act as a censor of unorthodox ideas and theories in books, whether they deal with politics or health. We should not forget that, in both fields, today's heresy may become tomorrow's dogma." (Ibid.)

19. FTC commissioner Elman, a Kennedy appointee and former law clerk to Supreme Court Justice Felix Frankfurter, wrote in his dissenting opinion: "It is the glory of a free society that a man can write a book contending that the earth is flat, or that the moon is made of green cheese, or that God is dead, without having to 'substantiate' or 'prove' his claims to the satisfaction of some public official or agency. . . . It is arrogance to presume that in any field of knowledge, whether dealing with health or otherwise, all the answers are now in." (Ibid.)

20. While most of the alchemists failed in their quest to make gold and discover the elixir of life, many laid the foundation for modern science (pharmacy, medicine, metallurgy, physics, chemistry, etc.), which today has accomplished exactly what the alchemists hoped to achieve: pharmacy and medicine along with the potential for unlimited prosperity.

21. Although Ponce de León failed in his quest to find the Fountain of Youth on the Island of Bimini in the Bahamas, he more than paid for his expedition by accidentally discovering Florida in March 1513—much as the alchemists themselves ultimately succeeded by discovering, not gold, but chemisty.

22. Later research identified that there are 13 such critical substances and that they are not all ammonia-based substances, but the term *vitamins,* with a changed spelling in recognition of this research, has remained.

23. The story of Edward Jenner's discovery of the cowpox vaccine to prevent smallpox is well known. But it is not well known that the actual process of inoculation itself (deliberately infecting someone with a disease to prevent that same disease from occurring) was developed in the East hundreds of years earlier and that this was well known in Jenner's time.

24. Behe, Michael J., *Darwin's Black Box: The Biochemical Challenge to Evolution.* The Free Press, 1996, p. 10.

Chapter 2: Understanding and Controlling the Demand for Wellness

1. Prior to age 40 I typically reduced my caloric intake by skipping meals without ensuring that my body was receiving the minimal daily required amount of vitamins and minerals. This led to my having colds on a regular basis, winter respiratory infections, and not functioning at my optimum level. Worst of all, since I had done this all of

my adult life, I had no idea what I was missing until I began eating healthy food throughout the day, exercising regularly, and taking vitamins and supplements.

2. A similar phenomenon exists in Western Europe, where there is a bulge in the population of those born between 1946 and 1964, although there it is related more to a severe decline in the birthrate that began in the late 1960s rather than a dramatic increase in the birthrate following World War II.

3. *Retro*—"relating to, reviving, or being the styles or esp. the fashions of the past : fashionably nostalgic or old-fashioned <a retro look>." © 1996 Zane Publishing, Inc., and Merriam-Webster, Inc.

4. Russell, Cheryl, *The Baby Boom: Americans Aged 35 to 54,* 2nd ed., New Strategist Publications, Inc., 1999, 2000, Foreword.

5. Most people think that Keynes had a greater impact during his time than he actually did. Many of the government programs of the 1930s and 1940s attributed to Keynes's recommendations were actually part of a larger phenomenon—active government involvement in the economy—and Keynes's *General Theory* was merely used after the fact to justify their continued existence. The actual New Deal programs of the 1930s preceded the *General Theory* by several years.

6. The first electrically powered washing machine was invented in 1910 by Alva J. Fisher, but the product did not become widely available until the invention of an electrically powered agitator-type washer by Howard Snyder in 1922.

7. U.S. Department of Commerce, Bureau of the Census, *Statistical Abstract of the United States: 1991* (Washington: Government Printing Office, 1991), pp. 1272, 1275.

8. Unfortunately, as we will see in Chapter 4, as this occurred the profit opportunity in agriculture shifted from producing healthy foodstuffs (e.g., wheat, milk, fruit) to manufacturing these foodstuffs into terribly unhealthy name-brand foods with long shelf lives (e.g., cereals, condiments, processed cheeses, canned foods, frozen foods, and junk or snack foods).

9. Today, this terrible disease has been almost completely eradicated through the addition of vitamin D to commonly consumed foods.

10. The cause of beriberi was discovered by Casimir Funk in 1912. It has been eradicated through the addition of vitamin B_1, or thiamine, to dehusked grains.

11. Vitamins contain no energy directly, but are required catalysts in order to produce the hundreds of chemical reactions required for sustaining life. Since they generally cannot be manufactured by the body, they must be obtained elsewhere on a daily basis.

12. Our bodies age or decay over time due to molecules called *free radicals,* which cause them to oxidate or "rust." Certain vitamins may be able to slow or retard oxidation.

Chapter 3: What You Need to Know about Food

1. Genesis 2:9 King James Bible.
2. Proteins are typically not digested into energy because they are the most difficult to digest and because the body needs these building blocks to constantly replace its organs.
3. Data compiled from Healthstatus.com (http://www.healthstatus.com).
4. "Forward into the Past: Eating as Our Ancestors Did," *Eating for Health,* www.obesity.com.
5. Genesis 2:9 King James Bible.
6. The chemical composition of a catalyst is not altered by the reaction, and thus a single catalyst molecule can be used over and over again. This explains why we need only a small quantity of each vitamin— although we do need to ingest these small quantities daily, because most vitamins do not remain in the digestive system.
7. Pasteurization is the application of heat to "destroy pathogenic (disease-producing) microorganisms, to inactivate spoilage-causing enzymes, and to reduce or destroy spoilage microorganisms" ("Food Preservation," *Encyclopaedia Britannica,* 2000), www.britannica.com.
8. "Betcha Can't Eat Just One" is the name of a television commercial for Lay's potato chips, re-released starring baseball great Cal Ripken (www.ripkenbaseball.com/pr_frito_lay.shtml) on April 2, 2001.
9. McDonald's Corporation, www.mcdonalds.com.
10. Schlosser, Eric, *Fast Food Nation: The Dark Side of the All-American Meal,* New York: Houghton Mifflin Company, p. 6.
11. Lin, Biing-Hwan, Joanne Guthrie, and Elizabeth Frazao, "Nutrient Contribution of Food Away from Home," *America's Eating Habits: Changes and Consequences.* Edited by Elizabeth Frazao, Food and Rural Economics Division, Economic Research Service, U.S. Department of Agriculture. Agriculture Information Bulletin No. 750 (AIB-750), www.ers.usda.gov.

Chapter 4: Making Your Fortune in Food

1. The traditional seven deadly sins are (1) vainglory, or pride; (2) covetousness; (3) lust, understood as inordinate or illicit sexual desire; (4) envy; (5) gluttony, which usually included drunkenness; (6) anger; and (7) sloth. They were identified during the early history of Christian monasticism and grouped together in the sixth century by St. Gregory the Great. (*Merriam-Webster's Encyclopedia of Literature,* Zane Publishing, Inc., and Merriam-Webster, Inc., 1996.)
2. This $45 billion includes approximately $20 billion paid through USDA price support programs to tens of thousands of farmers for

not farming. None of this $45 billion is included in the rough $1,000 trillion total, as it is all either exported or is a subcomponent of the other categories.

3. As of 8/03/01 the National Restaurant Association expected 2001 sales in the nation's 844,000 restaurants to be $399.2 billion (www.restaurant.org/research/index.asp).

4. Approximately half of this $70 billion is in products sold to food processors and thus may be double counted.

5. These are 1999 state population figures. Statistical Abstract of the United States, 2000.

6. Sperry, Peter, "How 'Emergency' Farm Spending Squanders the Surplus," The Heritage Foundation Executive Memorandum, 3 September 1999.

7. Becker, Elizabeth, "Corporate Welfare Fuels Big Farms," *The New York Times,* 14 May 2001.

8. The age of menarche has been dropping rapidly over the past few decades in the United States, occurring as early as age 10 in many girls. In civilizations that don't use bovine growth hormones, menarche typically occurs around age 15. (Yoffe, Emily, "Got Osteoporosis? Maybe All That Milk You've Been Drinking Is to Blame," *Slate Magazine,* www.slate.com, 2 August 1999.)

9. In 2853 B.C., Emperor Sheng-Nung of China named five sacred plants: soybeans, rice, wheat, barley, and millet. (North Carolina Soybean Producers Association, www.ncsoy.org.)

10. A breakthrough study at the University of Illinois at Urbana concluded that consuming soybean isoflavones can increase bone mineral content and bone density. As little as 40 grams of soy protein, consumed each day for six months, led to positive results in a test group of postmenopausal women. Forty grams of soy protein can be found in two ounces of soy protein isolate (www.unitedsoybean-board.com).

11. *Merriam-Webster's Collegiate Dictionary,* ©1996 Zane Publishing, Inc., and Merriam-Webster, Inc.

12. Soy-beverage marketers petitioned the FDA to use the term *soymilk* three years prior to NMPF's complaint. The FDA decided not to rule on the petition, which allowed soymilk producers to operate under an umbrella of protection as long as they don't deceive the public in their labeling or advertising. (Frank, Paula, "Soy's Evolution," www.foodproductdesign.com.)

13. Fiscal years ending March 31.

14. The original Gardenburger didn't contain soy because Wenner didn't like the taste and thought that many consumers had a negative view of soy-based products. Today, most Gardenburger varieties (except for the original style) contain 12 to 14 grams of soy protein per patty.

15. Wenner, Paul, *Garden Cuisine: Heal Yourself Through Low-Fat Meatless Eating,* Fireside, New York, 1998.

16. The original company Wenner founded was called Wholesome and Hearty Foods, Inc. The name was changed to Gardenburger, Inc., when it went public in 1992.
17. As a result of its share price on Nasdaq remaining below $5 for several months.
18. Restaurant Industry Forecast, National Restaurant Association (www.restaurant.org).
19. In 1999, average household spending on food away from home was approximately $2,583 for persons 35 to 54 versus $1,245 for persons 65 and older. (Restaurant Industry Forecast, National Restaurant Association, www.restaurant.org.)

Chapter 5: Making Your Fortune in Medicine

1. Behe, Michael J., *Darwin's Black Box: The Biochemical Challenge to Evolution,* The Free Press, 1996.
2. Trepanned skulls from prehistoric times have been found in Britain, France, and other parts of Europe and in Peru—many of them showing evidence of healing and, presumably, of the patient's survival. The practice still exists among primitive people in parts of Algeria and in Melanesia (www.britannica.com).
3. Although Hippocrates is said to have been born in 460 B.C. and a great many books bear his name, modern scholars attribute this collection of books to several individuals writing under this same name over several lifetimes.
4. The *Theory of Natural Selection* and the more recent *Theory of Intelligent Design* both posit that all living creatures evolved from prior-existing organisms due to changes in their DNA. Natural selection advocates believe these changes came from statistical random mutations that improved an organism's chance of survival (e.g., a leopard growing spots for camouflage). Eventually, the nonmutated organisms became extinct and the mutated organisms survived. Intelligent design advocates believe that these changes were not random but occurred across the board at the same time by all members of a species due to an already existing code written in the DNA (e.g., all leopards grew spots in 5 million B.C.).
5. Behe, Michael J., *Darwin's Black Box: The Biochemical Challenge to Evolution,* The Free Press, 1996.
6. Behe, Michael J., *Darwin's Black Box: The Biochemical Challenge to Evolution,* The Free Press, 1996, p. 10.
7. Personal interview with Carl S. (Sam) Rehnborg, Ph.D., son of Carl F. Rehnborg, September 7, 2001.
8. Telephone interview between author and Dr. Tod Cooperman on August 10, 2001.

9. An *intrapreneur* is an entrepreneur working within a large organization.

10. *Executive Health Program,* brochure, The Fitness Institute at LDS hospital, Salt Lake City, UT.

11. Adams, Fisher, Hansen, and Yanowitz, *Maintaining the Miracle: An Owner's Manual for the Human Body.*

12. Dr. Yanowitz also lights up when he talks about being a performing jazz pianist—having recorded an LP and several CDs, not only of standard jazz pieces but of his original compositions.

13. "Physical Activity and Public Health," *Journal of the American Medical Association,* February 1, 1995, vol. 273, no. 5.

14. Wee, Christina C., M.D., M.P.H., "Physical Activity Counseling in Primary Care," *Journal of the American Medical Association,* August 8, 2001, vol. 286, no. 6.

15. "Jill Stevens Kinney—America's #1 Female Club Entrepreneur," *Club Insider News,* May 1999, vol. VI, no. 5.

Chapter 6: What You Must Know about Health Insurance

1. Wellness Insurance™, the subject of the next chapter, is health insurance that covers expenses incurred to prevent disease—like weight control, vitamins, supplements, and exercise—along with major medical expenses above an annual deductible. Traditional health or "sickness" insurance pays only for medical expenses when you are sick and pays mostly for treating the symptoms of disease rather than for the prevention or disease. Wellness Insurance is a trademarked term of Wellness Services, Inc.

2. This occurred because a single additional dollar in income could push some taxpayers into a higher bracket on all of their income.

3. We will soon examine new tax regulations taking full effect in 2003 that will begin to level the playing field for some self-employed individuals.

4. IRS Rev. Rul. 68-433, 1968-2 CB 110, says that insurance premiums for drugs are reimbursable as a health insurance expense only if they are for *prescription* drugs. Of course, some savvy pharmaceutical firms get around this regulation by making much more expensive "prescription" versions of their over-the-counter products.

5. Patients without PPOs or those who pay cash sometimes never get appointments, because it is mostly assumed that they cannot afford to pay anything at all.

6. In a health maintenance organization (HMO) the provider is paid a flat annual amount per patient instead of being paid for each service rendered.

7. Many states limit the ability of insurance carriers to raise premiums

for "small employers" (generally 50 employees or less) due to high-loss experience, or they limit the size of such premium increases to be within predefined "rating bands" for small employee groups.

8. Technically, the federal Health Insurance Portability and Accountability Act of 1996 (HIPAA) limits insurance companies from excluding most preexisting conditions on new employees provided that, among other things, the individual employee was covered for this condition at a prior employer and has not had a lapse in healthcare coverage for more than 63 days. HIPAA has created a cat-and-mouse game where insurance companies do their best to get a group policyholder to drop their policy while technically following HIPAA and other federal regulations. For example, HIPAA requires insurance companies offering individual policies to accept former group applicants, but does not specify at what rates. Insurance companies offering individual policies typically get approval for a high-rated, extremely expensive policy that few could afford, and then, in order to comply with HIPAA, "offer" this too-expensive policy to HIPAA applicants with preexisting conditions.

9. This 22 percent figure is from verbal estimates I have culled while interviewing insurance executives and brokers. There are roughly 225 million people in the United States with health insurance, broken down as follows: 23 million Medicare (of which 80 percent purchase supplemental policies), 15 million Medicaid, and 187 million employer. This 187 million figure consists of 40 million with large corporations that self-insure and 147 million with large (and small) businesses that purchase third-party health insurance (including 16 million with individual health insurance purchased policies covering 24 million insured).

10. A study completed six years after COBRA was passed showed that only 21 percent of workers who qualified elected COBRA continuation coverage. (Mark C. Berger, Dan A. Black, Frank A. Scott, Carolyn Looff and Associates, Health Insurance Coverage of the Unemployed Final Report, April 17, 1996. Prepared for the Pension and Welfare Benefits Administration, U.S. Department of Labor, Washington, D.C.)

11. U.S. citizens become eligible for Medicare at age 65, although in this case Medicare would not cover their under-65 dependents.

12. Some states apply such individual premium protection to small employer groups (2 to 50).

13. Generally, the states requiring guaranteed-issue are New York, New Jersey, Massachusetts, Vermont, New Hampshire, Maine, and Kentucky. Washington and Oregon recently repealed their guaranteed-issue requirements.

14. A self-employed individual (as defined in Code Sec. 401[c][1]) may deduct as a business expense a statutory percentage of the amount paid for medical insurance on himself, his spouse, and his dependents (Code Sec. 162[l][1]).

15. Noting that large corporations have always been allowed to deduct 100 percent, Congress passed H.R. 2488, the Taxpayer Refund and Relief Act of 1999, which would have allowed immediate 100 percent deductibility for self-employed businesses. It was vetoed by President Clinton.

16. IRS code limits the self-employed health insurance deduction to net earned income (there is no such limitation for corporations paying health insurance premiums).

Chapter 7: The Gold Mine in Wellness Insurance

1. Traditional health or "sickness" insurance pays only for medical expenses when you are sick, and pays mostly for treating the symptoms of disease rather than for the prevention of disease. Wellness Insurance, a trademarked term of Wellness Services, Inc., is used with permission.

2. Wellness Savings Account and WSA are trademarks of Wellness Services Corporation, Inc.

3. Raising the deductible on an automobile policy from, say, $500 to $1,000 often reduces the annual premium by $500 or more—the insured typically pockets the $500 per annum and loses out only if he or she has more than one major accident per year on a regular basis. The only ones who definitely lose in such a situation are the insurance agents—who are paid a percentage of the total premium and sometimes paid lesser percentages on less-profitable products like high-deductible insurance.

4. Approximately 20 percent of healthcare insurance premiums go toward overhead.

5. In fact, the insurance company typically requires the insured to use the PPO in order to keep a record of, and maintain an approval process for, the amounts spent under the deductible in case the $2,500 annual limit is reached.

6. "Seventy percent of any population spends $150 or less on health-care in a year," according to Mark Weinberg, Group President at California's Blue Cross unit, which covers 850,000 individuals. ("Consumers Facing Sharp Rise in Health Costs," *New York Times,* 10 December 2000.)

7. Perspicacious healthcare benefits managers should be able to get around this income tax roadblock. The employer could pay the insurer $2,500 of the $3,000 saved in premiums per employee and then request that the insurer simply automatically (without processing) pay any employee "under-deductible" claims up to $2,500 per annum. But, as we will see in a moment, this would not work in a group policy environment, since typically 22 percent of the employees would not qualify at all for high-deductible, reduced-premium health insurance.

8. Such an indirect financial arrangement might entail converting an employee with benefits to a higher-paid independent contractor paying for their own benefits. Or, as we examine later, it might entail switching just the employee's spouse and children to Wellness Insurance.

9. A $3,800 per year investment compounded monthly at 8 percent per annum would equal approximately $58,000 in 10 years.

10. The original legislation for the MSA experiment was passed in 1997 and scheduled to expire on December 31, 2000, but was extended in December 2000 until December 31, 2003.

11. In such cases the medical insurance expense can be carried back or forward to other taxpaying years.

12. It is estimated that the single largest group of individuals opening MSAs to date have been physicians. Most insurance executives are surprised at the low number of taxpayers opening MSAs to date—these executives universally blamed the insurance brokerage community, noting that switching a family from a zero-deductible to a high-deductible policy typically reduces the brokerage commission from $850 (17 percent of $5,000) to $340 (17 percent of $2,000).

13. Initially, Congress passed a law authorizing such interest-bearing savings accounts, then called NOW accounts (for negotiable order of withdrawal), for just the New England Federal Reserve District. The law was expanded to include the rest of the nation a few years later.

14. 60 percent in 2001, 70 percent in 2002, and 100 percent in 2003 and beyond.

15. IRS Rev. Rul. 68-433, 1968-2 CB 110.

16. In the aforementioned example, switching from the zero-deductible to the $2,500 deductible HDHP would lower the agent commission from $996 (20 percent of $4,980 premium) to $382 (20 percent of $1,908 premium). Agent commissions on health insurance policies are typically about 20 percent of the first-year premium.

Chapter 8: Making Your Fortune in Wellness Distribution

1. At this point I also ask the class about the economic implications of inviting a passing ship of 50 destitute foreigners to come live on our island and share our newly developed wealth. During the ensuing debate the students realize themselves that they, and the new immigrants, will both become even richer when the newcomers are welcomed with open arms into our island society.

2. Readers of my prior books may note that I estimated distribution costs in 1990 at 80 percent (versus 70 percent today). This is because distribution costs as a percentage of retail sales fell throughout the 1990s due to the advent of the Internet (or real-time information sharing), but the same advent of the Internet lowered manufacturing costs at an even greater pace.

3. Not every department store owner was asleep at the switch. The century-old Dayton-Hudson Corporation (i.e., Marshall Field, Mervyn's, Dayton Hudson), successfully retooled its existing department stores toward more-fashionable merchandise while simultaneously building Target stores from scratch in 1962 into one of the world's largest mass merchandisers. In fact, they were so successful that the Target division exceeded 78 percent of their $33 billion in sales in 1999, and the company changed its name to Target Corporation in 2000.

4. Home Depot has since "institutionalized" such innovation by requiring existing vendors to submit a plan annually on how they will lower costs, or increase quality, by 20 percent per annum. If the existing vendor cannot meet these guidelines, their entire relationship is opened to competitive bidding by other vendors. This forces the manufacturers to innovate on a continual rather than on a when-it's-almost-too-late basis.

5. U.S. retail sales increased 27 percent from $2,359 billion in 1995 to $2,995 billion in 1999. (Statistical Abstract of the United States, 1999. U.S. Census Bureau.)

6. It is fascinating to note, almost theologically, what happened when the Pentagon hired three different groups to begin working on the concept of the Internet in the early 1960s—at MIT, at Rand, and in the United Kingdom (at NPL). When they all came together in Washington to agree on a standard in 1968, they had all come to the same conclusion regarding packets and independent client/servers, even though they had all proceeded under strict security guidelines and without ever knowing of each other's work.

7. Although he is rarely remembered that way, the late Sam Walton was really the first information age CEO. After starting his company in 1962 at the age of 44, Walton attended an IBM school in computers in 1966 with the goal of hiring the smartest person in the class.

8. To put it another way, the majority of the economic value or cost in finished goods today is in the tools used to make them rather than in the traditional labor and raw material costs.

9. Kaufman, Leslie, "As Biggest Business, Wal-Mart Propels Changes Elsewhere," *New York Times*, October 22, 2000.

Chapter 9: Staking Your Claim

1. *Merriam-Webster's Collegiate Dictionary*, Zane Publishing, Inc., and Merriam-Webster, Inc., 1996.

2. Henry Wells worked as a freight-forwarding agent in Albany, New York, before cofounding Livingston Wells, and Pomeroy's Express in 1843 to handle freight between Buffalo and Albany, and hiring Daniel Fargo as an agent.

3. Cronan, Carl, "Art the Revelator," *The Business Journal of Tampa Bay,* Sept 28, 1998.

4. Depositing $300 per month ($3,600 per year) in a federally insured 5.25 percent interest savings account would yield a balance of $185,474.03 in 25 years. At an interest rate of 7 percent, which might equal the rate of long-term bonds issued by the same insurance company, the balance would be $243,021.51—far more than the $100,000 paid back by the life insurance company on a whole life policy.

5. Since then he has been active as a philanthropist and a backseat coach: In 1998, Williams purchased the Tampa Bay Lightning hockey team for $117 million and donated $70 million to Liberty University. (Cronan, Carl, "Art the Revelator," *The Business Journal of Tampa Bay,* September 28, 1998.)

6. In the 1960s Sam Walton (the founder of Wal-Mart) often spoke of how he admired W.T. Grant—then the largest department store chain in the United States and a model for efficiency and growth. In 1975, when W.T. Grant filed bankruptcy, 1,073 stores were closed, 80,000 people were thrown out of work, and creditors had to write off approximately $334 million in bad debts and loans. The repercussions of this major failure were felt by communities and small businesses worldwide for years to come.

7. Genesis 2:9 (King James Bible).

8. Zohar I, 196A.

9. "Since by keeping the body in health and vigor one walks in the ways of God—it being impossible during sickness to have any understanding or knowledge of the Creator—it is a man's duty to avoid whatever is injurious to the body, and cultivate habits conducive to health and vigor." (Moses Maimonides (1136–1204), Mishnah Torah.)

10. Mead, Rebecca, "Slim for Him: God Is Watching What You're Eating," *The New Yorker,* January 15, 2001.

Chapter 10: Epilogue: Unlimited Wellness

1. Our bodies manufacture 200 billion red blood cells each day, replacing all the blood in our body every 120 days. Skin is completely replaced every one to three months. It takes 90 days for old bone to be broken down and replaced by new bone.

2. Watson and Crick received the Nobel Prize for discovering DNA in 1953, and Dr. J. Craig Venter of the Celera Corporation announced that they had completed mapping the human genome on April 6, 2000.

3. Robert Bazell, "Scientists Map Human Chromosome," 1 December 1999, *NBC Nightly News.*

4. Ibid.

5. In 2000 there were approximately 5 million U.S. households with a total net worth exceeding $1 million, and this number is projected to grow approximately 50 percent by 2005.

6. This mistake as a young man led to "a fruitless quest that occupied the rest of his life." (Albert Einstein, *Encyclopaedia Britannica*, 2000.)

7. Although Einstein's discoveries as a physicist may have been fruitless from this point forward, Einstein certainly more than distinguished himself in his later years as a statesman and champion of world peace. Einstein was professionally ostracized by other leading physicists because of his refusal to accept the probabilistic laws of quantum mechanics—although they later successfully used his fame and political connections during World War II. Einstein was called upon by them to get President Roosevelt to endorse the Manhattan Project to build the atomic bomb, but then Einstein was kept in the dark about their progress until the bomb was actually detonated over Hiroshima.

8. My friend and colleague Norman Beil disagrees with me that Einstein was incorrect on this point. Beil contends that statistics are used to make decisions only when we do not have the right answer—as in meteorology, where we use statistical data to predict a "28 percent chance of rain" even though whether or not it will rain is a binary outcome. Beil feels that Einstein was saying we should not give up searching for a unified field theory and rely on statistics, but rather that we should keep searching, and rely on statistics only when we have given up all hope of finding the correct answer.

9. Job 42:12–17 King James Bible.

10. Keynes, John Maynard, *The General Theory of Employment, Interest, and Money* (San Diego: Harcourt Brace Jovanovich, 1964), p. 383. Keynes's great work was first published in England in 1936.

Appendix A: Fat: What Is It, How Do We Get It, and How Do We Define It?

1. In addition to simply weighing underwater and dry, adjustments must be made for the amount of water displaced (Archimedes' principle), water temperature, water density, and lung capacity (using helium).

Appendix B: The Impact of U.S. Healthcare Reform on the Wellness Industry

1. The very poor in the United States receive Medicaid—a $200 billion program that pays virtually all medical expenses for U.S. citizens under age 65 who live below the poverty line.

2. It could be argued fairly that seniors deserve these special benefits, since our seniors are the ones who built the great economy that now pays for their medical expenses.

3. The U.S. Census bureau in 2000 defined $17,050 as the "poverty line" for a family of four in the 48 contiguous states ($21,320 in Alaska and $19,610 in Hawaii), plus or minus $2,900 for each additional or subtracted family member. ("The 2000 HHS Poverty Guidelines," U.S. Department of Health and Human Services.)

Appendix C: Summary of Wellness Insurance

1. In certain states they can be rerated annually into the next higher class with a controlled (e.g., 10 percent, 15 percent) increase in premium.

Appendix D: Frequently Asked Questions about Wellness Insurance

1. Wellness Insurance™ is a trademark of Wellness Services, Inc. All rights reserved.
2. In certain states they can be rerated annually into the next higher class with a controlled (e.g., 10 percent, 15 percent) increase in premium.
3. Wellness Savings Account™ is a trademark of Wellness Services, Inc. All rights reserved.
4. This rule does not apply for health plans covering: accidents; disability; dental care; vision care; long-term care; benefits related to workers' compensation laws, tort liabilities, or ownership or use of property; a specific disease or illness; a fixed amount per day (or other period) of hospitalization.
5. Super-MSA™ is a trademark of Wellness Services, Inc. All rights reserved.

Alternative Medicine: The Definitive Guide. Puyallup, WA: Future Medicine Publishing, Inc., 1993.

Anders, George. *Health Against Wealth: HMOs and the Breakdown of Medical Trust.* New York: Houghton Mifflin Company, 1996.

Andrews, Charles. *Profit Fever: The Drive to Corporatize Healthcare and How to Stop It.* Monroe, ME: Common Courage Press, 1995.

Andrews, Sam S., M.D., Luis A. Balart, M.D., Morrison C. Bethea, M.D., and H. Leighton Steward. *Sugar Busters!: Cut Sugar to Trim Fat.* New York: Ballantine Books, 1998.

Bailey, Covert. *The New Fit or Fat.* Boston: Houghton Mifflin Company, 1991.

Balch, James F., M.D., and Phyllis A. Balch, C.N.C. *Prescription for Nutritional Healing.* Garden City Park, NY: Avery Publishing Group Inc., 1990.

Behe, Michael J. *Darwin's Black Box: The Biochemical Challenge to Evolution.* New York: Simon & Schuster, 1998.

Berman, Louis A. *Vegetarianism and the Jewish Tradition.* New York: Ktav Publishing House, Inc., 1982.

Binzel, Phillip E., Jr., M.D. *Alive and Well: One Doctor's Experience with Nutrition in the Treatment of Cancer Patients.* Westlake Village, CA: American Media, 1994.

Brown, Montague, Everett A. Johnson, Richard L. Johnson. *The Economic Era of Healthcare: A Revolution in Organized Delivery Systems.* San Francisco: Jossey-Bass, Inc., 1996.

Castro, Janice. *The American Way of Health: How Medicine is Changing and What It Means to You.* New York: Little Brown and Company, 1994.

Dauner, C. Duane, with Michael Bowker. *The Healthcare Solution: Understanding the Crisis and the Cure.* Sacramento, CA: Vision Publishing, 1994.

Diamond, Harvey and Marilyn. *Fit for Life.* New York: Warner Books, Inc., 1985.

———. *Fit for Life II: Living Health.* New York: Warner Books, 1989.

Eddy, Mary Baker. *Science and Health with Key to the Scriptures.* Washington, D.C.: Office of the Librarian of Congress, 1934.

Follard, Sherman, Allen C. Goodman, and Miron Stano. *The Economics of Health and Healthcare.* Upper Saddle River, NJ: Prentice-Hall, Inc., 1997.

Fraser, Laura. *Losing It: America's Obsession with Weight and the Industry That Feeds on It.* New York: Penguin Books USA Inc., 1997.

Frech, H.E., III. *Competition and Monopoly in Healthcare.* La Vergne, TN: American Enterprise Press, 1996.

Gaesser, Glenn A. *Big Fat Lies: The Truth About Your Weight and Your Health.* New York: Fawcett Columbine, 1996.

Herzlinger, Regina. *Market Driven Healthcare: Who Wins, Who Loses in the Transformation of America's Largest Service Industry.* Reading, MA: Addison-Wesley Publishing Company, 1997.

Kalechofsky, Roberta, Ph.D. *Vegetarian Judaism: A Guide for Everyone.* Marblehead, MA: Micah Publications, Inc., 1998.

Katahn, Martin, Ph.D. *The T-Factor Diet: Lose Weight Safely and Quickly Without Cutting Calories—or Even Counting Them!* New York: W. W. Norton & Company, Inc., 1989.

Kunnes, Richard M.D. *Your Money or Your Life: ℞ for the Medical Market Place.* New York: The Cornwall Press, Inc., 1971.

Millenson, Michael L. *Demanding Medical Excellence: Doctors and Accountability in the Information Age.* Chicago: The University of Chicago Press, 1997.

Morreim, E. Haavi. *Balancing Act: The New Medical Ethics of Medicine's New Economics.* Washington, D.C.: Georgetown University Press, 1995.

Muller, H.G., and G. Tobin. *Nutrition and Food Processing.* Westport, CT: The Avi Publishing Company, Inc., 1980.

Ornish, Dean. *Dr. Dean Ornish's Program for Reversing Heart Disease.* New York: Random House, Inc., 1990.

Osmani, S.R. *Nutrition and Poverty.* New York: Oxford University Press, Inc., 1992.

The PDR Family Guide to Prescription Drugs. New York: Crown Trade Paperbacks, 1996.

Pilzer, Paul Zane. *God Wants You to Be Rich: The Theology of Economics.* New York: Simon & Schuster/Fireside, 1995/1997.

———. *The Next Trillion: Why the Wellness Industry Will Exceed the $1 Trillion Health Care (Sickness) Industry in the Next Ten Years.* Dallas, VideoPlus, Inc., 2001.

———. *Unlimited Wealth: The Theory and Practice of Economic Alchemy.* New York: Crown Publishers, 1990/1994.

Pilzer, Paul Zane, with Robert Dietz. *Other People's Money: The Inside Story of the S&L Crisis.* New York: Simon & Schuster, 1989.

Porter, Roy. *The Greatest Benefit to Mankind: A Medical History of Humanity.* New York: W. W. Norton & Company, Inc., 1997.

Powter, Susan. *Stop the Insanity: Change the Way You Look and Feel— Forever.* New York: Simon & Schuster, 1993.

Reid, Daniel P. *The Tao of Health, Sex, and Longevity: A Modern Practical Guide to the Ancient Way.* New York: Fireside, 1989.

Roberts, Marc. J., with Alexandra T. Clyde. *Your Money or Your Life: The Healthcare Crisis Explained.* New York: Doubleday, 1993.

Rodwin, Marc A. *Medicine, Money and Morals: Physicians' Conflicts of Interest.* New York: Oxford University Press, 1993.

Schlosser, Eric. *Fast Food Nation: The Dark Side of the All-American Meal.* New York: Houghton-Mifflin, 2001.

Shaouli, Rabbi Moshe Cohen, and Rabbi Yaakov Fisher. *Nature's Wealth: Health and Healing Plants Recommended by Professors of Science and Medicine.* English edition edited by Ruth Steinberg. Copyright Rabbi Jacob Fisher, 1999.

Simon, Julian L. *The State of Humanity.* Cambridge, MA: Blackwell Publishers, Inc., 1995.

Skidelsky, Robert. *John Maynard Keynes: Hopes Betrayed, 1883–1920.* Harmondsworth, Middlesex, England: Penguin Books, 1986.

———. *John Maynard Keynes: The Economist as Savior, 1920–1937.* Harmondsworth, Middlesex, England: Penguin Books, 1994.

Starr, Paul. *The Social Transformation of American Medicine: The Rise of a Sovereign Profession and the Making of a Vast Industry.* Basic Books, 1982.

Tips, Jack, N.D., Ph.D. *The Pro Vita! Plan: Your Foundation for Optimal Nutrition.* Austin, TX: Apple-A-Day Press, 1993.

Weil, Andrew, M.D. *Eating Well for Optimum Health: The Essential Guide to Food, Diet, and Nutrition.* New York: Alfred A. Knopf, 2000.

Weiss, Lawrence D. *Private Medicine and Public Health: Profit, Politics, and Prejudice in the American Healthcare Enterprise.* Boulder, CO: Westview Press, 1997.

Wyke, Alexandra. *21st-Century Miracle Medicine: RoboSurgery, Wonder Cures, and the Quest for Immortality.* New York: Plenum Press, 1997.

Much has happened since the first edition of *The Wellness Revolution* was published in 2002.

Wellness food sales continued their exponential growth—the soymilk manufacturer for whom I predicted $140 million sales in 2002 actually enjoyed sales in 2002 of $280 million. Unhealthy foods came under attack—a class-action lawsuit was filed against fast-food companies seeking damages for deliberately selling addictive, unhealthy products.

Wellness-based financial reforms accelerated even more than I predicted. For individuals, medical savings accounts, which were scheduled to expire by 2003, were extended by Congress in 2002. For employees, the IRS revised the rules on corporate medical plans to allow healthy employees to accumulate unspent sickness funds for their future wellness.

Soon after the book was first published, hundreds of readers wrote of their experiences as consumers within this emerging $1 trillion industry. Hundreds more wrote with questions about specific wellness products and business opportunities. The sheer volume of these inquiries, and the fact that some of their questions could be best answered by other readers, led to my creating a free online forum where wellness revolutionaries could share ideas and meet each other. Check in to www.TheWellnessCommunity.NET to keep up with the latest news on the wellness revolution.

As an entrepreneur, I too have set out to stake my own claim in the wellness industry. Along with my lifelong friend and partner Anthony Meyer, I founded Wellness Finance LLC, an online bank and insurance business dedicated to helping consumers finance their wellness. Like most of my past businesses, I discovered this opportunity first as an unsatisfied consumer—my wife was unable to find wellness-based health insurance and a good deal on a medical savings account for our own family.

The first automobile dealers sold only luxury vehicles to the very rich and thus didn't need to help their customers finance their purchases. But once Henry Ford's Model T made the automobile a mass-market product, car dealerships needed to know as much about automotive finance as they did about the actual vehicles they sold. This same thing is happening today in the wellness industry, as wellness products become more affordable and wellness providers seek to help their clients finance their wellness.

Of all the mail I've received, the most gratifying has been from individuals who changed their diet or wellness behavior after reading *The Wellness Revolution.* One of these individuals told me that before reading my book he had simply accepted his obesity and ill health as his lot in life. Although he picked up my book to learn about a new business opportunity, the overall explanation of the sickness and wellness industries provided him the motivation to change his diet, his health, and soon his life and the lives of those he loved.

Vive Le Revolution!
Paul Zane Pilzer

Just before his death at age 83, former president Richard Nixon was asked about the most important experience of his life. He replied, "Bebe never asked me about the eighteen and a half minutes." Nixon was referring to the missing minutes of the Watergate tape recordings that eventually forced his resignation, and the fact that his best friend, Bebe Rebozo, had never once asked him about the most unanswered historical question of his era.

Looking back two decades at the acknowledgments in my previous books, I see some of the most important experiences of my life—the names of the friends who have supported me through the good times and bad. Some of these include Ed Ames, Michael Ashkin, Norman and Carol Beil, Reed Bilbray, Jerry Coffee, Julie and Randy Fields, Deborah and Mitch Gaylord, John Grillos, Kenny Griswold, Richard and Kimberly Jaffe, Stephen Jarchow, John and Meg Hauge, Don and Jan Held, Ann Mather, Anthony Meyer, Dr. Stanley Pearle, Tony Robbins, Paula Sepulvado, and Caroline Zemmel.

John Hauge especially stands out as the person who first explained to me what now seems so obvious—that all we really have of value are the people we love.

One of the joys of a new book is the new relationships it fosters and the opportunity to work again with old friends. Here are some who come to mind on this project.

There is Karen Risch and Richard Poe, who each helped me organize the original proposal. There is the eminent professor Michael Behe (coincidentally now teaching at my alma mater, Lehigh University), who helped me understand the biology I should have learned in college. There is the visionary, Stuart Johnson, who first saw the potential benefits of this research

There are hundreds of people I've consulted—some of whom include Dr. David Bergman, Brandon Benson, Richard Bizzaro, Kendall Cho, Blair Feulmer, Rita and Stanley Kaplan, Michael Kleinman, David Koren, Ken Mabry, Alex Mastoloni, Dr. Mary Parsons, Jim Smith, Bryce Williams, Don Wilson, Gregg Wurster, Karen Wynn, Dexter Yager, Doyle Yager, and Steve Yager.

There is my researcher Joey D'Allesandro, who has transitioned from employee to close friend, and my former researcher, Brandon

Williams, who planted many of the theological seeds that continue to sprout in my work.

There is my business partner, Anthony Meyer, and my CEO Reed Bilbray, both of whom since the 1980s have selflessly allowed me to shine by their achievements.

There is the Los Angeles–based trainer Lisa Goldenthal, also known as the "sculptor" to her celebrity clientele. And there is my Utah-based trainer, Kat Jonsson, who has picked up where Lisa left off.

There is my mountain bike partner, Mel Lavitt, the epitome of wellness at age 65. Mel leaves me far behind going uphill, but tells me not to worry as he couldn't come close to biking like he does now when he was only my age.

There is my editor, Airié Dekidjiev, who was the first person to see how much more this book could be than just an exposé of the food and healthcare industries. I am especially grateful to Airié, just like my trainers Lisa and Kat in the gym, for continually driving my work to higher levels than I previously thought possible.

There are also my former editors, Allan Mayer (*Other People's Money*), Jim Wade (*Unlimited Wealth*), and Bob Asahina (*God Wants You to Be Rich*)—all of whom have taught me so much.

There is my literary agent, Ms. Jan Miller, about whom I can only say what I've said several times before: Jan is commonly known as "the dreammaker" to the many authors, including me, on whom she was the first one to take a chance. Now, after more than 20 years together, Jan's original role as just my trusted agent has taken a backseat to her role as my cherished friend. I also owe special thanks to Jan's assistant, Michael Broussard, mostly for introducing me to Airié.

After 20 consecutive years of teaching college students at New York University, I now teach Sunday school to teenagers in my local community. Looking back at NYU, I am grateful to the thousands of students who helped me find my main purpose in life: to teach. And I am equally grateful for the close friendships that developed from teaching with outstanding colleagues like George Stone and Morris Sutton.

God Wants You to Be Rich (Simon & Schuster 1995/1997), was dedicated to my most important mentor, Charles Jay Pilzer. Since that dedication, I had the honor of officiating at Uncle Charlie's fiftieth wedding anniversary, where the real star was his wife Geraldine. Aunt Gerry, a model for health and fitness, added as much to this project as her husband has added to my previous works.

And as always, there are my brothers, Stephen and Lee, and their wives, Donna and Meryn, and my brother-in-law Brian Dang. There are my in-laws, Linda and Kieu Dang—Kieu's pharmaceutical and international background was a great asset in my research. And of course, my mother, Miriam, and my father, Elias, to whom no amount of praise could do justice.

But, going forward, all of this pales in comparison to the gratitude I feel to my wife, Lisa, a former biochemist who stayed up many nights editing my manuscript, our daughter Miriam, and to our next child who should be born by the time this book is published. To all three of you, when I stop and contemplate my past, I can only think of the immortal words of John Lennon, who wrote, "In my life I love you more."

Paul Zane Pilzer is a world-renowned economist, a multimillionaire software entrepreneur, a lay rabbi, an adjunct professor, and the author of three best-selling books.

Pilzer completed college in three years and received his MBA from Wharton in 15 months at age 22. At age 24, he was appointed an adjunct professor at New York University where he has taught for 20 consecutive years. While employed as Citibank's youngest officer at 22 and its youngest vice president at 25, Pilzer started several entrepreneurial businesses—earning his first $1 million before age 26 and his first $10 million before age 30. Over the past 20 years, he has started and/or taken public five companies in the areas of software, education, and financial services.

He was an appointed economic adviser in two presidential administrations and warned of the impending $200 billion savings and loan crisis years before official Washington was willing to listen—a story that he later shared in *Other People's Money* (Simon & Schuster, 1989), which was critically acclaimed by *The New York Times* and *The Economist* magazine.

Pilzer's *Unlimited Wealth* (Crown Publishers, 1990) explained how we live in a world of unlimited physical resources because of rapidly advancing technology. After reading *Unlimited Wealth,* the late Sam Walton, founder of Wal-Mart, said that he was "amazed at Pilzer's business capacity" and his "ability to put it into layman's terms."

Pilzer's *God Wants You to be Rich* (Simon & Schuster, 1995/1997) explained how the foundation of our economic system is based on our Judeo-Christian heritage. This *New York Times* business best-seller was featured on the front page of *The Wall Street Journal* and on television shows ranging from *60 Minutes* to *First Person with Maria Shriver.* It has been published in 18 languages.

And now, in *The Wellness Revolution* (Wiley, 2002), Pilzer identifies the newly emerging wellness business and explains how wellness entrepreneurs can find their fortunes in this soon-to-be $1 trillion industry.

Pilzer, a former commentator on National Public Radio and CNN, has appeared three times on *Larry King Live!* He has also been featured on the cover of several national magazines. He speaks live each year to approximately 500,000 people, and more than 10 million audiotapes of his speeches have been sold.

He lives in Utah with his wife and children where they are all avid snowboarders, mountain bikers, and chess players.

To contact Paul Zane Pilzer visit www.thewellnessrevolution.info.